Andre Malraux:
The Human Adventure

Andre Malraux:
The Human Adventure

Violet M. Horvath

New York • New York University Press
London • University of London Press Limited
1969

PAGE	LINE	FROM	TO
3	1	"D'Une Jeunesse	"D'Une jeunesse
	28	Action and that individualism	Action and individualism
4	23	--individualism and of death--	--individualism and death--
5	12	party	Party
	17, 26	Tcheng-Daü	Tcheng-Daï
	18	Borodin's	Borodine's
	13	that marked	that marks
	17	and, by extension of	and, by extension, of
8	21	Katóv	Katow
	26	...--to make	...to make
3	18	Clappique, the buffon,	Clappique, the buffoon,
222	6	Kassner the experience of his ascent from the hell of	Kassner catches a glimpse of Prague, not a single street of
225	25	fellow begins in	fellow beings is
229	13	and at end of the novel	and at the end of the novel
239	24	no more voices	no more voice
242	29	Liarens	Linares
248	3	pressence	presence
252	24	the Malraux's cycle.	the Malraux cycle.
254	12	convoked to present	convoked to be present
258	29	Greek sculptor	Greek sculpture
262	10	often though unknowingly,	often, though unknowingly,
274	11	arms of descent	arms of a descent
280	23	miraculous revelations	miraculous revelation
294	10	let time flow	lest time flow
295	2	Antimemoires	Antimémoires
310	26	their month	their march
324	6	(trans. Beth Archer)	[omit]
331	12	Griselidis	Griselidis
335	21	La Douanier	Le Douanier
	23	La Temps du mépris	Le Temps du mépris
336	4	Picon, Gaëton	Picon, Gaëtan
	6	Shiva, in AM, 309	Shiva, 19; in AM, 309

ANDRÉ MALRAUX: THE HUMAN ADVENTURE
by Violet M. Horvath

ERRATA

PAGE	LINE	FROM	TO
half-title		Andre	André
title		Andre	André
half-title		Andre	André
viii	1	Metamorphose	Métamorphose
1	4	Gaëton	Gaëtan
19	11	toward a power beyond,	toward, a power beyond
29	8	[those of the East are]	[those of the East]
35	14	into questions by Socrates	into question by Socrates
65	6	"metamorphosis'"	"metamorphosis"
68	18	Cross and Black Death	Cross and Black Death
84	29	roccoco	rococo
101	25	Lunch on	Luncheon on
106	1	pseudo-romanesque, pseudogothic	pseudo-Romanesque, pseudo-Gothic
116	26	that each style	than each style
121	18	mere survival	mere revival
127	3, 4	old man	Old Man
	9	with him today	with Him today
	15	his place	His place
	26, 27	"he has already changed his	"He has already changed his
136	14, 15	In an account to the narrator and the reader of his earlier experiences,	In an account of his earlier experiences to the narrator, the reader,
141	28	Bulgarians ordered	Bulgarians, ordered
143	8	Royaume fairfelu (supra, p. 000)	Royaume farfelu (supra,
151	23	call Man something	call Man, something
152	22, 23	the Western now, abandoned by God and isolated from his fellows is thrown	the Western individual, by God and isolated from fellows, is now thrown
154	14	"D'Une Jeunesse européenne"	"D'Une jeunesse européenne"
156	13	wisdom and serenity, in the West	wisdom and serenity; in

For my mother

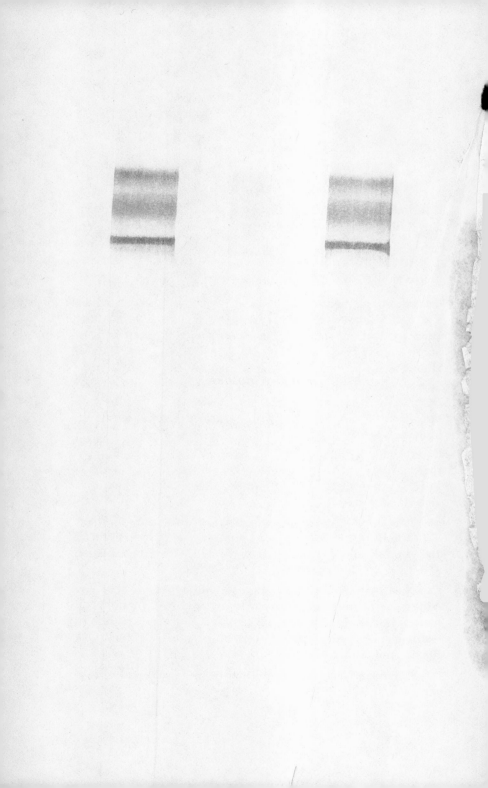

Acknowledgments

I wish to express my profound gratitude to Leon S. Roudiez, Justin O'Brien, Edward Said, Erika Ostrovsky, and Oscar Cargill for their helpful comments and suggestions.

In addition, I would formally like to express my gratitude for the permission to use the material below.

Excerpts from André Malraux's *Anti-memoirs,* translated by Terence Kilmartin, copyright © 1968 by Holt, Rinehart and Winston, Inc. and Hamish Hamilton Ltd. Reprinted here by permission of Holt, Rinehart and Winston, Inc. and Hamish Hamilton Ltd.

Excerpts from André Malraux's "D'Une jeunesse européenne," *Ecrits* (Les Cahiers Verts, No. 70), copyright © 1927 by Editions Bernard Grasset. Reprinted here by permission of Editions Bernard Grasset.*

Excerpts from André Malraux's *La Condition humaine,* copyright © 1933 by Random House, Inc. and Hamish Hamilton Ltd. Reprinted here by permission of Random House, Inc. and Hamish Hamilton Ltd.*

Excerpts from André Vandegans' *La Jeunesse littéraire d'André Malraux: Essai sur l'inspiration farfelu,* copyright © 1964 by Editions J.-J. Pauvert. Reprinted here by permission of Editions J.-J. Pauvert.*

Excerpts from André Malraux's *La Lutte avec l'ange: Les Noyers de l'Altenburg,* copyright © 1943 by Editions du haut pays, 1945 by Editions Albert Skira, and 1948 by Editions Gallimard. Reprinted here by permission of Editions Gallimard and André Malraux.*

* Translated here by Violet Horvath by permission.

Excerpts from André Malraux's *La Metamorphose des dieux,* copyright © 1957 by Editions Gallimard. Reprinted here by permission of Editions Gallimard and André Malraux.*

Excerpts from André Malraux's *La Création artistique* (Vol. II of *La Psychologie de l'art*), copyright © 1949 (France) by André Malraux; published for Bollingen Foundation by Pantheon Books, Inc.; produced by Editions Albert Skira, Geneva. Reprinted here by permission of Bollingen Foundation (through Princeton University Press) and Editions Albert Skira.*

Excerpts from André Malraux's *La Tentation de l'Occident,* copyright © 1926 by Random House, Inc., *La Voie royale,* copyright © 1928 by Random House, Inc., and *Les Conquérants, copyright* © 1928 by Random House, Inc. Reprinted here by permission of Random House, Inc.*

Excerpts from André Malraux's *L'Espoir,* copyright © 1937 by Random House, Inc., Routledge & Kegan Paul, Ltd., and Hamish Hamilton Ltd. Reprinted here by permission of Random House, Inc. and Hamish Hamilton Ltd.*

Excerpts from André Malraux's *Les Voix du silence,* copyright © 1951 by Editions Gallimard. Reprinted here by permission of André Malraux.*

Excerpts from Joseph Hoffman's *L'Humanisme de Malraux,* copyright © 1963 by Librairie C. Klincksieck. Reprinted here by permission of Librairie C. Klincksieck and Joseph Hoffman.*

Excerpts from André Malraux's *Lunes en papier,* copyright © 1921 by Editions Gallimard. Reprinted here by permission of Editions Gallimard and André Malraux.*

Excerpts from Charles Lucet's "Malraux et ses *Antimémoires,*" *French Review,* Vol. XLII, No. 1 (October, 1968), copyright © 1968 by Charles Lucet. Reprinted here by permission of Charles Lucet.*

Excerpts from André Malraux's *Royaume farfelu,* copyright © 1928 by Editions Gallimard. Reprinted here by permission of Editions Gallimard and André Malraux.*

* Translated here by Violet Horvath by permission.

Contents

Part III: *A Cyclic Spiritual Journey from Hell to Paradise*

Part IV: *Man's Open Future*

Part V: *Antimémoires*

A List of Principal Abbreviations and Short Titles

The only beings are those who create.
All others are shadows floating on the
earth, strangers to life. . . .
  To create, whether it is in the order
of the flesh or of the mind, is to leave
the prison of the body, to hurl oneself
into the hurricane of life, to be He who
Is. To create is to kill death.

—Romain Rolland

Andre Malraux:
The Human Adventure

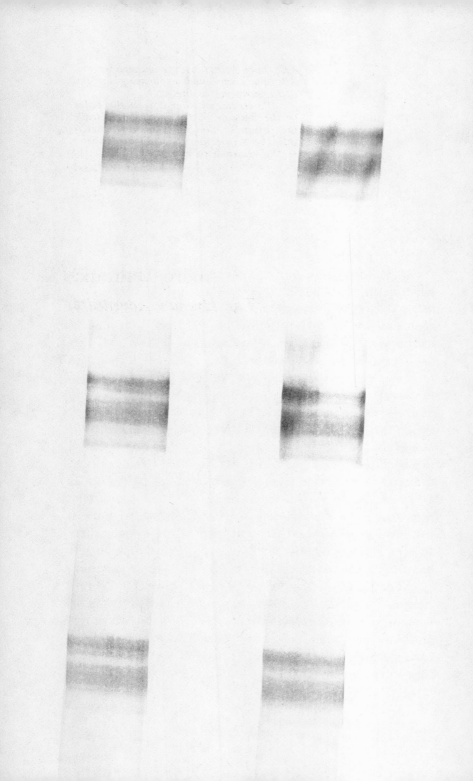

Introduction

Since the appearance of Malraux's books on art, which have shed much light on the themes treated in his fiction, many critics have sought the unifying idea of his literary creation. Gaëton Picon found it in the quality of man or in the positing of history as the new absolute. W. M. Frohock suggested the hero's experience of withdrawal and return as the unifying element. Edward Gannon expressed the essence of Malraux's hope for mankind in a portion of the title of his book, "The Honor of Being a Man." Gerda Blumenthal's *André Malraux: The Conquest of Dread* concentrates on the anguish pervading the world of the twentieth century, and on the need for both man and the artist to reach out toward a new transcendent. Charles D. Blend posits tragic humanism as the essence of Malraux's vision of life and defines the purpose of his work as the formulation of a new ethics for contemporary man. In a more recent study on Malraux, Joseph Hoffman sees the theme of destiny as the center of Malraux's vision.

This study attempts to present Malraux's literary creation to date as an organic whole from the point of view of an all-embracing subject, "the human adventure," and a unifying idea, the cycle of constant flux. My aim is to suggest the combination of this subject and unifying idea—the human adventure unfolding according to the cycle of incessant destruction and re-creation—as the key to Malraux's vision of the world.

To realize this aim and justify the title of my study, I have endeavored, first of all, to present Malraux's complete works as an epic of man, and second, to trace the presence of the cycle, in many forms, through his literary creation to date.

The idea of the cycle as the law of creation governing the life span of individuals, generations, epochs, and man's temporal existence in its entirety is ever-present in Malraux. It appears in the history of the human soul in the volumes on art, in the allegorical vision of the human adventure in the early *contes,* in the evolution of the contemporary hero and his world in the novels, and, finally, in the one volume of Malraux's *Antimémoires* that has already been published.

In Malraux, a harmony between the human and cosmic cycles often serves to set the tone and create the physical atmosphere for a human adventure unfolding on earth against the canvas of the cosmos, and in time against a backdrop of eternity. The stars, the constellations, the moon, the sun, and the earth play prominent roles in suggesting an interplay between the hero's inner world and other elements in the created universe. The various time cycles—the day, the week, the month, the season, the year, the generation, and the epoch—often govern both the structure of the works and the evolution of the heroes.

As early as *Lunes en papier,* his first published volume, Malraux's vision of the world in terms of the cycle is compounded of anguish and hope, for the cycle implies not only a beginning and an end—or death—but also the idea of resurrection and renewal. In *Lunes en papier* it is the figure of Death's valet, an "old man" resembling a "foetus," [1] who suggests the connection between death and rebirth. This close association between life and death as part of a continuous cycle of creation is a recurring theme in Malraux, one which governs his vision of both human life and civilizations.

The Malraux cycle has two movements: one winds from death to new life and the other from death to resurrection after the passage of centuries.

Malraux's overall vision is one of creation in continuous progress. In accordance with this vision, change emerges as the new "absolute," with a consequent rejection of all closed systems and an emphasis on the relativity of all human knowledge and values. Malraux enjoins man to remain unreservedly open to the infinite possibilities of human destiny as the creation of man by man continues with the unfolding of the human adventure in time.

The cycle of constant flux as the scheme of things is at the heart of Malraux's tragic humanism, at least insofar as the flux is in direct opposition to man's perennial yearning for eternity and stability. Awareness of the impermanence of both human life and human values, including the succession of absolutes man has set up in an attempt to defy destiny, engenders the sensibility of the absurd, which is the point of departure of Malraux's hero.

For Malraux's early heroes the cycle represents a wheel of fate, an order of life over which man has no control and to which he must submit. When consciousness of the absurdity of this state of affairs becomes acute, it leads to a violent eruption out of the historical cycle into which the heroes are born—to a rupture between the heroes and their world.[2]

It is this sensibility of the absurd that fires Malraux's imagination and leads to his relentless drive to transform the absurd into the significant by illuminating the past achievements of man, by forging for him a new *raison d'être* in the rapidly changing world of the present, and by opening a vista to a future which man himself must fashion.

More and more Malraux sees man as a being who must make history rather than submit to it, and here the ethical aspect of his work flashes into focus. He envisages man making history directed toward a definite goal: the promotion of the dignity of all men everywhere. The vision extends far into the future—perhaps beyond the human adventure.

The cycle which begins as the source of the hero's anguish gradually becomes the source of his hope. To an ever-increasing extent the hero regards himself not as a victim of the flux but as an active participant in its creation and perpetuation. Effecting change becomes a creative act, an outlet for man's creative potential, the *sine qua non* of progress. In Malraux, absurdity is transformed into significance as both the man of action and the artist contribute to the formation, transformation, or elaboration of the civilization of the epoch into which they are born.

Consciousness of imminent death—the end of the human life cycle—is the source of man's greatest anguish. This consciousness explains the predominance of the theme of death throughout Malraux's works and also his reference to man as "the only animal who knows he must die." [3] In Cartesian terms the anguish in Malraux's cyclic view of creation might be: "I was born, therefore, I must die," but the anguish is assuaged when he seemingly adds: "but I can survive myself in works that may endure and bear witness to my participation in the creation."

If the final vision is still one of tragedy, it is the tragedy of Malraux the agnostic, haunted by the obsession that time, and with it the human adventure, will eventually come to an end, and that all the effort and striving of man's earthly existence might some day prove to have been in vain. But there can be no doubt that Malraux continues to see his world through "a Christian grating"; religious terminology and numerology occur throughout his works, beginning with the seven deadly sins in *Lunes*. If the vision is a Christian one, it is darkened by the doubt of an agnostic who envisages time flowing "certainly toward death" and only "perhaps toward eternity." The interpenetration of time and eternity definitely exists in Malraux; it occurs in those moments when man's creative spark is kindled into activity—either artistic or heroic. It is experienced by the artist especially when he discovers a new "truth," and by the hero particularly after a direct confrontation with Death, over whom he emerges victorious. Malraux beckons contemporary man, alienated from God, to seek this spark—his link with the divine—within his own being.

The choice of *The Human Adventure* as the title of this book and as the subject of Malraux's literary creation as a whole was inspired by the phrase "the human adventure" encountered in *Les Noyers de l'Altenburg*, Malraux's last published novel. The phrase struck me as an appropriate title for Malraux's complete works (and hence for a study of them) because it expresses the monumental task to which Malraux has dedicated his life and art: the penetration of the mystery and significance of man's sojourn on earth—his past, his present, and his possible future.

The justification for an interpretation of the human adventure as one unfolding according to the cycle of constant flux is derived from the same novel, or more specifically, from the title of its colloquium, "The Permanence and Metamorphosis of Man." The paradox created by the terms "permanence" and "metamorphosis" is resolved when we reword the title to read: "the metamorphosis of fundamental man." In other words, man is a being whose fundamental powers (those which all men have in common) are revealed as he undergoes one metamorphosis after another in the course of his journey through history. The conjunction "and" (rather than "or") of the original title permits the rewording; the revised title is the key to Malraux's notion of man as an evolving being. The connection between metamorphosis and the idea of the cycle is revealed in an applied analogy between the walnut trees of the title of the novel and fundamental man, both of which manifest, with the passage of time, the infinite diversity that may emanate from a single source. In the case of the walnut trees, suggestive of the tree of life, metamorphosis refers to the infinite variety of branches, leaves, and nuts which the same tree may bear with each successive revolution of the annual cycle—to say nothing of the different statues which successive generations of artists may carve out of its logs. In the case of fundamental man, or the first man, Adam, the same term refers to the infinite forms of expression which the powers inherent in the species may assume in the course of a single lifetime, a generation, an epoch, or the human adventure in its entirety as the cycle of time winds on its way.

The term "metamorphosis" reappears in the title of Malraux's latest volume on art, *La Métamorphose des dieux,* where it refers more specifically to the evolution of civilizations in terms of the changing "absolutes" according to which man has successively oriented his existence. "Metamorphosis" is not limited to the concept of a continually changing present; it also involves the idea of a continually changing past viewed from the perspective of an ever-changing present. A full interpretation of the title suggests a metamorphosis of man coinciding with the metamorphosis of the gods as manifested in the history of art.

The foregoing elucidates the reason why perhaps no contemporary writer is so open as Malraux to misinterpretation when an attempt is made to ascertain his metaphysical, ethical, or political views on the basis of isolated works. Since the appearance of his volumes on art, few would doubt that Malraux's prime concern is and always has been man. He is concerned with what man has been and with what he has done, with what he might be and with what he might do, with his origins and his ultimate destiny, with the forces which seek to destroy him and with his struggle to transcend them.

But it becomes increasingly clear that Malraux's vision is centered on the fundamental in man. His focus is directed to what men of all ages and regions have in common, rather than to what differentiates one man from another. His concentration is centered on man's *misère* and on his *grandeur,* and on his capacities for good and evil. As a compound of *misère* and *grandeur* Malraux's fundamental man is Pascalian; in his capacity for good and evil, he is Augustinian. In terms of his human condition, which involves him in a struggle between the opposing forces of human nature both within his own being and in the world, he is a combination of both: his life is a compound of anguish and hope.

Malraux's view of the human adventure unfolding in time bears much in common with St. Augustine's theory of human history as an endless struggle between the forces of good and evil or between the "City of God" and the "City of Earth" inhabited by the descendants of Abel and Cain respectively. Both Malraux and St. Augustine conceive of man's temporal existence in terms of one grand cycle (within which there are innumerable secondary ones) beginning with man's fall from a state of innocence. They do, however, differ as to where and how the cycle will end. Neither deems it possible to penetrate the ultimate meaning of human suffering and striving.

According to St. Augustine, the cycle beginning with the Fall (and the ensuing struggle between the forces of good and evil) will end with man's temporal existence and the separation, at the Last Judgment, of the two "Cities" into Hell and Paradise for all eternity. The originality of Malraux's vision lies in his far-off hope that man's *grandeur* will ultimately conquer, or at least subdue, the demon in him sufficiently to make it possible for all men to exist in unity in one human society modeled on St. Augustine's "City of God." Joseph Hoffman, in his book *L'Humanisme de Malraux,* informs us that Malraux himself named Pascal and St. Augustine as two of his main sources of inspiration: "When, in 1955, I informed Malraux of my plan to dedicate a study to his work and indicated to him my intention of doing it in a Pascalian perspective, he approved: 'You are right to begin with Pascal'—adding: 'But don't forget St. Augustine.' " [4] It is therefore surprising to find that Hoffman concentrates solely on the Pascalian aspect. The three capital events in Malraux's cycle, as in St. Augustine's, are the Fall, the Redemption, and the resurrection of mankind at the Last Judgment.

Malraux's literary creation as a whole embodies the hope that man will ultimately remember that the purpose of his sojourn on earth is to destroy Satan, the task forgotten by the seven deadly sins of *Lunes.* Foolishly they destroy Death, and with her the cycle of creation (in which the role of death is just as important as that of life —the one flowing endlessly into the other), leaving Evil, or Satan, rampant without the possibility of change and renewal as the means by which the creation or redemption of man by man may be completed in history. Malraux's hope is focused on Pascal's *homme-grandeur;* his aim is to awaken man everywhere to a consciousness of a *grandeur* hidden in the deepest recesses of his soul, to a divine spark ever-ready to be kindled into creative activity. This activity includes all acts that serve to defy a destiny imposed upon man; it comprises any action that manifests man's freedom in terms of a refusal to submit to forces denying his dignity or to a world offering no outlet for his creativity. In NA (169) Malraux speaks of "the nobility that men are unaware of in themselves," and of the soul as "the victorious part of the only animal who knows he must die."

The subterranean voices in Malraux are a metaphor of the constant *inquiétude* of Pascalian man, and of the forces within man which urge him to continue to grow and refuse him calm and repose. Life is movement—creation in perpetual progress. Malraux does for man throughout the ages what Montaigne does for the individual: he urges him to remain open to the infinite possibilities of his destiny. To man's quest for stability, Malraux opposes the cycle of constant flux without which the evolution of man would cease before the creation of man by man could be completed.

If Malraux's vision begins with his fundamental man as a combination of Pascal's and St. Augustine's, his ultimate hope is that *l'homme-grandeur* will triumph. If, in the world of the twentieth century, the evil in man finds full expression, and if "man against God" has become "man against man," there emerges from Malraux's works the nascent hope that "man against man" may, in the not-too-distant future, become "man for man."

Malraux's complete *oeuvre* spans the whole of man's

earthly existence, from the dawn of recorded history to a glimpse of the end of time. Viewed in their entirety his works constitute an epic of man.

The opening section of this study presents Malraux's volumes on art as a history of the human soul coinciding with a history of art in three cycles—from the sacred to the sacred, from the divine to the divine, and from the profane to the profane—up to the contemporary period, which sets the stage for the fiction where the human adventure, and hence Malraux's epic of man, enters a new phase.

As we venture into Malraux's fictional world, which runs parallel to the real world in that each novel centers around one or more of the crucial events of the first half of the century, we are increasingly convinced that Malraux's literary creation as a whole is dedicated to the penetration of the mystery of man living in a universe where everything, including man, is subject to the relentless cycle of flux from life to death.

The evolving contemporary setting of the novels destroys the comforting sense of tranquility provided by the traditional novel. It transmits to the reader an underlying mood of uncertainty and anxiety which emanates from characters embarked on a quest for meaning in a restless, turbulent world.

If the volumes on art reveal how men of distant ages and places have defied the implacable cycle of time which flows "certainly to death and only perhaps to eternity," Malraux's fiction—his novels in particular—enables the reader to witness contemporary man as he renews the age-old struggle against time and death. Malraux's seven novels are set forth as an organic unity; the first, *La Tentation de l'Occident,* discloses the crises and prepares the setting for the struggle which engages the heroes of the other six. The six full-fledged novels, which are presented as a "divine comedy" in an existential setting, form a cycle based upon an analogy between contemporary man's quest for identity and the spiritual journey of "everyman." It is a journey that begins with the hero's descent into hell (the prison of the self no less than that of the world) and ends with his intimation of a far-off Earthly Paradise. If there is tragedy in the implication that the "journey" or cycle will have to be repeated by each man and each generation throughout the course of human history, there is also the hope that progress is being made toward the ultimate creation of a world society where men may live in peace and dignity.

Thematically speaking, the cycle winds from the hero's discovery of the tragic finality of death to his rediscovery of the secret of life; as the two ends of the cycle meet, both life and death are viewed as parts of the incessant cycle of creation. This accounts for the recurring close association of the two concepts in Malraux's imagery and thought, not only in the novels, but in his works as a whole.

The six-novel cycle may be divided in half: three are set in the Orient and three in the Occident. The hero who unifies both halves is contemporary Western man. In the novels set in the Orient the hero's descent into hell begins; in the first two of these novels, *Les Conquérants* and *La Voie royale,* the focus is on the absurdity of life intensified by the finality of death. With the transformation of death into a meaningful part of life by the heroes of *La Condition humaine,* the first half of the cycle ends as the ascent is about to begin. In the novels set in the West the accent shifts from death to life. The ascent from hell begins with the hero's rediscovery of the simple life of every day; it progresses with a revelation of the secret of life; it culminates with an intimation of eternity and a fleeting glimpse of an Earthly Paradise marking the end of "the human adventure" in time. By the end of the cycle both life and death are viewed as playing equally important roles in the cycle of creation.

In order to fully appreciate the cycle of Malraux's novels, it is important to bear in mind that the entire spiritual journey of the contemporary hero takes place in time against a background of eternity, and that the metaphysical significance of the journey—viewed from the perspective of eternity—transcends that of the immediate temporal situations in which the hero is involved along the way. Considered thus, Malraux's cycle of novels forms part of the incomplete epic of man's life on earth, with the twentieth century as but a flash or close-up on the screen of eternity.

The structure of the six-novel cycle, in terms of historical time, winds roughly from World War I to World War II, which is also the time cycle of the last novel, *Les Noyers de l'Altenburg;* in terms of place, it begins with the hero's departure from France and ends with his return. The action of the cycle begins with the hero's break out of the closed prison cycle of a meaningless world and ends with his vista of a new world in the making—an everchanging world which he himself must fashion.

Malraux's hero changes names many times as his quest for identity continues from novel to novel. Inevitably—with the possible exception of *Le Temps du mépris*—there is the *cyclic* master-disciple relationship. As the disciple breaks with his master at the end of one novel, he prepares us for the next stage of the hero's journey in the following novel. It will be noted that the dominant theme or themes usually coincide with the hero's changing view of his world as his journey continues. From novel to novel, one theme moves into sharp focus while another fades into the background; one theme grows in intensity as another diminishes in importance.

Preceding the cycle of six, as mentioned above, is the epistolary novel, *La Tentation de l'Occident*. Counting this novel, which is set simultaneously in both East and West, there is a total of seven novels. The number seven points to an analogy with the seven days of the biblical account of the Creation. If the biblical account ends with a day of rest, Malraux's last novel ends with a war-weary hero longing for peace in the bright sunshine of the fields of Chartres.

The spiritual cycle of Malraux's fiction as a whole may be said to wind from darkness to light. The hero, who begins his existence with a basic concern for things of the world—he is born of the moon *(Lunes en papier)*, symbol of earth, night, and darkness—ends it with a spiritual revelation. The symbol of the spirit is the bright sun which intermittently permeates the darkness of *Les Noyers de l'Altenburg,* which ends with the hero's revelation of the secret of life and an intimation of "The Earthly Paradise." With this novel, first published in 1943, the divine comedy of the first half of the twentieth century is complete.

The fourth portion of this essay is dedicated to a study of "Le Musée imaginaire" and "La Monnaie de l'absolu" of *Les Voix du silence,* where the evolution of Malraux's history of art continues with the transformation, in the contemporary period, of the cycle begun in the Renaissance into a spiral winding upward and outward to embrace the globe. The spiral embodies both the possibility of a universal humanism emanating from the civilization of the West and the hope of the ultimate fusion of the numerous civilizations now existing simultaneously on different levels into one universal society which will make it possible for all men to experience "the honor of being a man."

The fifth and final portion of this book is a study of the cyclic patterns that link Malraux's latest work, Volume I of his *Antimémoires,* to its antecedents. The emphasis is on the metamorphosed vision of the future that emerges from Malraux's reexamination of his basic themes in the light of recent history (the end of World War II to 1965) and new experiences.

As one of the main objectives of this study is to present each work as a whole within the perspective of the total plan, I have sought to maintain the essentially linear progression of my structural design by avoiding, wherever possible, not only retrogression to works already analyzed, but also references to works in anticipation of their presentation within the plan of the whole. While the fiction is presented in the order of the date of publication, the sections on art follow the chronology of history. This means that the three cycles of Part I—from the sacred to the sacred, from the divine to the divine, and from the profane to the profane—are set forth horizontally—sacred, divine, profane, sacred, divine, profane—so as not to disrupt the continuity of history.

Notes

1. (Genève: Skira, 1945), p. 180. Henceforth cited as *Lunes.*
2. The break out of the cycle is "the gesture" in Albert Sonnenfeld's "Malraux and the Tyranny of Time: The Circle and the Gesture," *Romanic Review,* LIV, No. 3 (October, 1963), 199.
3. André Malraux, *La Lutte avec l'ange: Les Noyers de l'Altenburg* (Genève: Skira, 1945), p. 169. Henceforth cited as NA.
4. (Paris: Klincksieck, 1963), p. 27.

Part I
*The History of the Human Soul
in Three Cycles*

I.

The Sacred Art of Ancient Egypt

In *La Métamorphose des dieux,* Malraux links the earliest manifestations in art of the creative spark in man with the dawn of the human adventure; he maintains, "the power of artistic creation was initially that of giving form to what enabled man to become man, to escape from chaos, from animality, from his instincts, and from eternal Shiva." [1]

By way of elaboration one might say that Malraux's history of art begins with the exteriorization of the divine faculty in man in works of art expressing the latter's "awareness" of, or reaching out toward a power beyond, the world of time and appearances. Every masterpiece of art, according to Malraux, contains intimations of a transcendent world, even though the same work might also, and even primarily, reflect the visible world. The artist who succeeds in capturing and manifesting this absent world in his creation has found a truth, and in that truth both his soul and his style. In the successive worlds of truth which artists for thousands of years have erected in opposition to the world of appearances, André Malraux has traced the history of the human soul.

Corroborating the foregoing interpretation of the volumes on art is Malraux's own statement of purpose in Part I of *La Métamorphose des dieux* where he makes it abundantly clear that "the eternal part of man" (MD, 35) is to be the protagonist of his work, with other considerations playing necessary but secondary roles in aiding him to elucidate the mystery of his protagonist's incessant struggle to comprehend and transcend the human condition—to defy destiny:

> The purpose of this book is neither a history of art— although the very nature of artistic creation often obliges me to follow history step by step—nor an esthetics, but rather an inquiry into the significance of the presence of an eternal response to the question posed by the eternal part of man (MD, 35).

As will be seen later, each metamorphosis of the gods corresponds to a stage in the history of the human soul, whose richness and complexity are yet to be revealed as man continues his voyage through time.

What makes Malraux's books on art particularly rewarding is that he has achieved his purpose; he has succeeded in elucidating the mystery of "the eternal part of man," which emerges as the power which both enables and impels man to transcend his human condition, to break through the world of time and appearances to a truth whose discovery affords him a glimpse of eternity.

Nor is the discovery of such truths the exclusive privilege of either the artist or Pascal's man of faith aided by grace. Included along with them are all the heroes, saints, philosophers, scientists, and poets who have succeeded in transforming the chaos of experience from absurdity into a significance, that is, into a truth according to which man might, for a time, orient his existence.

The reproductions in the volumes on art range from

primitive to contemporary; they were chosen, Malraux tells us, for their power to manifest successful attempts at capturing intimations of the interpenetration of time and eternity: great works of art contain "reflections of mortal appearance but also those of another world"; they express "deliverance from the human condition and from time" (MD, 24).

The number and quality of Malraux's insights, which are the result of the energy, intuition, and knowledge he undoubtedly poured into gathering, assimilating, presenting, and interpreting his materials in his kaleidoscopic history of art as an "anti-destiny," provide the reader with a stimulating spiritual, intellectual, and esthetic adventure as he discovers, in art, one means by which man, throughout the centuries, has managed to transcend, in time, the limitations imposed upon him by destiny.

Malraux's history of the human soul unfolds in three cycles—from the sacred to the sacred, from the divine to the divine, and from the profane to the profane—set forth here, as indicated above, in the linear progression— sacred, divine, profane, sacred, divine, profane—to coincide with the chronology of history.

The first of the three cycles begins with the glimmer of the divine spark that brought Ancient Egypt out of the prehistoric night. The truth born of that glimmer was the revelation—in Egypt's tombs, sculpted figures, and mummies—of the eternity of death in a realm conceived as a metaphor of the positive aspects of the world of time and appearances. Ancient Egypt's world view revealed one of man's great triumphs over a destiny which would limit the significance of life to the brief span of man's earthly existence. In his interpretation of Egypt's truth, Malraux places the accent on her "discovery of eternity" rather than on death, and he urges us to do the same, lest the true significance of her sacred art elude us; the point is made in the following passage:

> . . . since we have ceased to make sepulchres of her tombs, our tendency is to think of them as country villas of the beyond, where her mummies, a people buried with its toys of clay or gold, enjoy an everlasting childhood. Yet this country is eternity, a time which is not that of man, not even the longest time of man. Egyptian art . . . grants the dead access to the eternal. . . . it transmutes appearance into Truth (MD, 9).

This art of Ancient Egypt and, indeed, any art whose forms suggest the existence of a universe separate and distinct from the manifest world, Malraux calls sacred art. He speaks of the sacred statue as "a figure delivered from the world of appearances" and of the sacred temple as "a place freed from the world that surrounds it" (MD, 18). Malraux maintains that Egypt's art represents a negation of the world of concrete reality, and hence of man's life in it, for its forms partake of the eternal, where death is truth, and life is appearance; he refers to the inhabitants of the Egyptian artist's world as "the living-dead of the Orient" (MD, 56).

Of particular significance, we shall soon find, is Malraux's qualification of the world view embodied in Ancient Egypt's art (and in that of the East in general) as static rather than dynamic: "The artists of the immobile civilizations of the Orient address themselves to a continuity without history, where generations succeed one another like generations of horses" (MD, 27).

Note

1. André Malraux, *La Métamorphose des dieux* (Paris: Gallimard, 1957), p. 25. Henceforth cited as MD.

2.

The Divine Art of Ancient Greece

The history of the human soul continues, and the second of the three cycles begins, with a revelation of the divine element of the universe in the art of Ancient Greece. While the East sought the secret of what lay beyond the cosmos, the Greek quest was directed to the secret of the cosmos itself. Malraux defines this secret as the essence of all that exists, as "the inalterable part of ephemeral appearance, the divine part of all life, as Man is the divine part of man" (MD, 80).

While the sacred communicated man's subjection to the eternal, the divine expressed man's declaration of freedom from that subjection—a declaration which marked the birth of Western civilization and the Western image of man. Whereas the Egyptians, who had opened the gates of eternity to the dead, considered the problem of destiny resolved for all time, the Ancient Greeks, who conceived of death as the end of the human life cycle, posed the problem anew: they shifted the focus to the domain of the living; they reduced all things to "the measure and intensity" of a human life.

In reopening the question of destiny—the forces over which man feels powerless—Greece gave birth to the first rebel hero, Prometheus, the archetype of Western man, determined to turn life to account, to emerge victorious over Destiny rather than submit to her. In place of the passive being of the East, Greece introduced the active hero of the West; in lieu of the unhistorical world view of the East, Greece introduced the concept of the future and the germ of an evolving vision of life in time. The following passage describes the birth of man as a creative being conscious of his ability to alter the scheme of things: it is the image of a man no longer content with "being" (*être*) but insistent upon "doing" (*faire*):

> What appears then for the first time—and not for the last—is a world in which man dares to draw his supreme values from his dreams and demands of himself what he can *do* in order to harmonize with them, rather than what he must *be* in order to harmonize with the eternal. "Future centuries," proclaims Pericles, "will say of us: they have constructed the happiest and most illustrious city state!" What king of the East would not have been surprised by that fraternal pride? Eternity is little concerned with the future (MD, 59–60).

As Malraux's study of art progresses it becomes increasingly apparent that his esthetics is inseparable from his notion of man as an evolving being. It is an esthetics directly related to the successive truths which man, in the course of history, has set up in defiance of Destiny. Malraux enables the reader to arrive at an intuition of the esthetics of a period or of an artist by providing a series of insights into the nature of the truth manifested in the art in question, and by indicating the means by which the expression of this truth may be recognized. Of paramount importance is the relation of a particular truth to the question of time. In his history of art, Malraux reveals that man's hopes, in a given period, are focused on one of three worlds of time: the eternal, the immortal, or the temporal (the ephemeral), corresponding, in art, to the sacred, the divine, and the profane, respectively. All art in Malraux's study falls, to a greater or lesser degree, into one of the three categories: sacred, divine, or profane.

It has already been noted that the sacred manifested the antithesis of the real: it depicted eternity rather than time, or truth in the world beyond as opposed to appearance in this one. The divine incarnates a realm situated between the profane and the sacred, that is, between time and eternity: "Greece, who knows no true sacred, knows no real profane: all life is imbued with the divine, and all that is divine enhances the life that embodies it" (MD, 52–53). This intermediate realm is that of the immortal, where Malraux situates the forms of the divine along with the gods that inspired them.

Since the immortal is the source of the artist's inspiration, it is not surprising to find Malraux rejecting the term "anthropomorphism" traditionally used with reference to the Greek gods: "The word 'anthropomorphism' explains nothing, because the nature of the ancient gods rests on a fundamental ambiguity: they are humanized but not human; they live neither in time nor in eternity" (MD, 53). Some pages later Malraux reinforces this rejection when he asserts that the divine emanated not from the human, but from the immortal, and that the Greek artist conceived of the domain inhabited by the gods as an inaccessible realm which lay beyond his reach—one whose existence he strove to manifest in his creations:

We have long believed that the Greek sculptors had wanted their gods to resemble men; the whole evolution of Hellenic art indicates the contrary. The

divine proceeds from the gods to man, not from man
to the gods; in all the arts that claim Athens as their
birthplace, human figures resemble the gods; the gods
do not completely resemble mortals (MD, 64).

In Ancient Greece, the gods represented the external
or internal forces of Destiny over which man felt powerless. Knowledge of these gods came to the Greeks through
two of their greatest poets, says Malraux, and he identifies
his source as Herodotus: "It was Homer and Hesiod who
gave the Greeks a theogony, the gods their names, their
realm of activity, and their powers; it was they who made
the gods' faces familiar" (MD, 57). As far as this theogony
is concerned, Malraux maintains that if the Greeks practiced a religion, as evidenced by their recourse to prayers
entreating divine assistance or intervention, they never-
theless had no sacred book and no concept of eternity.
Nor did they have a Judge or a Creator. Homer's epics,
in which the Greeks discovered the nature of their gods,
became their national book. In Homer, these gods were
depicted as humanized but not human, and as powerful,
but not all-powerful, for they, as well as the men over
whom they so capriciously ruled, were subject to the same
thrall of Destiny. According to Malraux, their powers
were superior in degree but not in kind to those of human
heroes. Immortal but not eternal, these gods were granted
an extended existence of doubtful duration in the shades
of the underworld.

Having no concept of eternity, the Greeks sought the
divine element in the universe—"the inalterable part of
ephemeral appearance" (MD, 80). As a concept, the "universe" was inseparable from its "order" and its "beauty,"
hence, the Greeks used the same word "cosmos" to designate all three. To those of their creations which embodied

the divine element, the Greeks granted a share in the immortality allotted to their gods. This attribution of the value of immortality to the products of human creativity must have struck a resounding chord in the soul of Malraux, for it emerges as one of the dominant themes not only of his volumes on art, but of his literary creation as a whole.

> After the arts [those of the East are] distractedly installed in eternity, the people whose gods are but immortal, and who know of no survival other than that of the shades, invent the immortality of great human creations, because they partake of the divine which they embody (MD, 80).

Creations imbued with the divine are by no means limited to the plastic arts; they are found in the literature of Ancient Greece as well. Indeed, Malraux traces the origin of the vision of the divine to Homer, the author of the Greek epics. How does Malraux enable us to arrive at an intuition of the divine? At one point he maintains that while any epic poet might have recounted the incidents of the Trojan War, it required Homer's genius to fuse them into a creation revealing the divine. On another occasion, he describes the statue of Aphrodite—an illustration from the plastic arts—as "a radiant figure, inseparable from her splendor" (MD, 53). "Radiance" and "splendor," then, are qualities emanating from figures imbued with the divine. Elsewhere (MD, 59), Malraux distinguishes the attitude engendered by the divine from that inspired by the sacred. He uses the term "adoration" to define the Eastern attitude toward the sacred or the world of "eternal truth," and the word "admiration" to describe the feeling of the Greeks for their gods who were merely immortal. Malraux deepens our insight by contrasting the reactions of the beholder of the divine with those of the beholder of the sacred: he suggests the term "enthusiasm" to define the emotion aroused by the divine, and the word "prosternation" to describe the attitude to which the sacred beckoned its beholder.

Of even greater importance than the role of Homer's epics was that of Greek tragedy, which, according to Malraux, for the first time in the history of the human soul, succeeded in breaking the thrall of destiny which had held man in its sway in the East for over three thousand years. Malraux's interpretation is original both in terms of the poet's achievement in his creation and in terms of the effect of tragedy upon the spectator. He rejects the term "catharsis," widely used since Aristotle to define the experience of the observer after witnessing a tragedy, at least insofar as this term implies an identification of the spectator with the tragic hero. To the notions of depression and despondency generally regarded as descriptive of the viewer's reactions to tragedy, Malraux opposes the term "exaltation" to describe the emotion with which the spectator leaves the theater; it is this emotion which explains the latter's eagerness to return again and again to see the same play. But why should a tale depicting human bondage or man's subjection to his fate exalt the spectator? The answer, Malraux intimates, is that the poem has transformed the poet into a master of destiny—into the positive counterpart of his tragic hero: "Its cause [that of exaltation] is far more profound than a participation in thrilling legends; it is the discovery that poetry—poetry, and not what the poet relates—speaks to Destiny as one equal to another" (MD, 62). The implication is that the spectator who experiences exaltation identifies himself not with the submission of the tragic hero to his destiny but rather with the poet's victory over, and subjection of, destiny in his creation: "In tragedy destiny becomes the subject of art, in both senses of the word" (MD, 63). Thus, the image of man born of Greek tragedy marks an advance over the one born of the Homeric epics; Malraux is very eloquent on the subject:

> But it is striking that for the first time, through the Atrides, lyrical power confronts what no human power had ever confronted. The capital event is the appearance of tragedy itself, of the world in which tragedy is transformed into poetry for the first time— of the world in which man sets himself on a par with destiny, master of the gods, as he had formerly set himself on a level with the gods, masters of men, in the world of Homer (MD, 63).

To the imaginative powers in man which set him first on a level with the gods and then on a par with destiny, Greece gave the names of the Muses, which have since been used to designate man's creative powers.

In terms of the history of the human soul, the contribution of Ancient Greece might be expressed as the emergence of *man* as a being distinct from the universe— a being on a par with destiny by virtue of his creative powers. The word "man" is emphasized to suggest the "species," because Malraux is emphatic about the fact that Greece did not give birth to the individual: "in spite of the inscription of Delphi and the injunction of Socrates, the Greek knows himself but little, and is little concerned about knowing himself" (MD, 59).

What Greek tragedy actually seems to have discovered, according to Malraux, who, however, does not state so explicitly, was the power and dignity of Pascal's "thinking reed," as the following variation on the Pascalian theme will attest: "In a world where that which is not governed by man has assumed, through him, so many radiant forms, tragedy chooses to give form to that which crushes him; but in it [tragedy], he ceases to be crushed" (MD, 62).

To comprehend the power of man expressed in Ancient Greece and appreciate the striking contrast between two world views, one need only call to mind the pyramids, the sphinxes, and the mummies of Egyptian art and set them side by side in one's "imaginary museum" with one of the supreme contributions of Greece—her *Winged Victory (Niké de Samothrace).*

Malraux expands his acknowledgment of our indebtedness to Greece when he says that though "Greece invented neither joy nor youth she was the first to celebrate their glory [in art]" (MD, 56); and he further heightens the distinction between the Greek world and that of Asia in speaking of the dance: "Seen from Asia, Greece is a flutter of veils. We owe her the dance—what we call the dance, and not ritual ballet" (MD, 56).

Thus far the movement away from the sacred has been expressed in terms of the greater closeness of the divine to the human, but Malraux makes it clear that the divine is still in the realm of the inaccessible—a realm above and separate from that of man:

The gods are at once the Others and the Admirable Ones. Were they but others, they would not be the Olympians; were they but admirable, they would be no more than heroes.

The goddesses partake of a beauty of a divine order

(a beauty which marks their distance from mortals, not their resemblance to them) in the same way that they partake of a power which can not be confused with royal power (MD, 63–64).

Yet, by virtue of the creative act, Greek man not only shared the immortality of the gods but also achieved victory over Destiny, the master of the gods. Indeed, Malraux's oft-quoted phrase, "with the destiny of man, man begins and destiny ends" [1] expresses precisely what happened in Ancient Greece.

With reference to the world view born in Greece, Malraux suggests that while it may be considered an advanced stage in the evolution of the human soul, it must also be viewed as simply one of many human possibles, since both the sacred and the divine emanate from the same source: "The Eternal and the immortals are not born of the *same part of the soul;* but the immortals and the heroes *who rival them,* can be born only of a *soul* forgetful of the Eternal" (MD, 57) [italics mine].

Not until the sacred world of "eternal truth" had receded into the background could the Greek rebel hero have made his appearance:

Before its evidence [that of the sacred] as despotic as original sin will be in the Middle Ages, the exaltation of a rebel hero was inconceivable—even Aeschylus' Prometheus would have been sacriligeous. Never had the awesome silence of the sacred heard laughter before "the inextinguishable peals" of Olympus (MD, 57).

Note

1. André Malraux, *Les Voix du silence* (Paris: Gallimard, 1951), p. 73. Henceforth cited as VS.

3.

The Profane Art of Hellenistic Greece and Ancient Rome

The movement away from the sacred continues as Ancient Greece is superseded by Hellenistic Greece, where the divine is slowly conquered by appearance. Art, which hitherto had been inseparable from the transcendent world it incarnated, was now becoming a value in its own right. Once this happened, profane art, which might be defined as an art independent of any religious orientation, was born. Even before the fall of Athens, the age of the makers of the gods was gradually drawing to a close. Malraux refers to Praxiteles as "the last maker of goddesses at a time when the makers of the gods were disappearing" (MD, 89).

The validity of the gods of the city had been called into questions by Socrates, by Euripides, and by the sophists even prior to the conquest of Greece by Alexander. With the advent of Alexander and the Hellenistic period, mystery again took root in Greece. As the Hellenic Greeks began to participate in the orgies and ecstasies of the Dyonisian cults, they gradually relinquished their position as the equals of Destiny. Their gods, stripped of the divine, became statues, and the images of their gods, which were once those of a religion, became those of a culture.

*

Art, which no longer served the divine, began to serve appearance. Athena, once a goddess, was now looked upon as an idealized woman. Little by little "resemblance to appearance" became the sole criterion for determining the worth of all art: "Behold appearance promoted to the rank of respected judge of images stripped of the divine, as it will be promoted scornful judge of sacred images stripped of the sacred" (MD, 91).

It was during the Hellenistic period, too, that the canons for art criticism were set down. These canons, which were first adopted by Rome and later by classical Europe, resulted in the rejection of, and disdain for, any art which did not have as its aim the imitation or idealization of the real. The severe style of the sacred was looked upon as a stage toward illusionism, and the genius of Olympus as an awkward attempt at representation. Statues which had been gods were now looked upon as objects, independent of the visions of which they were born.

The Hellenic Greeks hailed Lysippus as their greatest sculptor, for it was he who aimed at suggesting life by depicting movement; it was he who declared: "I depict what I see" (MD, 95). With Lysippus, says Malraux, the creation of the divine ceased. Statues which succeeded in communicating the illusion of life became works of art. One cannot help being struck by the distance between this art and that of Egypt which, in the rigidity and monumentality of its forms, sought to destroy appearance and create the illusion of a world of truth and eternity.

Speaking of Lysippus, Malraux says that the stiffness (*raideur*) he sought to destroy was that of the divine just as the early Greeks had sought to destroy that of the sacred. But the life that Lysippus sought to suggest was only that of mortals, for "one cannot imagine a sacred god similar to the figures of Lysippus, nor even an Olympian: he would have lost his divinity" (MD, 92).

With the sculpture of Lysippus, art as an independent value superseded art as an expression of the sacred or the divine, and with this supersession, the first world of esthetics, based upon a concept of beauty derived from the world of statues, came into being. It was not long before a wide variety of figures from the visible world were first idealized by the new world of esthetics and then granted entry to it. Malraux designates this transformation of the profane (the visible) by the world of beauty to which it was to belong as the most significant contribution of Hellenistic Greece to the evolution of art:

> [The statue] acquires significance only in the world of sculpture, and the artist could not undertake his work without reference to it; the statue does not pretend to capture reality except in order to belong to an esthetic world—to a world of fiction unknown to humanity up to that time (MD, 96).

The movement away from the divine, well underway in Hellenistic Greece, was completed in Ancient Rome, where the eternal and the immortal were obliterated by the world of time. Malraux says that "for the first time, a major art recognized the world of appearances as the order of the world, for the first time the order of appearances coincided with Truth" (MD, 106).

When Malraux asserts that Roman art did not endeavor to manifest transcendent truth and was not art in the true sense of the word, he seems to restate what he deems to be the essence of all real art—its power to forge a link between this world and a transcendent world. Malraux's denigration of Roman art is forcibly expressed when he states that "Rome conquered Greece and Olympus, but she did not conquer the divine; she will invent, without suspecting it, a parody of divinization. . . . she makes sacrifices to unknown powers, but knows no communion with them" (MD, 100). And, on the same page, he continues: "Without Greece, her gods would be without images; for her, no secret soul of the world calls forth Apollo or Aphrodite."

What, then, did Roman art express? What became of art in Rome? In Hellenistic Greece the world of esthetics constituted its own *raison d'être,* but Malraux declares that, in Rome, art was legitimized by the object, and the object by its function. As examples, he cites Rome's invention of the arch of triumph, whose purpose was to remind the vanquished of her victories, and of the column, by means of which she recounted these victories to herself.

Malraux makes a distinction between the "realism" of the Hellenic Greeks and the "reality" of the Romans. In the following passage he seems to imply that while the Hellenics sought to create the "illusion of the real" or to suggest life, the Romans endeavored to "embellish reality" —to enhance the image that served as the model: "In spite of what Roman sculpture owes to Greek, in spite of idealization, the former is separated from the latter by a reality which is not related to illusionism . . ." (MD, 105). "Art's goal is no longer to destroy the order of appearances, but to adorn it" (MD, 108).

The "reality" of the Romans is mentioned particularly in connection with the special type of portraits which they invented—portraits of the dead resembling the living: "a reality which all art had rejected for three thousand years, and for which the word "realism" by no means accounts—a reality which we reëncounter, present but invincible, in the most idealized Roman sculpture" (MD, 102). While the artists of both the sacred and the divine considered the portrayal of the individual as the work of artisans and therefore as unworthy of their powers, those of Rome made "objects of art" of the portraits of their illustrious dead men.

In Rome, the gods who had once formed parts of sanctuaries or temples were used to adorn gardens. Art, which had been religiously oriented for centuries, now became theatrical. The State became the supreme value, and Roman art, such as it was, was dedicated to it. Malraux says, "the superficial stylization which Rome derived from appearances put propaganda, battles, and ceremonies to the service of the decor of the state" (MD, 108). But if Malraux denigrates Roman art, he does not depreciate Rome's contribution to the grandeur of the human adventure: "Her theatrical Hellenism expresses in its style neither the grandeur of Rome nor the implacability of the Romans . . ." (VS, 614).

Rome's main contribution to the history of art was her conquest of appearance—a conquest which proceeded from the Hellenistic texts containing the standards of beauty according to which all art was supposed to be judged.

With the barbarian invasions and the collapse of the Empire from within, a whole world was passing out of existence, but as it did, and in the ensuing darkness, the light of the sacred was being rekindled by the spread of Christianity, which was to bring the wheel from the sacred to the sacred full cycle.

4.

The Rebirth of the Sacred

The focus remains on man's evolving view of his position in the scheme of things as Malraux's history of the human soul continues in the period which witnessed the rebirth of the sacred.

The Greek image of man on a par with the gods and Destiny, and the art, first divine and then profane, which had manifested that image, died with the empire. As the world structure which had sustained man's victorious image of himself crumbled about him, man once again became a victim of Destiny, a victim seeking release from his human condition. Threatened with destruction in the chaotic age of imperial decline, man began once again to reach out for the Other World of the sacred.

Malraux links man's quest for deliverance during the Great Regression which spread over the world of the dis-integrating Roman Empire with three major forms of expression in art: Buddhist,[1] Byzantine Christian, and Western Christian or Romanesque. These three forms of expression coincided with the aspirations of the respective religions. Now that man and his world had been devalued, all three strove to reject the world of appearances and to depict once again the Other World of the sacred. Reality, which had been equated with truth in Rome, was now declared a mystery. Christian and Buddist artists alike began to transform the profane forms they inherited into sacred forms embodying the world visions of a new epoch.

> Over the dying empire, the gods reëstablish their invincible domination. What died with the Empire was profane art. The smiling faces of Attica, the self-assured faces of the Capitol were as foreign to the desert, the forest, the catacombs, and to the nocturnal world of the stars and of blood, as Plutarch was to Saint Augustine. Art, which was once again seeking sacred forms, sought to escape the human as stubbornly as it had wanted to attain it in the sixth century.[2]

The dialogue between East and West, begun by Egypt and Ancient Greece, enters a new phase with the metamorphosis of the gods of antiquity into Christ and Buddha. But the dialogue is not limited to Buddhism on the one hand and Christianity on the other; it is also maintained between the Christian East (Byzantium) and the Christian West. Malraux reveals how three world visions—Buddhist, Byzantine Christian, and Western Christian—all born, at least in part, of the death of the Empire, ultimately diverged. While Western Christian art evolved in a cycle beginning with the decline of the profane and ending with its rebirth, art in Byzantium and in the nascent Buddhist world of Hellenized India continued, for more than a thousand years, to manifest the eternity of the sacred, to express a relatively static world view expressing a single solution to the human predicament.

Byzantine and Buddhist art began with the metamorphosis of the Greek god Apollo, while the Roman god Hermes served as the model for the West. In each case the metamorphosis began with the sign, proceeded to the human, and culminated in the divine: in Hellenized India, Apollo became first a sign representing a sage, then the human Siddhartha, and finally the divine Buddha; in the Christian world Apollo (in Byzantium) and Hermes (in the West) became first a sign representing the good shepherd, then the human Jesus, and finally the divine Christ.

Photographs of the sculptures illustrating the metamorphosis of Apollo into Buddha [3] offer cogent evidence in support of Malraux's thesis suggesting the continuity (though not steady) of civilizations as opposed to Spengler's thesis affirming their isolation. According to W. M. Frohock,[4] Malraux had declared his intention of refuting Spengler to Emmanuel Berl as early as 1928. In *La Métamorphose des dieux*, Malraux reaffirms his determination to repudiate Spengler by advancing not only the idea of continuity but also that of progress in human history: "Perhaps the first planetary civilization will produce the first history of the human race. But a 'continuous' history, whether it be that of the conquest of the elements by man, or that of the creation of man by man, postulates a progression, though it be interrupted by tragic setbacks . . ." (MD, 31). Charles D. Blend, in his book *André Malraux: Tragic Humanist*, submits Malraux's repeated use of the terms "metamorphosis," "resurrection," and "renaissance" as evidence of his intention to refute Spengler's theory of closed cycles of civilizations,[5] and W. M. Frohock maintains that *La Psychologie de l'art* is Malraux's *"rational refutation"* [6] of Spengler. I hope to show even further that Malraux's complete works are a rejection of the Spenglerian thesis.

The photographs of the metamorphosis of Apollo into Buddha are especially persuasive in confirming Malraux's theory of historical continuity, since they reveal the combined influences of three civilizations—Chinese, Greek, and Buddhist—before the transformation is complete.

In their quest for the Other World of the sacred, Buddhists and Christians alike began with a determination to annihilate the world of appearances. They sought to destroy the illusion of freedom in the Greek forms and to obliterate any suggestion of the human from the art of the ancient world. Of this attempt Malraux says, "they do not imitate life badly, they refuse to imitate it; they insist upon metamorphosing or transcending it" (CA, 36). Malraux is even more explicit with regard to the Byzantine artists:

> The latter represent neither what they see, nor a chosen fragment of the world surrounding them, they represent their possession of an imaginary world—a supreme negation of the ephemeral.
>
> Their style is born of the compelling need . . . to represent the superhuman by means of the human (CA, 51).

The Buddhist artists pursued this course in an attempt to depict the sage, who, through meditation, finds serenity, which enables him to forget the world of time and experience the sensation of merging with the cosmos—with the absolute or the eternal. In order to achieve their purpose, the Buddhist artists transformed a "living" Apollo into a serene, motionless Buddha. They eliminated the Greek smile and illusion of movement; they transformed the rounded contours of the Greeks into sharp ridges. The lowering of Apollo's eyelids to express meditation, says

Malraux, was perhaps the supreme revelation and final expression of the Buddhist view of the world, for it was through meditation that the sage achieved a sense of temporary liberation from the thrall of destiny in the guise of the endless cycle of reincarnation in time:

> Reincarnation—unknown to primitive India—had dissolved everything in the limits of time; it had diluted all life in its eternity. And Indian destiny had been so heavy (how forcefully the Buddha had uttered: "Escape the Wheel" . . .) (CA, 25).

Once again the human soul had found a means of defying destiny, of releasing man from his human predicament: "The expression on the faces of the Buddhist statues is that of a deliverance, and that of a man who has found deliverance . . ." (CA, 25). In the following passage Malraux describes the gradual completion of the metamorphosis of Apollo: "From the life of one sculptor to that of another, Apollo hardens or thickens his planes which become more and more abstract; he lowers or closes his eyes, and refines his world-forgetting smile" (CA, 37).

And the theme of liberation from the cycle (though not that of reincarnation as in the case of the Buddhists) is the starting point of Malraux's heroes—men of action and artists alike. For them the cycle represents a destiny imposed from without rather than one forged by themselves; it represents a prison from which they must escape. This is true both of the historical cycles into which they are born and of their own life cycles which physical death would terminate.

If the Buddhist found release from the world of time in the sensation of merging with the absolute, the Christians were to see in Christ their means of escaping the ineluctable flow of time toward death. Through Him, they would pass from time to eternity in the hereafter: "for all, Christ was the One *against whom the irremediable could not prevail*" (MD, 224).

What the Byzantine Christian artists set out to achieve, in their attempt to release man from his human predicament, was the elevation of the human toward the divine in the hope of reaching God. They considered it pointless to portray either man or appearance now that both had been stripped of value; they endeavored instead to manifest, once again, that Other World of truth. Malraux illuminates the whole concept of the sacred when he says that, for Byzantium, "*God* is elsewhere . . . out of the world" (MD, 185).

In order to achieve their aim, the Byzantine artists had to discover a new style, and, far from belittling their achievement, Malraux maintains, "as much genius was necessary to forget man in Byzantium as had been required to discover him on the Acropolis" (CA, 50).

In Byzantium the Eastern sanctuary was to reappear as the incarnation of the Other World toward which man's striving was now to be directed. Saint Sophia, with her cupola, symbolized that world set apart from the manifest world—Saint Sophia, which Malraux designates as an "outpost" of another world:

Before being the discovery of a style Saint Sophia is the creation of a place delivered from the world of appearance, though that world might be majestic.

The different techniques by means of which churches will become outposts of another world matter little: mystery has found a medium of expression though that mystery was in the soul before it became a style (MD, 136).

Even within the sanctuary, the Byzantines, in their paintings, pursued their negation of the "reality" of the Ancient Roman world:

> And in order that Truth be represented, it had to escape the real world. It was no longer a question of depicting the world, but the Other World. . . . Whence the gold background, which creates neither real surface nor real distance, but another universe; whence that style which remains incomprehensible as long as we insist upon seeing in it a pursuit of the real, for it is always an attempt at transfiguration (CA, 54).

For more than a millennium this use of dark and gold backgrounds suggestive of the eternal was to be one of the dominant expressions of Byzantine Christian art. And the figures of this art were further set free from appearance by virtue of both their size and the abstractness of their bodies. Malraux cites two examples as supreme expressions of Byzantium's attainment of the sacred: the *Torcello Virgin,* sunk into the "other universe" of a dark cupola where she stands majestically aloof from the world, and the gigantic *Christ Pantocrator,* who seems to dominate the whole creation. He goes on to say that "these two figures for which the art of representation could do nothing, . . . could only have been born of its death . . ." (CA, 56).

In Byzantium, Christ and the Virgin were completely

transfigured, entirely liberated from their human biographies; they were transformed into symbols of the Other World where they were destined to remain while the West gradually broke away from the sacred and thus resumed the dialogue with the East. Comparing the Byzantine Virgin with ours, Malraux says:

> Our art will show us . . . all that Byzantine art at first refused the Virgin: the maternity of the manger and of the cross. And also what it gave her: the pathetic symbol it made of her by stripping her of her biography (CA, 55).

The implication in the following quotation is that Byzantium was removed from the West not only because of its affinity with the spirit of the East but also by virtue of its greater closeness to the Orthodox world of the Old Testament:

> The spirit of Byzantium is the relentless striving to flee appearances, the reaching out toward a Nirvana where man attains God instead of blending with the Absolute. In Dostoyevsky, as in our Middle Ages, this absolute will become charity. In the West, the prophets will become saints: the saints of Byzantium were prophets.
> That is why Christ, who is so different from the saints in Rome, becomes so like the prophets in Byzantium; Christ is the absolute Prophet (CA, 56).

The Virgin, in Byzantium, underwent the same transformation: "she became the feminine expression of the Prophet" (CA, 56).

In counterdistinction to the lamplit darkness of the Byzantine sanctuary—that world apart—Malraux speaks of the role the stained-glass windows of Western cathedrals were to play in establishing a communion between the Church and the whole of the created universe. He refers to these windows as a prelude to the manifestation of God in His entire creation: "With the unchanging glimmer of the lamps, with the eternity of *Being (that which is)*, the stained-glass window mingles the intrusion of the sun, of the seasons, the eternity of the ephemeral (that which passes) . . ." (MD, 184). The eternal "that which is" and the ephemeral "that which passes" represent the polarities of the dialogue between East and West. While they remain separate worlds in the East, they eventually fuse in the West.

Malraux begins his study of Western Christian art by revealing the new notion of man which gave rise to it and which it in turn revealed. He does this by contrasting the Christian view of man and his relation to the absolute with the Ancient Roman way of seeing the world. Malraux's study of Western Christian art also sheds more light on the dialogue that developed between East and West—between Byzantine and Western European Christianity.

Perhaps the most striking and enduring contribution of Western Christianity to the evolution of the human soul was its internalization of destiny, that is, its awakening of man to a consciousness of his dual nature: evil as a result of original sin, and good by virtue of the divine origin of his soul. Through this revelation, which gave rise to a private struggle within each man, Malraux implies that Western Christianity (not Greece or Rome) gave birth to the individual: "the western Christian bears the most imperious fatality within him, and it is in the deepest

recesses of each heart that the hands of Christ, still crucified by the very nature of man, bring anguish and pity
with the individualization of destiny" (CA, 61). The
image of man engendered by this revelation was to direct
the course of our art toward an increasingly greater
emphasis on life in time, for salvation had to be won on
earth:

> This individualization of destiny, this involuntary or
> unconscious trace of a private drama on each face,
> was to prevent Western art from becoming similar to
> either the ever-transcendent Byzantine mosaic or to
> Buddhist sculpture, ever athirst for unity (CA, 61, 64).

Malraux had already voiced his view of the Christian imprint on man's soul in his "D'Une jeunesse européenne,"
where he affirmed that "of all the marks we bear, that of
Christianity, made in our flesh, in our very flesh, like a
scar, is the most deeply traced." [7] In the same passage, he
continues with the awakening of man by Christianity to a
consciousness of his divine origin on the one hand, and
of his fall on the other. The resulting inner conflict
(*désaccord*) is the essence of his own Pascalian-Augustinian
image of man:

> With the vestiges of the soul, the Christian scar
> imposes upon us the idea of the unity of man, the
> idea of his permanence and of his responsibility; with
> original sin, . . . this same scar founds its strength on
> the acute consciousness of our inner discord (JE, 135).

Christianity transformed the free man launched by
Greece and emulated by the Romans, who endeavored

through some form of steadfastness (courage, intelligence, decision, fortitude) to stand firm against the cosmic flux of forms, into a being who looked upon himself as a sinner dependent solely upon Grace for defense against the impermanence of all earthly things subject to the cycle of constant flux from life to death. It becomes increasingly apparent that Malraux views the history of the human soul as an incessant struggle against mortality, against a destiny which would limit man's significance to the brief span of his temporal existence.

In addition to the internalization of destiny through the revelation of man's dual nature, the strong individualism of Christianity is also due, and in no small measure, to Christ's historicity—to his human biography. Christianity was founded on specific events which had as their purpose the redemption of all men. Jesus was born of a fully human woman and He Himself combined the human and the divine—both man and God. The ancient Romans had equated truth with reality, while the Christians equated appearance with life, but declared that truth was a mystery. This mystery could be penetrated only through grace, through participation in divine love. To assuage man's consciousness of original sin, Christ brought his message of love, with the result that anguish and hope were to be the dominant and conflicting emotions underlying the life of every Christian—and of Malraux's heroes. Man's thoughts now went beyond the Roman world of appearances and even beyond the mystery of the cosmos, which the Greeks sought to explain, to the possibility of eternal life in the hereafter through salvation, which Christ's death made accessible to all, from the lowest to the highest. The success and rapid spread of Christianity is attributed to the fact that it introduced what amounts to the equality of all men before God:

The first Christian preaching in Rome was invincible
because it told a slave, the daughter of a slave, who
hopelessly watched her child, born in vain, die:
"Jesus, the Son of God, died, crucified on Golgotha,
so that you might not be alone in this agony"
(CA, 118).

Western cathedral art, says Malraux, brought a similar
message to the faithful in disclosing the Christian mission
to reach all men: "the tympanum portrays the sending
of the apostles to the nations . . . they proselytize the
pygmies, the dog-men . . ." (MD, 195). The authors of
these scenes are also credited with bridging the gap between man and the Eternal by "introducing men into the
world of God" (MD, 198).

In the following passage Malraux defines and illuminates the supreme message of Christianity to the world:

The revelation is expressed in three flashing words:
God is love. But this love is not human love, it is
sacred love; it partakes of the mystery of the Eternal.
The Revelation brings not an elucidation of this
mystery, but rather a communion with it (MD, 134).

Elaborating on the widening of the schism between
East and West, Malraux points out that Byzantium ig-
nored the human aspects of the Christian story, aspects
that were to be depicted in Western art as it evolved:

This theology [that of Byzantium] does not recognize
a biography of Jesus, but rather a series of manifestations of God through Christ. It therefore condemns,
in Arianism, the movement toward a man called

Jesus and insists that the Virgin is the mother of God, and not the mother of Jesus (MD, 146–47).

Romanesque art, the first main phase of the Western Christian cycle, like Byzantine art, began with the evolution of the sacred sign into the sacred symbol: the figure of Christ emerged as a symbol superseding the signs of the cross and the fish. As in Byzantium, the Romanesque Christ was set free from appearances; he was a symbol of that Other World from which man felt alienated and toward which he reached out: "the great Romanesque work of art was created to release the sentiment of the sacred, to manifest the inexpressible" (MD, 211). The Romanesque Christ in the West is described as a figure "ten times greater than the other personages, [a figure who] imposes the necessary Presence and the fundamental meaning. At Moissac, at Autun, and at Vezelay, he dominates the tympanum by virtue of his size . . ." (CA, 73).

Malraux's disclosure of the spirit of Romanesque art is achieved by relating it to, and distinguishing it from, both that of Byzantine art and that of the Gothic art that followed it. He puts the spirit of Romanesque in an intermediary position more or less equidistant from both: "Compared with Byzantium, Romanesque art is of the New Testament, and compared with Gothic, it is of the Old . . ." (CA, 73).

The remoteness of God manifested in Romanesque art is attributed to St. Augustine, for whom "original sin (and its consequence, the human condition) had separated man from the 'incommunicable mystery' of the Eternal, which reached him only through Grace. This mystery had governed Carolingian faith; it was still governing Romanesque faith" (MD, 223–24). Whereas Byzantine art tended toward abstraction, where it remained, Romanesque began with the abstract but gradually moved toward a humanization of the sacred by way of the saints. Malraux reminds us, however, that the Romanesque world was still a sacred world in which God remained aloof from men. It remained for Gothic art to bridge the gap, that is, to bring God to man through the intercession of Christ, a figure no longer symbolic of the sacred, but at once wholly human and wholly divine: "it is not the human which is to disappear in the art of their Gothic successors, it is the sacred" (MD, 213).

Notes

1. Malraux refers to the emergence of Buddhist art in Hellenized India where Apollo was metamorphosed into Buddha.
2. André Malraux, *La Psychologie de l'art*, Vol. II: *La Création artistique* (Genève: Skira, 1949), p. 20. Henceforth cited as CA.
3. These photographs appear in both *La Psychologie de l'art* and VS, but not in MD.
4. *André Malraux and the Tragic Imagination* (Stanford University Press, 1952), p. 151.
5. (Columbus: Ohio State University Press, 1963), p. 168.
6. *Op. cit.,* p. 151.
7. *Escrits, Les Cahiers Verts,* No. 70 (Paris: Grasset, 1927), p. 135. Henceforth cited as JE.

5.

The Rebirth of the Divine

As we move from the Romanesque world to the Gothic, we enter the second phase of the Western Christian cycle: the Romanesque sacred gradually evolves into the divine (imaginary) Gothic. The gap between the world of God and the world of man disappears through the mediation of Christ, who suffered and died to redeem all men. Gothic art evolves from a manifestation of Christ's tragedy to a manifestation of His victory. As the emphasis shifts from the Fall to the Redemption, mystery gives way to love, and adoration to communion.

The Christian man of the early Gothic period is portrayed as a tragic figure conscious of the Fall and of his responsibility for the suffering of Christ, and Gothic art seeks to manifest this tragedy in its style:

> The face of each man bears its trace of original sin; the form of wisdom [in Buddhist art] was unique, but the forms of sin have the infinite multiplicity of creatures; carved on every Christian face is a pathetic experience, and the finest Gothic mouths resemble the scars of life (CA, 61).

In fact, Malraux maintains that until the great period of Christian art, the face was but a mask from which all evidence of life was absent: "When, in a museum, we arrive at the Gothic halls, we seem to encounter the first real men . . . Gothic art unmasked man" (CA, 65). In contrast to the stamp of suffering on the Gothic face, Malraux maintains that the faces of classical statues "meet in the same assured triumph, in the self-same conquest of what were once fatalities" (CA, 61). And he compares the portraits of Roman patricians, whose faces bear no sign of suffering, to those of prematurely aged children.

As Gothic art evolves, Christ Crucified gradually becomes Christ King—a king who is portrayed crowning the Virgin; Malraux makes particular mention of "Christ crowning the Senlis Virgin" (MD, 222).

Paradoxically enough, Malraux draws an analogy not between the world views of the apogee of Greek art and the Renaissance, but between the Ancient Greek world view and that of the great period of Gothic art which brought the wheel from the divine to the divine full cycle. He designates the thirteenth century, the period of the apogee of Gothic art, as an era of peace on earth—at least to the extent that man viewed life and his role in it as meaningful and comprehensible. The disorder and subdivision of feudalism, which characterized the Romanesque period, gradually gave way to the order and stability which the Church and monarchy were to attempt to bring to man's existence, the former to his inner life and the latter to his life in the world. The Gothic world was an ordered hierarchy with the king as its temporal head, the pope as its spiritual head, and God at the summit of all. The world order was dedicated to, and in large measure modeled after, the world of God. This included the orders of the knights of chivalry.

The transition from the Romanesque world to the Gothic world also represents a transition from the world

of "being" to the world of "action," the latter representing, for Malraux, the true spirit of the West. The implication is that with Gothic art the break with both the Old
Testament and the Eastern world of being is complete:

> The Romanesque Christ is; he appears on the tym-
> pana as God, a symbol of the ineffable and a mani-
> festation of the world of Being. Beginning with
> Senlis, he *acts;* and the crowned Virgin replaces the
> *Majesté.* What belonged to God as God has
> disappeared (MD, 218–19).

With the Gothic reduction of Christ's figure (Chartres)
to human dimensions, Romanesque symbolism in Christian art came to an end:

> The Christs of the Romanesque tympana dominated
> the human figures that surrounded them—and not
> only by virtue of their size; that of Chartres does not
> dominate his prefigurations, but blends in with them.
> The liberation that the Chartres Christ summons
> will mark the end of symbolic expression . . .
> (MD, 218).

The canonization of St. Louis (a human figure in
whom the temporal and the spiritual were combined) is
in harmony with a vision of a sanctified humanity. The
world of God and the world of man have been fused and
henceforth art will seek to manifest the divine element
(as had Greece) in all that exists. Gothic at its apogee is
once again a world of human values. Contrasting it with
the Romanesque revelation of God's world apart, Malraux
writes:

But sacred art manifested the world of God, not that of man; sentiments which had no reference to God were absent from it, as they are from the sacred (MD, 244).

Whereas the imaginary [Gothic] is a world of human values. In the imaginary world of Truth these values become the privileged means of praising God (MD, 246).

It is in relation to the reappearance of the smile at the apogee of Gothic art that Malraux indicates the completion of the cycle from the pagan divine to the Christian divine: "The metamorphosis is complete: the smile is going to regain its right of access to the City of God" (VS, 242).

Malraux identifies the figures of Gothic art with the inhabitants of one of the cities in St. Augustine's *magnum opus:* "It is the City of God that Gothic sculpture brings to the faithful, as Romanesque sculpture had brought it the sacred: Gothic art is populated by the redeemed" (MD, 233). Elaborating on the subject several pages later, Malraux says, "Gothic art is the first revelation of the City of God, and, for this reason, it is far removed from any art that preceded it and from all art that will follow it. When this revelation ceases to be its goal, the function of art will change. Even if Gothic cathedrals continue to be built" (MD, 250).

In spite of the smile on its angel, Rheims already foreshadowed the Renaissance in its figure of Christ as a King marked by suffering. The smile, according to Malraux, represented a brief glimmer of concord before the dissension of the Renaissance was once again to disrupt man's ordered concept of his world: "Although Rheims is the

divine city transformed into a Sanctified Fairyland, its
Christ King already bears the signs of the suffering majesty
that will supersede him" (MD, 257).

Two figures, St. Francis and Giotto, are designated
as the precursors of humanism. Each introduced into the
prevailing world view of the period something which was
to overshadow, for a time, the smile at Rheims and un-
settle the hierarchic structure of the Medieval world. St.
Francis in his teachings, and later Giotto in his paintings
(including the cycle of St. Francis' life) injected into the
age a new spirit which began to shift the focus to man's
terrestrial existence, to his suffering no less than his joy.
This new spirit, which effected a transformation in man's
attitude toward God and the world, was to culminate in
the elevation of man's estate; it was a spirit that marked,
at one and the same time, the culmination of Gothic and
the beginning of the Renaissance. The widespread influence of St. Francis is attributed to the fact that he was
"a saint independent of theology" (MD, 243): his teachings inspired an all-encompassing love for God, man, and
the whole creation; they breathed new life into an age
characterized by a consolidated hierarchy of values.

The saint of Assisi's vision, embracing both a humanization of grief and a pantheistic view of the creation, had
the effect of increasing the importance of man's life in
time—its sorrow no less than its joy. While St. Francis'
humanization of grief tended to draw men together into a
Christian brotherhood striving for communion with
Christ's victory, his pantheistic vision of the world nour-
ished the growing sense of Gothic exaltation which prefigured the humanists' emphasis on life in this world. The
depth of St. Francis' love is perhaps most fully expressed,
says Malraux, in his *Canticle Blessing Our Sister Death*—
a blessing which could emanate only from a being deliv-

ered of fear and inspired by trust in the victory of Christ's
Redemption of all men.

Giotto, whom Malraux hails as the first independent
artist in the modern sense (he was also the last master
craftsman), represents, at one and the same time, the culmination of Gothic art and the art of transition leading
to the Renaissance. In Giotto, the emotional energy of
Gothic found release. It was he who discovered, in the
South, what had already been done in the North; namely,
that emotions could be rendered by depicting their external manifestations. The smile at Rheims found its companion in the "tear" which appeared for the first time in
Giotto's portrayal of St. Francis' sorrow: "the fourteenth
century discovers for suffering what the smile is for joy"
(CA, 87). And Malraux refers to Giotto's Christ Crucified
as "the sad brother of the Angel of Rheims" (CA, 87).
Psychology began to replace the symbol in Giotto's paintings; his figures openly express their emotions; they look
at each other and employ dramatic gestures. Giotto's paintings, no less than the art of the cathedrals and St. Francis'
teachings, manifested the evolution of the Gothic spirit
from a concentration on the tragedy of the Crucifixion to
a focus on the hope made possible by Christ's suffering and
death: "Nothing was more alien to the Romanesque soul
than this sentiment of an accomplished Redemption, this
effacement of the Eternal through communion in Christ's
victory" (MD, 232).

The Christ against Giotto's early gold and later blue
backgrounds is a savior uplifted from the world of men:
he is a savior reminiscent of the aloofness of the Byzantine figures of Christ. But the human is also uplifted to
the divine in scenes depicting man's role in aiding Christ
in the continuation of the Redemption; the faces on all
of Giotto's figures, including the humblest, are idealized

and radiate a divine light. Whereas early Christianity interiorized destiny, Giotto, Malraux seemingly implies, interiorized the divine in his paintings. When he imbued his figures with a divine light expressive of communion with the sacred love of God, Giotto introduced a new phase in the evolution of Western Christian art:

> Medieval art had been the first great art of the particular: Giotto's figures no longer depict the individual. Idealization, by means of which each face tends toward the divine, is substituted for the divine stamp that Gothic art had imposed upon each face (CA, 102).

When Giotto united Byzantine reverence (Christ aloof from men) and Gothic love, he did so by proclaiming the dignity of man's estate: "he was perhaps the first Christian artist whose faith granted each Christian his share of majesty" (CA, 102). Malraux speaks of the divine light emanating from Giotto's figures as though it represented a Christianization of the radiance and splendor shining through the figures of the Golden Age of Greece and maintains that the completion of the cycle from the divine to the divine, foreshadowed at Rheims, is realized in Giotto's Padua:

> Idealization reappears each time that man is reconciled with destiny: on Olympus as at Rheims, at Rheims as at Padua, at Padua as in the China of the Tangs. . . . The fraternal world of which Franciscanism was but the clearest symptom joined the fleetingly reconciled world of the apogee of Gothic art (CA, 102).

Giotto's idealized Christian is a man in harmony with his world, a man who has reacquired the mastery, but not the pride, of the Roman. While the ancient Roman sought to cultivate virtues which would make him self-reliant, the Christian is ever conscious of a power higher than himself.

The most significant contribution of Giotto to the spirit of the new epoch was perhaps his depiction of scenes "suggestive" of natural ones. Giotto's scenes marked the introduction of the sacred, heretofore represented as a separate universe, into a world "resembling" the earth. The terms "suggestive" and "resembling" are indicative of Malraux's distinction between what he refers to as Giotto's "suggestion of nature" and what the Renaissance artists misinterpreted, in the light of the new age that was coming into being, as Giotto's "imitation of nature." Malraux asserts that natural scenes were not the direct source of Giotto's inspiration. His mountains were said to have been modeled after rocks set up on a table, while the intense, solid blues of his skies, which descended the length of his paintings without any indication of a horizon line, represented not the natural skyscape but rather its transfiguration into an imaginary realm in which elements of the sacred and the profane were fused to concreate the divine.

> Giotto does not copy the sky of man, he makes of it, for the first time, the sky of Christ. He discovers a *power of painting* unknown in Christian art: the power to situate, without sacrilege, a sacred scene in a world resembling that of men (MD, 337).

Because of the "suggestion" of the world of men in

Giotto's scenes, the Renaissance was to confuse his "religious fiction"—scenes situated in a *divine* realm and manifesting events partaking of the sacred—with an attempt at imitating, in painting, dramatic scenes enacted on earth. This pictorial fiction of the master of Padua, says Malraux, not only supersedes the narrative art of cathedral sculpture but also fulfills it.

Malraux also credits Giotto with the inauguration of composition and the introduction of figures into "photographically" centered scenes bordered by window-like frames. His statue-like figures not only contributed to the revival of antiquity (an age which had excelled in sculpture) but also anticipated the third dimension, the conquest of which was to establish the goal of Western painting as representation for a long time to come.

Giotto's "suggestion of nature" as the setting for scenes radiating the divine had a special appeal for the artists of the nascent epoch, for it not only heightened (even if unintentionally on the part of Giotto) the importance of man's world, but also harmonized with the changing faith of the early Renaissance—a faith from which the world of transcendence was being eclipsed by the visible world.

The artists of the new age were to admire Giotto mainly as a forerunner of illusionism (imitation of nature), which they came to regard as the true goal of the art of painting and hence as the criterion according to which excellence was to be judged: "The Renaissance recognized Giotto as having genius, but it considered him awkward—and it attributed everything that brought him close to illusionism to his genius, and everything that separated him from illusionism to his awkwardness" (MD, 322–23). It will be remembered that a similar criterion came into existence with the profane art of Hellenistic Greece.

6.

The Rebirth of the Profane

The entire Christian cycle which began with the death of the profane in Ancient Rome is completed in Renaissance Rome—after an initial phase in Florence—with the rebirth of antiquity. Rebirth here is meant as renewal rather than mere revival: Malraux uses the term "metamorphosis'" as distinguished from "return": "With Florence on the decline, *the cycle* opened by the death of Ancient Roman forms *closes in Rome,* after more than a thousand years, not with a return to antiquity, but with its metamorphosis" (CA, 106).

The Renaissance came into being between the wane of Medieval Christendom and the Reformation, between the breakdown of feudalism and the rise of national monarchies, and during the transition from a predominantly rural to an increasingly urban way of life. If the thirteenth century brought the Gothic period to its point of highest fulfillment, the fourteenth century, says Malraux, was characterized by a breakdown in all phases of the world structure, religious, political, social, and economic. There was a movement away from the religiously oriented Medieval world structure to a much greater concentration on the mundane.

The rise of new monarchies, which were largely a consequence of the growth of cities, soon relegated the

Holy Roman Empire to history; the monarchs, who had begun by defying imperial authority, ultimately challenged papal authority as well. It was Philip the Fair who exchanged places with Pope Boniface VIII as head of the social structure. Malraux explains how this switch from a spiritual to a temporal ruler at the summit of the hierarchy was made possible:

> The conflict between Philip the Fair and the Papacy would probably have taken a different course if the Italian banks had not assisted the king: Western Christianity discovered the power of money. This capital event is, however, linked to the end of the civilization in which the domain of the mind was inseparable from that of faith (MD, 284).

Faith, which for centuries had governed and ordered men's lives, began to lose its creative force as the unifying element of human existence. More and more, faith came to be regarded as but one, albeit important, aspect of life and the Church as one, albeit important, part of the kingdom.

None of the Gothic cathedrals were ever completed; Malraux explains this phenomenon primarily in terms of the nature of the Gothic quest: "Gothic art is the expression of the divine only because its striving to conquer it is never completed" (MD, 267). Malraux also mentions the roles of the Hundred Years' War and the Black Death in bringing an end to the creative spirit of the High Gothic period.

New churches supplanting the Gothic cathedrals soon came into existence. These churches with their radiating chapels and honeycombs of oratories attested to a change from collective to private worship. Malraux draws an analogy between the breakdown of communal faith and the collapse of an empire.

The age of private versus collective devotion was one in which monasteries became places of refuge from the world, and in which hermits' huts made their appearances at the gates of Paris. The Christian individual was becoming increasingly aware of his separateness.

The secularizing trend was well under way by the end of the thirteenth century. As the heir of the knight was superseded by the royal heir, as national languages began to replace Latin, and as court figures (already playing a prominent role in the new literature of the time) began to appear in psalters, the world of transcendence receded into the background. Malraux refers to the Psalter of St. Louis as "the first Christian art that signifies nothing" (MD, 272). Psalters of the period, in general, attested to the victory of the court poet, Chretien de Troyes, whose literary figures—lords and ladies of noble rank—began to replace the denizens of the City of God. Christian art which did "signify something" began to focus, but not exclusively, on the theme of suffering. This theme, which was foreshadowed as early as the Christ of Rheims and deepened by the teachings of St. Francis and the paintings of Giotto, reached an intensity of expression in portrayals of the suffering and death of Christ—and of men.

Contrary to the age of the Church Triumphant (the Gothic age), which culminated in the transmutation of Christ's tragedy into the victory of His Resurrection, the new era was characterized by a growing obsession with personal sin and guilt which set the stage for the reappearance of the devil. In connection with the fourteenth-century Flagellants, Malraux says, "it seems that He [Christ] has just died a second time" (MD, 295). In art, the "Pieta" superseded images of Christ the King. With the growing emphasis on the human, the Son of God was looked upon, more and more, as the divine Son of Mary. With the shift in emphasis from His victory to His suffering and death, faith became compassion: "the world in which the Eternal appeared and the one in which Christ Crowned the Virgin were effaced by the world of men in which the Mother contemplated her dead Son" (MD, 295).

In addition to suffering, incarnate in portrayals of the Passion of Christ, art also depicted its antithesis, joy, and indeed combined both in manifestations of the life of His mother, Mary: "No order of grief succeeds the hierarchies governed by the Divine Majesty; this world in which the Mother contemplates her dead son is also the one in which she plays with her living child" (MD, 296). Fourteenth-century art manifested both the suffering and joy of earthly existence: images of the *Virgin and Child* offset images of the *Cross and Black Death*.

Of considerable importance to the evolution of art was the fact that the increase in private as opposed to communal worship was accompanied by the desire to possess the object of worship: crucifixes came to be admired for their "artistry." When the "object" of art—even though it was still religious—became as important as its "subject," the cycle from the profane to the profane was about to be completed: "All civilizations discover their profane art when they discover art as a value in its own right" (MD, 243). The artist was to become increasingly aware of his own creative power and begin to reveal his identity.

As the humanistic movement of the Renaissance progressed into the fifteenth century, the shift in the focus of man's hopes from eternity to time was increasingly manifest in the art of the period: religious subjects, formerly limited to divine personages or the redeemed of mankind, began to embrace the whole of creation; the divine, once an imaginary realm, began to figure in the world of appearances.

Malraux directs our attention to what amounts to an interpenetration of time and eternity; he points to a religious art which became increasingly profane on the one hand and to the emergence of a profane art which began to stake its claim on eternity—to transform art into an "anti-destiny"—on the other. Renaissance art began to depict a fusion of the here and the beyond, of the world of appearances and the eternal City of God. For the first time in the history of Western art, the sacred—God the Father—was annexed by the world of time.

In a passage contrasting the painting of the early Renaissance with the art that preceded it, Malraux enables us to intuit the spirit of the new epoch:

> Compared with both the cathedral, whose major figures represent only divine or redeemed personages, and the frescoes of the Campo Santo, fifteenth-century painting seems to portray a remission of the entire Creation, a redeemed world into which the trees of Flanders and the streets of the Florentines enter, with the procession following the Magi, to join the saints, the shepherds, and the chosen animals (MD, 351).

When Malraux ends the foregoing passage describing the optimism which characterized the new age by saying, "But it seems that the divine can no longer be expressed except through the world of appearances" (MD, 351), we know that the revolution of the cycle from the divine of the apogee of Gothic art to the profane art of the Renaissance is underway.

It was in the North—in fifteenth-century Flanders—that the world of transcendence finally yielded to the earth; it was there that Flemish painters began to represent "reality" by introducing geographically recognizable Gothic cities as backgrounds in their religious paintings. In Flanders, what concerned God transpired first of all in the world of man. Malraux points out that, as opposed to Giotto, "the Flemings who paint mountains do not imitate pebbles" (MD, 351). These painters also discovered the horizon line, a discovery which marked a significant step forward in the Renaissance conquest of "reality."

But it was not only the landscape *per se* that suggested the real world in Flemish painting—it was the depiction of time. Malraux suggests that the Flemings' discovery of the means of rendering light suggesting the time of day was perhaps their greatest contribution to the evolution of painting, and he points out that the Flemish artist's light differs from the natural or artificial light that had formerly illuminated religious figures; he makes it abundantly clear that the depiction of light suggesting a time, but not an hour of the day in the painting itself, was an original discovery of the artists in fifteenth-century Flanders—a discovery which probably occurred at about the same time in Italy. The emphasis on time (as opposed to eternity) in the Renaissance world view was now depicted in painting:

> For the mosaic, the light [candlelight] was that of the sanctuary; for the stained-glass window it was the living light of God, just as it was for the statues, for sculpture knows no hour other than the one that

illuminates it. In the fifteenth century, fictitious time joins fictitious space. Light passes from God to the painter (MD, 355).

This fifteenth-century light, which still formed the setting for religious scenes, did not yet forecast the profane time of the impressionists. The importance of the discovery lay in the fact that once religious scenes began to figure in time, the death knell of eternity as a separate universe was sounded: "Art invents a time that welcomes the figures of eternity . . . into space, shadow, and light" (MD, 356).

While it is true that Flemish settings, where the divine was expressed by appearance, no longer represented an imaginary world as did Giotto's "sky of Christ," Malraux maintains that the figures in Flemish paintings represented not a faithful rendering, but rather a metamorphosis of the models which no doubt served as a starting point. Van Eyck's painting of St. Joseph is cited as an illustration:

> One does not admire Van Eyck more than one admires Giotto, but differently: the admiration that Van Eyck inspires is addressed to his power both to express the divine through appearance and to introduce appearance into a world that metamorphoses it; his reality is not one in which St. Joseph is similar to a carpenter, but one in which a carpenter becomes St. Joseph . . . (MD, 361).

It was the statue-like appearance of their figures that continued to link the Flemings with the preceding age. Fifteenth-century art inaugurated not only the depiction of time but also the annexation of eternity by time. This happened when artists dared to portray the Eternal Being, God the Father, in a scene whose setting was the world of time. The significance of this event is interpreted in a passage comparing the figure of the Almighty with the spiritual and temporal rulers of the manifest world:

> At the beginning of the 15th century, there appears an image, without precedent, of a debonnaire or majestic Old Man whose attributes are sometimes those of the pope and sometimes those of the emperor: an image of God which marks one of the capital dates in the spiritual history of the Western world, for it goes without saying that this image expresses not the sudden entry of the Eternal into the world of art, but the annexation of the Eternal by the world of man (MD, 353).

Malraux reminds us that, antecedent to this event, the Son, but not the Father, figured in art: "God had been represented in a symbolic (the Carolingian hand) or allusive fashion; He had created man through the Word, and, even in Byzantium, Eve issued from the body of Adam before a figure of Christ" (MD, 353).

Malraux seems to suggest that the interpenetration of time and eternity characteristic of fifteenth-century art worked both ways: when religious scenes began to figure in time (represented by the light of the painter), portraits of living men, independent of any religious significance, began to stake their claim on eternity.

The Renaissance portrait painters were the first to deliver living figures from time. Time, here, is synonomous with history or with man's period of exile on earth as a consequence of the Fall. By granting his models—living beings—access to the world of art which transcends the historical time of the individual's life span, the artist was liberating them from the human condition; in so doing, he introduced a new phase into the cycle of Western Christian art that began with the fall of Rome.

Malraux underscores the metaphysical significance of these portraits by distinguishing them from the arts that preceded them:

> The portraits of the living were irreconcilable with the sacred, for through them man escaped time. For Christianity and Judaism, time is what is born of original sin; for all religions, it is the mark of the human condition. The sacred arts had liberated from time only those figures which belonged to the sacred— those of the priest-kings and the dead; and Christian art liberated only those which belonged to God (MD, 367).

Flemish portraits came into existence, not as the result of the artist's submission to reality, but as an outgrowth of religious fiction: they were born of the isolation of figures of donors from religious scenes. Malraux emphasizes the fact that the isolation of these figures preceded and eventually inaugurated the painting of portraits of living persons in a secular context. These portraits marked the rebirth of a profane art devoid of any religious significance:

> These pictures were destined neither for churches nor for Bibles . . . nor even for Books of Hours. Born of religious fiction, these portraits were no longer related to it: they no longer derived their value from any service to God (MD, 368).

Of considerable consequence for the history of art was the new type of painting that came into existence with the portraits of donors: "It was not reality that the painters discovered in the margins of religious fiction, it was the easel picture" (MD, 370).

It is in connection with several Flemish and Italian portraits that Malraux mentions the rebirth of a profane art independent of any religious significance and speaks of a metamorphosis of the role of art. He attributes this metamorphosis, defined as the artist's obscure consciousness of his power to rival the creation, to the admiration inspired by these profane portraits. Malraux makes particular mention of the portrait of Jean de Leeuw by Van Eyck, whom he qualifies as the first Christian painter to paint a donor who donated nothing. Malraux also designates Van Eyck as the first Christian painter who wished, or knew how, to represent his own wife. Before his time, images of living persons had figured in painting only by virtue of what related them to God: "When Christ and the Virgin disappear, the world of painting welcomes Margarite Van Eyck" (MD, 369).

Gradually the mysterious power of the artist will subsume the subject. Malraux refers to "the enigmatic power that the development of profane painting renders more and more apparent" (MD, 370).

The growing awareness of this power to create is accompanied by a metamorphosis of the role of art into an "anti-destiny," that is, into the artist's means of defying destiny by rivaling the creation. What is important at this point in Malraux's history of the human soul is the artist's consciousness of a power which all artists had always possessed, but which had been subsumed by the world visions their art embodied. This new consciousness will enable the "human" hero to achieve, in some measure, what has always been his aim: "The hero always wishes, to some degree, to escape from the human condition—the condition that Christ chose to assume" (MD, 373). Malraux explains why the concept of a "human" hero "consciously" rivaling the creation is without precedent in Western history up to this time:

> The military character of feudalism causes us to forget that the Bible is a sacred book *without heroes*. The hero, absent from the New Testament by its very nature, plays a very small role in the Old. The latter attaches less importance to the Maccabees than to the Prophets (MD, 372).
>
> The courage and strength of Roland and of Perceval, set them in opposition to obstacles or enchantments; the superhumanity of Hercules or of Prometheus sets them in conflict with the order of the world. For the Church, a conflict with this order could only be a struggle against original sin or Luciferian pride; the Church recognized no superhumanity other than sainthood and no sainthood without grace (MD, 373).
>
> Admiration was completely legitimate only when inspired by acts accomplished in the service of God: from the thirteenth to the fifteenth centuries, the Church condemned tournaments to the point of envisaging, on several occasions, refusing its assistance to those who succumbed in them. Man could be transfigured only through spiritualization. . . . We must be somewhat attentive in order to be consciously aware that the domain in which he [the unsainted knight] would become a hero did not yet exist (MD, 377).

The emergence of art as an anti-destiny is the outstanding achievement of the Renaissance both in the

North and in Italy. But Malraux maintains that Italy's contribution surpassed that of the North in this domain; he mentions this particularly with respect to the revival of the pagan themes of antiquity in the painting of each. He maintains that while Flemish painting recognized only what exists—and therefore could welcome Venus only as a woman—Italy painted Venus because she did not exist— in other words, as a creature of the imagination. Malraux singles out Botticelli's *The Birth of Venus* as the first painting in which creatures of the human imagination appear in the august company of the divine.

> . . . the Venus of Florence brings with her a domain which Christian art had never known: the unreal. It was the domain in which the Christian, for the first time, dared to set up the images of his dreams in rivalry with those of the world of God (MD, 379).
>
> It was the pictorial world in which Venus could become a rival of the Virgin, the nymph a rival of the angel—and the imaginary, a rival of the Divine City (MD, 382).

7.

The Elaboration of the Profane

The High Renaissance

It was in Ancient Greece that man first began to question the scheme of things; it was there that the human soul ultimately broke free of the subjection to the eternal imposed upon it by the static East. It was in Greece that man declared himself an equal of the gods and even of destiny by virtue of the creative act; and it was there that profane art—art as a value in its own right—was born.

The reemergence of the Greek spirit of inquiry became one of the distinguishing features of the Renaissance. Once again, man was to attempt to refashion the universe according to human laws. If the struggle of Greece was directed against the East, that of the Renaissance was directed against the Oriental elements of Christianity— elements which made of man a submissive rather than a creative being. As in Greece, art in the Renaissance was once again to become an end in itself; the cycle of profane art begun in the Hellenistic period was to complete its circle by the end of the Renaissance.

In "Le Musée imaginaire" of *Les Voix du silence* Malraux writes of the achievements of Greece in the most glowing terms. He begins with her discovery of the richness of the human spirit which marked the end of the single, static world view characteristic of the East—a view which held that man's only means of release from the human situation was to blend with the unity of the cosmos. He continues with a description of the man-oriented world view her art disclosed:

> Greek art is the first which seems profane to us. In it the fundamental passions acquired their human quality, exaltation began to be called joy, for even the depths became those of man; the sacred dance in which the Hellenic figure appears is that of man finally liberated from his destiny (VS, 73).

And of those statues which represented the culmination of the Greek liberation of the human spirit Malraux writes:

> The entire cosmos humanized its elements, forgot the stars; in contrast to the petrified slavery of the figures of Asia, the unprecedented movement of the Greek statues was the very symbol of freedom (VS, 74).

One of the most frequently quoted passages of *Les Voix du silence* is the one in which Malraux cites the Greek artist's acanthus as an example of man's capacity to equal or surpass the creation: "Every artichoke bears within it an acanthus leaf, and the acanthus is what man would have made of the artichoke if God had asked his advice" (VS, 74).

The same theme is reiterated in another frequently quoted passage in which Malraux refers to the Greek nude as "one a god might have created, had he not ceased to be a man" (VS, 74). During the Renaissance the nude was to

reemerge as the medium for the expression of the sublime.
The eclipse of the Greek smile was destined to last
almost a thousand years. During the initial phase of this
period, Ancient Rome was to strip the art it had inherited
of its spirit and produce one which had nothing in common with the image of man that Rome herself had
bequeathed to the world—an image of a man who had
mastered destiny by virtue of his own indomitable spirit.

In contrast with the materially oriented civilization
of the Empire, Christian culture in Medieval times was
essentially a culture of the soul; its sources were the Bible
and the writings of both the saints and the Church Fathers.
In terms of its orientation in time or history, it belonged
exclusively to a present opening only to eternity. The
Renaissance, on the other hand, harked back to the past
to emerge with that smile, refashioned in its own image,
which announced man's reconquest of a position he had
abandoned when what remained of Greece collapsed with
the Empire:

> Each time that the smile reappears, something of
> Greece is ready to burst forth—from the smile at
> Reims to that of Florence; and each time that he
> becomes king, man in harmony with his world has
> reconquered the fragile royalty of the obsessive and
> limited kingdom that he conquered for the first time
> on the Acropolis of Delphi (VS, 78).

But before man could reign supreme once again he
had to undermine, if unconsciously, the forces which had
held him in their sway. Malraux maintains that from the
eleventh to the sixteenth century man had been passing
from Hell to Paradise through Christ. The completion of

the cycle from Ancient Greek to Renaissance humanism required a metamorphosis of man's attitude toward himself and his world; this metamorphosis, underway for a long time, culminated with a proclamation of the perfectibility of man. Malraux says that the day Nicholas of Cusa wrote " 'Christ is perfect man,' *a Christian cycle closed* [italics mine] at the same time as the gates of hell; the forms of Raphael could be born" (VS, 84).

The forms of the High Renaissance represented a harmonious fusion of the Christian present and the pagan past. The path to this reconciliation of man with his world was achieved by a reconquest and transfiguration of the ancient forms that were most in accord with the Christianity of the period.

Regarding Renaissance art in general, Malraux asserts that there can be no doubt that the "imitation" of things and beings became a value, but he also maintains that there has been a tendency to confuse what was actually a "convincing expressing of fiction" with a representation of reality:

> That art, which was so concerned about its means of imitation and which attached so much importance to "rounding out" its figures, was not at all a realistic art: it strove to be the most convincing expression of fiction—of a harmonious imaginary world (VS, 70).

In this connection Malraux refers to Botticelli's and Lippi's works as "suppositions": "All fiction begins with 'Let us suppose' . . ." (VS, 70). He distinguishes them both from Medieval works, which he qualifies as "affirmations," and from those of Leonardo—especially his *Last Supper,* which he designates as a "sublime tale." The transition from Medieval "affirmation" to the "sublime tale" of Leonardo coincided with the transformation of Christianity from a "faith" into a "religion."

It must be pointed out, however, that if the themes of Renaissance art—that is to say, of its painting—were fictional, there can be no doubt that its settings and figures suggested an "illusion" of reality. According to Malraux, the influence of Leonardo was far-reaching in this domain: it was he who completed the conquest of space begun in the ninth century by virtually liberating his figures from the canvas: "The power of illusion that Leonardo brought to the painter, at the moment when a weakened, soon-divided Christianity ceased to subject the testimony of man to the invincible stylization that is inseparable from every presence of God, was to orient painting in its entirety" (VS, 69).

Surprisingly enough, Malraux treats Michelangelo only briefly and in passing, even though the few allusions made to the Titian's works leave no doubt that he is appreciated as the towering genius of the Renaissance. Malraux's limited treatment is centered mainly on Michelangelo the sculptor. No sculptor after him, according to Malraux, was able to rival the first place held by painting as the supreme medium of artistic expression from the Renaissance to the present. Malraux refers to the Titan's works as marking the end of great Western sculpture until the agony of academism. He designates Michelangelo as "the last sculptor that can compare with the masters of the Acropolis, of Chartres or of Yun-Kang" (VS, 87); he speaks of him as an artist who "exhausted his genius not in approaching the past but in breaking with it" (VS, 87). In "La Création artistique," Malraux asserts that this victory over the past is the mark of all true genius.

The equilibrium and harmony achieved by Raphael

in his works brought Renaissance painting to the point of its highest fulfillment—the point beyond which it ceased to be creative. The painting of Raphael represented not only a fusion of pagan and Christian themes (or a confusion of the imaginary and the religious) but also a synthesis of the techniques developed during the period. These techniques were designed to enable the artist to approach the attainment of a "fixed ideal of beauty" based upon the ordered harmony ("the divine proportion") of the human body.

Beginning in the midsixteenth century, academies of art which formulated the components of this "fixed ideal of beauty" began to appear on the scene in increasing numbers. As the constituents of the "ideal" were more and more clearly defined and accepted, the function of art, according to Malraux, was radically altered. Ceasing to give expression to any conception of the world that linked man to God or to the cosmos, art became culture, and culture, in turn, became the mistress of art. The logical corollary was the birth of art criticism with the cultivated man in the position of highest critic—"not because he loved painting, but because he loved culture" (VS, 85). Once culture became an absolute value, art was subordinated to an idea of civilization; its function was to adorn reality and dreams with the consequent abandonment of its own intrinsic values.

This "fixed ideal of beauty" which Malraux prefers to call the "fixed rationale of beauty" was not limited, as a criterion, to the plastic arts but was considered applicable to literature and music as well—indeed, even to life as a whole.

During the High Renaissance, then, culture emerged as *the* value directing the lives of the privileged few to whom it was accessible, and *le beau ideal* was set up as the goal "which the artist did not create but attained" (VS, 85).

It was not until the nineteenth century that art was to break free of the restrictions imposed upon it by this formulated esthetics—"founded on what one believed to be the Greek heritage" (VS, 15)—and rediscover that freedom which is the *sine qua non* of true creativity. The great artists of the intervening centuries—with the exception of Rembrandt—were guided by and, for the most part, judged, according to this "myth of beauty" established by the academies which came into existence during the High Renaissance of Italy and flourished until the advent of impressionism.

From the Late Sixteenth to the Nineteenth Century

The evolution of the human soul continues with the elaboration of the cycle of profane art as we move from the late sixteenth to the nineteenth century. Malraux directs our attention, during this period, to the gradual ascendancy of the individual, of a concept of man as a being distinct from his fellows. The capital impetus in this direction came from the Reformation's imposition of the individual in matters of religion. This was paralleled, in the domain of art, not only by the appearance of portraits of individuals in increasing numbers, but also by the artist's growing determination or struggle to impose his own personality—his own soul—on the portraits of his models. The intensification of this struggle until the advent of impressionism, which marked the final victory of the artist over his model, accounts for Malraux's treatment of the period as a unity. He is careful to point out, however, that only the great artists engaged in the struggle, while the others were guided by the standards imposed by the academies which dominated the cultural scene.

In the seventeenth century, which witnessed the consolidation of the absolute monarchy in the political sphere and of the authority of the academies in the domain of culture, man's defense against destiny was, once again, the ordered structure of his world.

Of inestimable consequence to the history of the human soul was the emergence in the eighteenth-century world of the *philosophes*—and for the first time in the history of man—of a deity born of the Goddess of Reason rather than of the soul. During the Age of Enlightenment, science and reason joined forces to disrupt the consolidated architecture of the seventeenth-century world. Both God and the monarch, the two figures who had occupied summit positions in its ordered hierarchy, were called into question; the consequence was a relativization of the absolute and a disintegration of Value into a host of values.

Malraux's treatment of the art of the period immediately following the High Renaissance is guided by the divergent religious orientations of the North and South of Europe as a result of the Reformation and Counter-reformation respectively. In fact, Malraux does not study the entire period between the late sixteenth and nineteenth century, as is customary with art historians, in terms of the evolution of style from classicism to mannerism, baroque, roccoco, neoclassicism, and finally modern art. His tendency is to treat in any detail only those artists—the independents—who remained aloof, or broke away from the dominant trends of academy-regulated art, which continued as the controlling force until the nineteenth century. His study is therefore fragmentary, and, as such, is in keeping with his concept of truly creative art as that which invariably springs from the artist's declaration of independence. More will be said about Malraux's esthetics in general in my discussion of his "La Création artistique" (*infra*, I, 8).

While Malraux proposes "theatricalized fiction" as the distinguishing characteristic of both religious and profane painting in the South, as manifested primarily in the paintings of the Venetian School (with which he also associates Rubens, a Flemish painter), he stresses realism as the dominant feature in the painting of the North, as evidenced primarily in the paintings of the Dutch School, whose center was Holland.

Following the tradition set by Michelangelo in the Sistine Chapel, both the Venetians and Rubens continued to paint vast surfaces, thereby creating a style of decor. The Venetians brought theatricalized fiction to its fullest fruition. Lyricism, too, was rediscovered in Venice by the leaders of what developed into the Venetian School. Malraux deals with the baroque striving to represent life in all its richness of detail and movement in his treatment of Titian, the master with whom El Greco finally broke in order to find his own soul.

With the exception of the paintings of El Greco, an artist regarded by Malraux as unique in his time and indeed in all time, the religious painting of the South is qualified, as indicated above, as "theatricalized fiction"; its purpose was to seduce the spectator. El Greco, who was as little concerned about the spectator as Michelangelo had been, broke with the prevailing trends of the Venetian School to achieve the most austere stylization in ten centuries of Western art. Malraux draws an analogy between the religious spirit emanating from the great religious works of Michelangelo and *The Burial of the Count of Orgaz,* El Greco's masterpiece:

> And *The Day* joins the *Crucifixion, The Pieta* and *The Count of Orgaz* on a tragic summit as separated from the theatre as from the earth, and in the haunting solitude where Rembrandt will join them. The spectator no longer counts (VS, 89).

In his combination of Gothic and baroque, rather than the prevailing Roman and baroque, El Greco stood apart from the accepted trends of the period and achieved a manifestation of pure spirit—the heights of mysticism—in his paintings. Malraux's study of the formation of El Greco, the artist, over a period that spans approximately a quarter of a century, will be discussed in the succeeding chapter dealing with the cycle of artistic creation.

The Reform movement, which challenged the hierarchy of Rome and sought to renew the authority of St. Augustine by replacing the accent on the individual, was distinguished by Dutch painting. According to Malraux, it was in Holland that the Italian image of man died and that painting was freed of idealism. Realism, which, before the Dutch, had been limited to Christian figures that the artists had not seen, now began to embrace a variety of subjects, including not only portraits of living individuals (inaugurated by the Van Eycks) but also isolated landscapes, still-lifes, and even interiors, which had previously served only as settings or parts of settings for figures sharing a scene.

As mentioned above in connection with the ascendancy of the individual in matters of religion, the individuality of the painter became an increasingly forceful presence in his works during the Reformation. This was true, of course, only of the great figures of the age—the independents—such as Hals, Rembrandt, Vermeer, and others whose works were atypical of the period trends. According to Malraux, Protestantism engendered, with few exceptions, only second-rate, bourgeois portraits.

In corroboration of his own persuasion of the rising importance of the individuality of the painter, Malraux cites Hals's statement of his intention to create paintings that would end all painting and asserts that it was indeed with Hals that the rivalry between the painter and his model began—a rivalry which marked the beginning of the end of the artist's subjection to his subject. The word "beginning" is important because the struggle was to continue, as indicated above, until the nineteenth century. This was true not only of Hals but also of other great portraitists of the seventeenth century, especially Rembrandt and Velazquez. Regarding the latter's portraits of Philip IV and the royal family of Spain, Malraux maintains that posterity has come to know the royal family as Velazquez transformed or deformed them.

Perhaps the most forceful individualist in Reform painting was Rembrandt, who carried the artist's struggle with his model beyond Hals and Velazquez. But the part of himself that Rembrandt strove to render, Malraux intimates, was his inner voice—the soul that linked him with the divine and enabled him to commune with Christ.

The Reformation is to rediscover that voice [Christ's] through the individual; and Rembrandt is haunted by his own face, for he will at first lay disguises upon it, not in order to adorn it, as has been said, but in order to multiply it. His women resemble one another because they resemble him.

For Rembrandt, to represent is neither to idealize nor to lend an expression; it is to give a soul (VS, 471).

From the foregoing, one might infer that, for idealization, Rembrandt substituted the penetration and manifestation of the very essence of the individual—his soul.

It is understandable then that Rembrandt, whom Malraux ranks among the greatest artists of all time, is credited with having kept the religious spirit alive when profane painting was born of the Reformation.

> . . . he [Rembrandt] rebels against the world of appearances with all his genius, against a society in which he sees only the wall of nothingness that separates him from Christ (VS, 469).
> It is singular that the dialogue of a single soul with God powerfully responds to man's immense appeal for communion. Rembrandt, in painting, discovers it (VS, 471).

As for idealization, under which designation Malraux would probably include figures born either of an imaginary transcendent realm or of the artist's attainment of such a realm through the deindividualization—and hence transfiguration—of real-life personnages, it was not totally absent from the period: it reappeared in the paintings of Vermeer, whose departicularized figures radiating an inner light induce Malraux to compare them, not to the "Italian" image of man, but to the idealized figures of pre-Hellenistic Greek sculpture:

> He always seems to de-individualize his models as if to departicularize the universe: to obtain, not types,

but a sensitive abstraction which is reminiscent of certain *Korés* (VS, 474).

But Vermeer's figures issued neither from an imaginary realm, as did the statues of the Greek gods, nor from the world of God, as did the idealized figures in Giotto's paintings: they were figures born of the real world and were represented in real-life situations in a secular context. Malraux further points out that in Vermeer's paintings it is the picture itself (no doubt the interrelationship of the colors, forms, and volumes) that arouses the admiration of the spectator, rather than the subject, whether it be a portrait or an anecdotal scene. He cites Vermeer's *La Lettre d'amour* as an example of such a scene—a scene which "announces" the birth of a new world: "The letter has no importance, nor have the women. Nor the world in which letters are delivered: the world has become painting" (VS, 478).

Malraux reveals his admiration for Vermeer by designating him the precursor of Manet and the impressionists, but he points out that neither Vermeer nor his contemporaries were aware that his art marked the beginning of a metamorphosis of the painter's world into one of pictures, which would someday rival the creation as the private autonomous world of the artist:

However, modern art does not yet begin. Because the transformation of the world into painting, far from being proclaimed, has, in Vermeer, as in the Velazquez of *The Maids of Honor,* the character of a secret. The real is not subordinated to the painting; the painting itself seems to be subordinated to the real, to be seeking a quality which is neither the slave of appearance nor in opposition to it—a quality which balances it. In 1670 Hals and Rembrandt are dead, and an era with them. Vermeer, who is alive and succeeds them, as modern art follows romanticism, opens another epoch. It will be discovered two hundred years later (VS, 478).

With reference to seventeenth-century culture in general, Malraux proposes, and we can certainly agree, that it was France which ultimately imposed an ordered structure on the chaotic disorder of the Renaissance. The culture of the age, which was primarily intellectual, sought to attain a well-balanced concept of man and the world, one that was first directed at satisfying the mind and later at merely responding to its pleasure. Academies of the period defined a myth of beauty, an eternal style, which guided all forms of artistic creations in both literature and the arts. It was believed that styles which did not measure up to this "ideal of beauty" (considered independent of history, though attained for the first time in Greece) were either primitive or decadent. This attitude explains the seventeenth century's misconstruction of the true value of Medieval Christian art:

> The seventeenth century's disdain for Gothic art lay not in a lucid conflict of values, but in the fact that the Gothic statue was then judged not on the basis of what it is, but as a failure to be something else: it was assumed that the Gothic sculptor had desired to sculpt a classical statue; and that if he had not succeeded, it was because he had not been capable (VS, 18).
> Louis XIV's "Remove these maggots" also applies to Notre Dame (VS, 18).

The rediscovery of life and movement begun in the Renaissance culminated in the baroque period of the seventeenth century. The painters of the period aimed at creating a sublime theater (the theater also reigned supreme in literature); they sought to combine baroque movement with Roman theatricalism; to the baroque illusion of movement in depth, they added the gesture.

By the last third of the seventeenth century, all of the great figures were dead—Hals and Rembrandt, Velazquez, and even Poussin, whose paintings were set up as models of *le beau idéal* by the French Academy. Dying, too, was a world order whose hierarchical structure still converged on God. This was also true of its music—that of Handel and Bach.

The eighteenth century welcomed science into the domain of culture just as the seventeenth century had welcomed art. This new scientifically oriented culture emphasized knowledge rather than self-awareness. Man, in the Age of Enlightenment, was oriented toward the future as contrasted with Medieval man, who looked neither back nor ahead in time (but only to eternity), and with Renaissance man, who fused what he judged the best of the past with the present in order to structure a world which would serve not only his own, but subsequent ages as well—a world whose structure was completed by the seventeenth century.

Malraux analyzes what happened when the eighteenth century's Goddess of Reason began to loosen the underpinnings of the established world order:

What Christian civilization was abandoning was not one or another of its values, it was more than a faith: man, once oriented toward Being, was being replaced by a man capable of being persuaded by ideas and actions; the supreme Value was being shattered into a multiplicity of values. What was gradually disappearing from the Western world was the absolute (VS, 479).

As Christianity passed from the absolute to the relative under the influence of the Enlightenment, it entered a new phase: what had been faith in the Middle Ages and religion during the Renaissance was now deteriorating into a formal piety devoid of any intimation of the sacred. What the *philosophes* were attacking, according to Malraux, was not Christianity or its intrinsic values, but the formal piety into which it had degenerated. He claims that the age, contrary to accepted opinion, was combative rather than skeptical, and that the zeal of attack acted as a substitute for religious fervor.

The conspicuous absence of religious sentiment from the new scheme of things conceived by the Goddess of Reason is singled out as the capital event of the Enlightenment; Malraux suggests that what passed for religion—Deism—was a creation of the mind, not of the soul.

The new fact, the consequences of which were to transform art and culture at the same time, was that this time, one religion was not being called into question *by the birth of another*. Religious sentiment all the way from veneration to sacred terror and love had changed forms many times; reason and science were not its latest metmorphosis, but its negation. It was negated by people who did not wish to know anything about it—and soon it was negated under the authority of a man completely absorbed in the Supreme Being (VS, 478).

The Jesuits, too, were combative. In their counter-attack on the *philosophes* they sponsored an art which Malraux qualifies as an art of propaganda. This art, which was furiously profane in spite of its religious subject matter, was the first of its kind in Europe. Although they were in accord with the *philosophes* both in adhering to the standards established by the academy and in their disdain for all art prior to Raphael, the Jesuits sponsored an art that put baroque gesture and movement to the service of a theatricality which was designed to seduce the viewer. Stressing this theatricality, Malraux describes the paintings as he sees them:

These feminine saints were neither wholly saints nor wholly women? [sic] without doubt: they were actresses. Whence the importance of the feelings and the faces: the painter's principal means of expression was no longer either design or color—it had become character (VS, 90).

Nor does art become less theatrical when neoclassicism begins its struggle to free painting of baroque gesticulation: Malraux says the theater remains, while its source is changed from Jesuit to classical. There is also a change in the source of pictorial inspiration: the neoclassicists break away from the highly emotional expressiveness of baroque figures and resuscitate the expression of detachment created in the fifteenth century by Piero della Francesca.

Underlying or accompanying the alteration in the method of characterization was a shift in the esthetics of the period. For the neoclassicists the psychological detachment of Piero's figures allowed more scope for the expression of the sentiment of the artist in his paintings. While the earlier esthetic was directed at satisfying the mind, the new esthetic was to appeal to the heart of the spectator; the expressive power of the picture itself, rather than the facial expressions on individual figures, was to constitute the source of this appeal.

If the Jesuits and the *philosophes* vied for control of men's minds in the realm of ideas, they were, according to Malraux, in accord as to what constituted art. Their criteria were the same and their emphasis was on the subject matter: "Good painting was that which pleased the sincere and cultivated man, not to the degree that it was painting but to the extent that it represented a fiction of quality" (VS, 92).

While this esthetic, based on a fiction of quality, had been evolving and spreading over most of Europe, truly creative artists pursued their own destinies. "Aging Rembrandt was the first *génie maudit*" (VS, 95).

From the Nineteenth to the Twentieth Century

As we enter, with Malraux, the age of the birth of modern art and the culmination of the profane, we find both the god of the Jesuits and the *philosophes'* Goddess of Reason receding into the background to yield first place to a new political deity on which man would focus his hopes for a better world. Politics stepped into the role of man's defense against destiny. But to little avail, for the Rights of Man proclaimed by the Revolution soon became the rights of the middle class, the first ruling class in history which had no transcendent values of its own.

In Malraux's view, the nineteenth century lived on two sets of myths—one revolutionary and one reactionary

—for the simple reason that the bourgeoisie created no new myth of its own. For the first time the truly creative artists and the ruling class parted ways. The bourgeois world, which acknowledged no transcendent values, inspired nothing but disdain in the artists of the time; hence, the dichotomy of society into two hostile worlds.

With regard to society the rebel artist now played a role analogous to that played by the revolutionary of the preceding century. In his struggle against what he considered the amorphous world of the bourgeoisie—a world oriented toward no value which elicited any response from the depth of the human soul—the artist found in creativity itself his *raison d'être*. He looked to the creators of the past—to all those who had attested to the presence of a divine spark in man—for inspiration. Together with his fellow artists, he built up a separate world sustained by a heroic attitude dedicated to the cult of genius:

> But, in uniting Shakespeare with Beethoven, and Michelangelo with Rembrandt in the Valley of the Dead, the nineteenth century was uniting them with all the sages, with the heroes and the saints. The illustrious dead were not only witnesses to a divine faculty in man, they were also the progenitors of the Man to be born (VS, 487–89).

The artist's sole defense against destiny was now his own creative spark, which might be kindled and then exteriorized and transformed into works which would light the way for the realization of the hopes which had sparked the Revolution. Though the artist scorned the present, he respected the past and projected into the future his aspirations for a better world.

In connection with the nineteenth-century artist's re-

jection of his world, Malraux cites, in *Les Voix du silence,*
Wagner's passage on the source of human creativity: "He
who has not been endowed by a fairy, from the cradle,
with the spirit of discontent with everything that exists,
will never succeed in discovering anything new" (491–92).
The works born of this "spirit of discontent," which permeated the artistic world of the nineteenth century, engendered the hope that man might, in some way, and
through his own efforts, be instrumental in creating, in
historical time, an earthly counterpart of the eternal City
of God—a utopia where men would live in peace and
dignity. Malraux draws a parallel between the hope stirred
in the nineteenth century and that kindled by the early
Christian martyrs:

> The great myths of that century: liberty, democracy,
> science, and progress converged on the greatest hope
> that humanity had known since the catacombs. When
> the tides of time have used up, in the fraternal depth
> of oblivion, the remains of that ardent searching, we
> shall without doubt discover that no century was
> more concerned about bringing to all men an aware-
> ness of their own grandeur. . . . These subterranean
> voices still murmur under what is best in our time . . .
> (VS, 489).

The rebel artist's break with society was not only
metaphysical but also esthetic in that it included a total
rejection of the officially sponsored academy art which had
evolved from Italian ecclecticism (culminating in the
works of Raphael) to the formation of an "ideal beauty"
aimed first at satisfying the mind and later at appealing
to the sentiments of the viewer. Malraux speaks of "the

immense cemetery of nineteenth-century academism . . ." (VS, 95).

Contrary to what we might expect, Malraux affirms that the voice of the epoch born of the aspirations of the French Revolution was first heard in Spain:

> . . . it was not in France that the hinge of the century was being hammered into position, and he who heard the age-old voice once again was indeed a "man of the Enlightenment," but he was Goya (VS, 480).

> . . . the break which separated the romantic from the classical writers had no equivalent in painting—except in Goya, whose profound influence was felt later (VS, 97).

Malraux interprets the expression of terror and the raised arms of the illuminated figure in Goya's *The Shootings of May Third* as an image of crucified humanity crying out "the anguish of man abandoned by God" (VS, 97). The voice of despair rising from the canvas echoes that of man across the centuries—even though the victim is dying not for the Kingdom of God but for deliverance from the French conquerors under Napoleon. In this painting Malraux hears "the cry of Spain," and in Goya's *Saturn,* "the age-old cry of the world" (VS, 97), which is to resound through the era right up to the present.

What Goya did in his paintings of human suffering and torture, of monsters and nightmares, and of man being swallowed up by time in his *Saturn,* was to strip the world of hypocrisy. He depicted aspects of existence which heretofore had not been admitted as fitting subjects for portrayal in art.

Malraux speaks of the freedom in Goya's art as the element that began the breakthrough to modernism; his evaluation of Goya's role in the evolution of painting is more fully developed in the volume *Saturne: Essai sur Goya,* dedicated exclusively to the Spanish artist of the late Enlightenment.

In France it was Daumier, the painter of the renowned *Chess Players* and mentor of Manet, who brought the art of painting to the threshold of the modern era. Both he and Goya are cited as transitional figures in the sense that their works contained elements of both museum art and of what was soon to become modern art. To the extent that their works were representational and belonged to the story-telling art of their predecessors, they continued in the tradition of museum art; to the extent that they repudiated all values that did not appertain exclusively to the picture itself, they looked forward to the modern era. Of Goya, Malraux writes: ". . . his language and his material remained in the service of representation. . . . but Goya, minus these voices and the element of shadow inherited from the museum, is modern art" (VS, 113).

We are reminded, however, that officially sponsored museum art continued to be produced. Corresponding to the two antagonistic civilizations—that of the rebel artists and that of the middle class—were two different schools of painting. While the artist in revolt sought a new style independent of the story-telling art of the past—a style which would make painting mistress of, rather than subject to, the forms of life—the artists backed by the Fine Arts Authorities continued to paint historical, fashionable, or anecdotal subjects which catered to the tastes of the middle class. The truly creative art of the rebel artist, who refused to conform, was bought by nobody. Haunted by his own "absolute," the sincere artist was destined to a

life of solitude and poverty, while the official "artists," who
satisfied the period taste without expressing any genuine
values, were acclaimed and their works purchased by the
new, bourgeois ruling class. Regarding this state of affairs,
Malraux says:

> How wrong it is to think that the painting of an
> epoch necessarily expresses its values! It expresses
> some of its characteristics, which is quite different;
> and some of its values, if it possesses any. Otherwise,
> it is content with pseudo-values, that is to say, at best,
> with tastes (VS, 490).

The rebel artist's deep commitment to his own creative power made art a specialized activity, an end in itself;
the creative act assumed the character of a mystical experience, and the poets, who stepped into the role of art
critics, borrowed the language of religious mystics to express their views. It will be noted that Malraux himself, especially in the divisions entitled "La Création
artistique" of both *La Psychologie de l'art* and *Les Voix
du silence,* often uses a religious, if not mystical vocabulary.
Even in "La Monnaie de l'absolu" of *Les Voix du silence,*
we find him speaking of the artist's "faith," and of his
"espousing poverty." Of the rebel artists as a group, he
says: "Rarely have so many great artists offered so many
sacrifices to an unknown god (VS, 493). Malraux also
mentions the artist's awareness of the power of his works
to both resurrect the past and transcend the historical
present. The creative experience itself is described in mystical terms as "the possession of something dazzling: the
frenzied conquest of terrestrial joy . . ." (VS, 61).
It was the growing consciousness of history in the

period as a whole that awakened artists to the survival value of art and its power to resuscitate works of the past. This same consciousness led them to rediscover two-dimensional art—that of Byzantium—which Malraux asserts is the art of the entire world with the exception of several hundred years of Western art. With the rediscovery of Byzantine art, all two-dimensional art, including that of the Middle Ages which had been disdained and neglected since the Renaissance, acquired significance.

What the nineteenth century sought now was a new definition of art completely independent of "the fixed ideal of beauty" formulated by the academies—one based rather upon a quality that all art had in common, and to which the artist or connoisseur of any age might respond. The following passages explain what actually happened:

Art and beauty separated, as at the time of the agony of Italianism, in a different but equally profound way (VS, 110).

And the striving of art, which for centuries had been aimed at wresting objects from their true natures in order to subject them to the divine faculty in man which had been called beauty, was now applied once again to wresting objects from their true natures in order to subject them to the divine faculty in man called art (VS, 118).

By "art" Malraux means, as he makes abundantly clear elsewhere, the manifestation of a "truth," the transformation of the world by the artist into a significance which serves as the soul's defense against destiny.

If Goya and Daumier paved the way to the modern era, Malraux credits Manet with effecting the decisive pictorial break, corresponding to the much earlier literary break, with the past. Manet's break resulted in the irrevocable separation of the artist's world from that of society at large.

The elimination of fiction as a subject from both painting and poetry was the first characteristic of modern art. Manet, in painting, and Baudelaire, in poetry, abandoned the story-telling art of their predecessors. It was the former's *Portrait of Clemenceau* that marked the final victory of the artist over his model in the struggle that had begun with Frans Hals:

> The subject must disappear because a new subject is appearing—one which is going to reject all others: the dominating presence of the painter himself. In order for Manet to paint the *Portrait of Clemenceau,* he had to resolve to dare to be everything in it, and Clemenceau, almost nothing (VS, 99).

It was also Manet who brought to fruition the pictorialization of the world which was dimly foreshadowed in the paintings of Vermeer. Painting became simply painting when Manet introduced his "dashes of color," which ceased to imitate or transfigure but insisted upon pictorializing. Specific reference is made to the "raspberry balcony" of Manet's little *Bar,* to the "pink dressing gown" of his *Olympia,* and to the "blue cloth" of his *Lunch on the Grass,* all of which "are quite evidently 'dashes of color' whose material is pictorial rather than representational" (VS, 114). These same dashes of color initiated the modern artist's rejection of all values foreign to painting, and, more immediately, ushered in the impressionist movement in art:

> It was at his [Manet's] expositions that the conflict
> that marked the origin of modern painting burst into
> the open—through the proclamation of the values of
> painting and not simply through their clandestine
> presence (VS, 100).

Manet's dashes of color also led to the discovery of the
specific power of the blending of colors freed of the dark
hues of the past, and to the employment of pure color
and the emergence of what Malraux qualifies as the modern "dissonant harmony" replacing the "consonant harmony" of the past.

Quoting Mallarmé's view of the "purpose" of the
world, Malraux suggests that what the poet says is equally,
and perhaps even more, applicable to the painter's art:
" 'The world is made to end in a beautiful book,' said
Mallarmé; it was created far more to end in these pictures" (VS, 115).

The question of style becomes central as Malraux
continues his discussion of nineteenth-century art. The
cult of genius, which exalted the creative power of the
individual, and which was already the subject of much
romantic poetry, was soon paralleled in painting when the
creative power of the artist took precedence over all other
considerations. The artist's talent was no longer employed
to express fiction or to faithfully "copy" models, objects,
or scenes from the real world, but rather to subject everything to his style, which became his "signature." This
signature served as evidence to posterity of the artist's presence in the world and of his power to equal or surpass the
creation. It is pointed out that this signature, of which
the modern artist is conscious, is not a new phenomenon,
but may be defined as the stylistic device or devices which
reveal the artist's identity:

Rubens and the thick broken arabesques of his sketches; Hals and his schematized prophets' hands characteristic of modern art; Goya and his accents of pure black; Delacroix and Daumier and their furious whip lashes. . . . Their vehement style was their signature (VS, 111).

Malraux indicates the glaring discrepancy between the declaration of fidelity to vision and the actual practice of Manet and his followers, the impressionists, whose works manifested the conscious imposition of the artist's signature on an autonomous pictorialized world:

At the moment when, the gates having been forced open by Manet, impressionism affirmed its virtues in the name of a closer accord with vision—as if it sought to be an open air art perfected by opticians—Cézanne, and soon Gauguin, Seurat, and Van Gogh, created the most brutally stylized art since El Greco (VS, 115).

In connection with Van Gogh in particular—and with special reference to his *Chair*, which symbolizes the triumph of the artist's will over the object—Malraux writes of the painter's *annexion* of the world superseding his representation of it. In passages dealing with the impressionists, postimpressionists, and expressionists, our attention is directed to the increasingly forceful presence of the artist in his style on the one hand, and to the diminishing importance of the subject, once the dominant feature of a painting, on the other. The subject is no longer chosen for itself, but as a vehicle for the expression of the artist's personality. With special reference to Cézanne, Malraux says:

If landscapes and still-lifes—as well as nudes and de-individualized portraits, which are themselves still-lifes—become major genres, it is not that Cézanne loves apples, it is because, in a painting of Cézanne which represents apples, there is more room for Cézanne than there was for Raphael in his portrait of Leon X (VS, 117).

What became of the art of fictional representation? Malraux tells us that "the representation of fiction, after fifty years of comfortable and derisory agonizing, was to find its luxuriant resurrection and veritable domain: the cinema" (VS, 119). In his *Esquisse d'une psychologie du cinéma,* Malraux points out that the history of photography as a conquest of movement culminating in the cinema paralleled the history of painting from the Renaissance to the baroque era, when the conquest of movement reached its frenzied peak.

The conscious struggle of the modern artist to subordinate everything to his picture, to subject everything to his style, and to use the universe as a means of expressing his own language, has culminated in the reduction of the world by the artist to his own private plastic world, a world in which the individual reigns supreme:

And the will to annex the world superseded the immense desire to transfigure it. The scattered forms of the world which had converged on faith or beauty now converged on the individual (VS, 119).

A note of nostalgia and regret, barely detectable in the foregoing quotation contrasting the intensely individualized character of modern art with the art of the past, is forcefully expressed in Malraux's diagnosis of the malady of contemporary civilization and contemporary man—a malady resulting from the deadening of spiritual values in the age of the machine. He speaks of twentieth-century culture as the first to have severed all bonds with the eternal, and as the first agnostic culture (though agnosticism is not new) where the absence of all sense of religious communion has abandoned every individual to his own resources, that is, to find his own means of defying destiny. Malraux looks upon twentieth-century man as a fragmentary being without essence, as the heir of a host of relativized "absolutes," as an individual thrown back on himself and growing increasingly aware of his inability to cope with the multiplicity of life. Malraux further maintains that if the last two centuries witnessed the relativization of the absolute, our century is facing a relativization of the individual. The twentieth-century individual, as Malraux sees him, is no longer an ally of the world at large, but its enemy; he is an individual who views his world as an adversary to be conquered, and whose failure as a conqueror is making him acutely aware of his own limitations: "the individual, left to his own resources, is discovering that he is nothing spectacular and that the 'supermen' that once exalted him have turned out to be all too human" (VS, 494).

The contemporary artist faces the same dilemma; the cycle of profane art, reborn at the close of the Renaissance, seems to have reached the extreme limit of its expression in the highly individualistic art of our time:

For each day the incapacity of modern civilization to give form to spiritual values becomes more apparent. Even by passing through Rome. In places where cathedrals were formerly built, they are building

pseudo-romanesque, pseudogothic, and modern
churches from which Christ is absent (VS, 493).

It has been said several times; but if it [individualistic
art] can go no farther, it can go elsewhere [2] (VS, 601).

A victim of extreme lucidity with regard to the state
of his world and of his contemporaries, André Malraux
has dedicated his life to communicating to his fellow men
his own vision of a possible solution to the dilemma of
twentieth-century man. His solution emerges as an ethical
one based upon the reintegration of the individual into
society and the world—a reintegration in the form of the
dedication of each to the promotion of the human dignity
of all. Malraux's solution is grounded in his faith in man,
in his conviction that the notion of man as an individual,
concerned with little outside himself, is but one, and by
no means either the last or the noblest, expression of the
human soul whose infinite resources are as yet largely
unexplored. After affirming that the myth of man not only
preceded but will also survive that of the individual,
Malraux goes on to say: "To ask whether 'man is dead' is
to affirm that he is man—and not his cadavre—and he is
man to the extent that he applies himself to ordering his
faculties according to what is noblest in him—and this
is rarely limited to himself . . ." (VS, 494). Malraux predicts an end, in the foreseeable future, to our individual-
centered culture:

A civilization focused on man alone does not last very
long, and the rationalism of the eighteenth century
ended in the gust of passion and hope that we know
all too well: but the culture of that century was resuscitating everything that reinforced its rationalism,

and ours is resuscitating all that reinforces our ir-rationalism (VS, 494).

Pervading all of Malraux's works is the distinction between the individual, whose lucidity has impelled him to defy a destiny imposed upon him from without, and the man who is living on a subhuman level under conditions that require the expending of all of his energies for mere survival, and who is, therefore, denied the possibility of experiencing "the honor of being a man."

It is important to bear in mind that it is an *individual* that Malraux would reintegrate into the society of men— a being who is fully aware of his stature as a man and who, by conscious choice, is willing to dedicate himself to elevating all men to a level of human dignity. This explains why all of Malraux's heroes are intellectuals who have broken with a society in which they themselves suffered humiliation or in which dignity was denied their fellow men; they are lucid heroes, conscious of their world, and activated by a desire to either escape from the imperfect world into which they were born or to refashion it.

Malraux's individual is born of a break with what he considers a world in need of rectification—a world conceived as a prison from which he must escape in order to forge his own destiny. Malraux himself is perhaps the chief protagonist of his own works. Whether the individual be a man of action or an artist, his origin is the same: he is born of a rupture with the world he has inherited. This world might be the political structure of society in the case of the former, or the world of pictures in the case of the latter. When the break occurs, man's creative potential is activated—he is ready to refashion his world, and this, according to Malraux, is how history is made. *To make history* is man's latest defense against destiny, his means of defying the human situation into which he is born. It is history that man must now combat and alter in order to escape his human condition: "The new adversary of Hercules, the latest incarnation of destiny, is history . . ." (VS, 633).

It will, however, be demonstrated in Part III of this book, that the evolution of Malraux's fictional hero makes it abundantly clear that when the hero's defiance is unrelated to any ethical goal, when it is simply defiance for defiance's sake, it leads to the autodestruction of the hero.[3]

Part III will also illustrate that the following quotation, dealing specifically with Malraux's view of the history of art, is valid for his concept of the human adventure as a whole as it emerges from his epic of man:

A history of art . . . could no more be one of constant progress than one of eternal return. When we discover that the key to creation is in a rupture with the past, art, without separating itself from history, links up with it inversely and in a different way. The whole history of art, provided it is that of genius, is a history of deliverance: for history seeks to transform destiny into consciousness, and art [action for the Malraux hero] to transform it into freedom (VS, 621).

The foregoing elucidates the significance of one of the most frequently cited passages of *Les Voix du silence* —a passage in which Malraux proclaims art the archenemy of destiny, while he extols art's masterpieces as manifestations of man's perennial victory over his fate:

Every masterpiece is a purification of the world, but the common lesson of each is that of its existence;

and the victory of each artist over his servitude joins, in an immense unfolding, that of art over the destiny of humanity. Art is an anti-destiny (VS, 637).

The "successive emancipations" leading to "purifications of the world" of which Malraux writes refer to the artist's breaking out of one cycle or phase of a cycle of art history to create a new one. The greatest geniuses are not those who bring to fruition a cycle in progress by introducing a new phase elaborating the preceding one, but those whose break with tradition is radical enough to alter the whole course of art history, or, in the case of the man of action, the history of the world.

Notes

1. Bernard Halda, in his comparative study *Berenson et André Malraux* (Paris: Minard, 1964), p. 15, explains the divergent approaches to art history and criticism of the two men on the basis of their separate attitudes toward this "fixed ideal of beauty": he claims that while Berenson accepted it as an immediate criterion, Malraux rejected it:

   Devant le désarroi du monde, Berenson reste calmement attaché aux valeurs qu'il juge éternelles et par conséquent soustraites au sort toujours mouvant, toujours précaire, parfois tragique des civilisations. Deux idéologies aussi contraires . . . ne peuvent qu'inspirer des psychologies de l'art bien différentes. L'une pèse avec des balances extrêment précises selon des unités absolument fixées; l'autre arpente à longeur de méridiens.

2. The possible course of our contemporary art will be discussed in Part IV: Man's Open Future.

3. The author acknowledges her indebtedness to Charles Blend who, in his excellent book on Malraux, traces the ethical evolution of the Malraux hero from novel to novel.

8.

The Cycle of Artistic Creation

The cycle continues as the unifying theme of Malraux's epic as he discusses the question of style, which for him is almost synonymous with art. In "La Création artistique," [1] Malraux discusses the cyclic evolution of the style of a whole period, of the artist in general, and of a specific artist, El Greco. He traces the cycle through the following phases: a link with the past in an initial stage involving the imitation of inherited forms; a break with the past as a new style is wrested from the imitated forms; the mastery and elaboration of the new discovery to the fulfillment of its expression; and finally the deterioration of the elaborated style into a spiritless convention calling forth the new art destined to destroy it.

The following passage outlines the cyclic evolution of great period styles:

> The lives of great styles untiringly stir up the past, because each of them leaves it "in suspense." A style is born as a revelatory expression; it is repeated as a conventional expression of what the civilization surrounding it believes to be its quality, and it dies in what this civilization believes to be its summit— calling forth the new genius that will destroy it (CA, 212).

As for the cyclic evolution of the individual artist's style, it is related to a master-disciple relationship. The existence of this relationship has already been indicated by W.M. Frohock, Gaëtan Picon, and more recently by Leon S. Roudiez, in their studies on Malraux. The purpose of reintroducing it here is to stress the connection between the evolution of this relationship and the unifying theme of the cycle.

Malraux makes a distinction between the final phase of a period style, which leaves any future life it may have to the whims of destiny in the guise of the new art which may recall it to life, and that of an artist, who often ends his career by introducing the germ of a new style into his own fully elaborated style:

> But the talent of painters rarely reaches the agonizing stage. Having first invented their language, then learned to speak it (it is the moment when they seem to be able to transcribe everything), painters often invent a second language (CA, 212).

The elucidation of this idea will be treated in connection with the artist's break with his own creation—the final phase of his cycle—after tracing his career through the stages of his formation.

The aspiring young artist discovers his vocation through his admiration for the works of a certain master (or masters). In the initial phase of the cycle he begins to imitate his masters; the second stage leads to a break with the master as the disciple wrests his own style out of his early imitations; the succeeding phase witnesses the emergence of the disciple as a new master as he conquers and eleborates his own discovery; in the final phase the new master breaks with his own fully evolved style, as it is about to die, by injecting into it the germ of a new style for a future disciple to discover.

By way of elaboration, Malraux traces the beginning of the artist's career to a *pastiche* of his chosen masters' works. This *pastiche* represents a "gesture of fraternity" representing the artist's *conversion* [2] from the real world to the world of painting. Gradually the artist wrests his own truth from his early imitations, but, before he can be considered a master in his own right, he must demonstrate his conquest of this truth by transforming it into a possession, that is, into a new style which becomes his signature.

Creation always *begins* with this struggle between the disciple and his master and *ends* with the triumph of the former who destroys the truth of the latter by wresting from it a new significance which imposes a new order on some aspect of the world. Malraux insists that the role of destroyer precedes that of creator in the formation of the truly great artist:

> If that which separates the man of genius from the man of talent, from the artisan, or even from the amateur is not the intensity of his sensitivity to spectacles, it is not exclusively the intensity of his sensitivity to works of art either: it is that he alone, among those whom works of art fascinate, he alone *also* wants to destroy them (CA, 152).

Malraux is emphatic about the fact that the artist's vision is educated, not in the world of nature, but in the world of art—that his formation begins with his *con-*

version from the real world to the world of pictures. He maintains that the incipient artist copies *not* an object of nature but rather another painter's reduction or *possession* of the world: "We know absolutely nothing about what a great artist would be if he knew no work of art and had before him only living forms" (CA, 118). Malraux pursues the idea and expresses his view concerning the task that would probably face an artist having at his disposal only the natural world:

> The young painter does not have a choice between his master and "his vision"; he has a choice only between his master and other masters, between canvases and other canvases. If his original vision were not that of one or more masters, he would have to re-invent painting (CA, 141).

The same conflict is the *sine qua non* for the emergence of a new period style: the new is born of the destruction of the old: "In Chartres as in Egypt, and in Florence as in Babylon, the raw material of an art about to be born is the previous art" (CA, 129). A specific example of this transformation of existing forms into new forms is cited in connection with the metamorphosis of Apollo by the Buddhists; once again Malraux insists that the artist's primary source is art itself, with life playing, at best, a secondary role in the creation of a new style:

> The Buddhist sculptor who watched a face grow meditative as its eyelids lowered perhaps imposed the meditative look on the head of a Greek statue by closing its eyes; but if he discovered the expressive value of those closing eyes, it means that he was instinctively searching, among all living forms, for a

means of metamorphosing the Greek face . . .
(CA, 174).

The eruption of the conflict opens the second phase
of the cycle and involves the disciple's break out of the
"prison" of the art of the school or master he has chosen
to imitate. The prison metaphor is one which pervades
Malraux's works. While his potential hero or man of
action is a "prisoner" of the society that formed him,
"the artist is born a prisoner of the style which permitted
him to cease being a prisoner of the world" (CA, 152).
The break out of the prison marks the ignition of the
creative spark and, in both the artist and the man of
action, generates a desire to transform the world—either
that of art or that of society. But the success of the artist
is by no means assured at this stage; "it is at this rupture
that art begins: it is not art, but there is no art without
it" (CA, 148).

The potential artist becomes a master only when he
has conquered his own style (which might have originated
as the result of a lucky accident) to the point where it is
detectable in all his canvases as his signature, representing
the new truth or significance he has imposed upon some
aspect of the chaotic multiplicity of the world: "A lucky
accident is but an accidental masterpiece; genius lies not
in the discovery of style but in its possession. All genius
is mastery . . ." (CA, 148).

In his interpretation of the essence of the art of four
great painters—Goya, Giotto, El Greco, and Van Gogh—
Malraux reveals his conception of the artist's "truth" as
a manifestation, in art, of a new vision of the world:

The genius of Goya strove to strip the world of its
mask of hypocrisy; that of Giotto to remove its mask
of suffering (CA, 148).

> The truth of this last one [El Greco] . . . stripped the
> world of its splendor to restore to it its soul . . .
> (CA, 149).

> The truth of Van Gogh was, for him, the pictorial
> absolute toward which he tended; for us it is his
> work itself (CA, 149).

As Malraux extends his discussion to other realms of
knowledge, he provides a clearer idea of what is involved
in the discovery of truth irrespective of the pursuer's
domain:

> And every artist of genius . . . becomes, as does every
> great style, a transformer of the significance of the
> world, which he conquers by reducing it to his forms
> as the philosopher reduces it to his concepts, and the
> physicist to his laws. And he is victorious not over
> the world itself, but over one of the latest forms that
> it has assumed in human hands (CA, 160).

And referring specifically to the artist, Malraux says:
"Every genius combats a previous possession—a style,
from the obscure sketch that animates him at the outset
to the proclamation of his conquered truth" (CA, 155).
    Once the artist has found his truth he enters the third
phase of the cycle, which is dedicated to the mastery
and elaboration of his new discovery. During this stage,
he evolves into a new master: "No sooner is it elaborated
that each style expands over all the forms that it can
annex; each artist seems to cast out his masters, step by
step, from his first decisive works" (CA, 158).
    The artist ends his career—and brings his cycle to

a close—by breaking with his own moribund style. As it is about to deteriorate into a convention and die, he introduces into it the seed of a new style for a future disciple to discover and bring to fruition:

> When the style of death touches them ever so lightly, the recollection of their earlier break with their masters impels artists to break with their own mature style. One then says they are deepening it. . . . The voice of the infinite becomes urgent when it assumes a funereal timber. . . . The artist builds his supreme incarnation on the ruins of his own creation as he had built his first on the ruins of his masters'. And soon, other painters, not yet free of his voice, will spend their lives wresting from him the accent that he had imposed upon the world. *The cycle is closed* [italics mine] (CA, 212).

As an example of the germ of a new style, Malraux cites the marginal bouquet of flowers in Velazquez' painting *The Infanta Marguerita*:

> . . . Velazquez would not have dared to isolate the bouquet that he played with in a corner of *The Infanta Marguerita* and which had to wait two hundred years for its posterity. But if the marginal innovation [the bouquet] of *The Infanta* struggled against the style of Velazquez, the marginal work of his apprentice years struggled against the masters of the past. . . .
> The art of marginal innovations is one of freedom, but it is not vagabond; it is, rather, similar to that which the artist finds at the end of his life (CA, 165–66).

The cycle of style which engenders something new as it is about to die is like a phoenix (one of Malraux's favorite symbols) rising from its own ashes. Life and death, death and rebirth, are closely associated in Malraux's vision of a creation in continuous progress. When a new cycle stirs up the past, as happened in the Renaissance, the result is not repetition, but rather renewal and metamorphosis of the old. One might describe what happens as an interaction of past and present resulting in a fusion which not only renews the past but also opens onto a new future:

> In art, the Renaissance made antiquity no less than antiquity made the Renaissance. With Florence dying, *the cycle* opened by the death of imperial forms *closes in Rome* [italics mine], after the passing of more than a thousand years, not with a return to antiquity, but with its metamorphosis (VS, 269).

The artist is unquestionably controlled by history both as regards his subject and his style, and he can belong to no other age but his own. The influence of history, however, may lead to entirely different forms of expression in different artists of the same period, depending upon whether they accept, reject, or remain aloof from the prevailing values of their age: "The fan of possible expressions of a culture, although limited, is wide open" (CA, 169). El Greco and Tintoretto are cited as prime examples of two artists who—though they lived during the same period and began by imitating the same master, Titian—extracted completely different "truths" from the art that formed them. Whereas Tintoretto tended to accept everything the world had to offer, thereby bringing the Venetian School to a brilliant climax, El Greco found his voice—his truth—in a rejection of everything but what he considered to be the soul or essence of the Christian spirit.

El Greco's career is presented as an illustration of the evolution of a specific artist who was influenced not only by history, but by geography as well. As his name indicates, the geographical influence—Greece, Italy, and Spain—was threefold: the article, *El,* is Spanish; the noun, *Greco,* is Italian, and the article and noun combined signify "the Greek." The two geographical changes —from Greece (his birthplace was the Island of Crete) to Italy, and from Italy to Spain—were responsible for two major *conversions* before El Greco found the truth which made him the unsurpassed genius of his age. The choice of El Greco's career to illustrate the influence of history (and of geography) on an artist was prompted by the existence of three versions, painted over a period of more than twenty years, of the same painting:

> He [El Greco] painted several versions of *Christ Chasing the Merchants from the Temple,* and the unity, not only of its subject, but also of a part of its composition, permits us to follow it [the evolution of his genius] (CA, 176).

It is an enlightening experience to examine the reproductions of these versions in conjunction with Malraux's text.[3] In the first version, representing El Greco's first *conversion* under the influence of Italy, we notice, and Malraux describes it, all the rich profusion of detail characteristic of Venetian baroque art. In the second version there is already convincing evidence of an attempt at simplification by virtue both of the omission of many objects present in the original painting and of the alteration of the composition. After a lapse of twenty years, during which there was a second *conversion* under the influence of Spain, and, according to Malraux, the intervention of genius, the third and final version, rejecting everything that might detract from El Greco's burning faith, appeared. El Greco had finally achieved, in a combination of Gothic and baroque never duplicated, the Christian style he sought.

Regarding the several extant versions of El Greco's *Toledo in a Thunderstorm,* Malraux indicates that a similar striving toward simplification produced "the first Christian landscape." This painting, depicting Toledo not as it was but as El Greco dreamed it might be, marked the culmination of the artist's genius. From version to version, Malraux envisages El Greco breaking with himself—replacing one of his own canvases with another—as he had earlier broken with his masters; in the process the role of nature (*l'univers*) is once again minimized: "He had greater need of some of his own canvases, which he conserved in order to struggle against them . . . than he had need of the universe" (CA, 191).

In some of his most inspired prose Malraux describes the transformation of the actual Toledo by El Greco in his masterpiece, *Toledo in a Thunderstorm:*

So many years and so much effort, so much solitude and semi-obscurity, to give rise to his city! Who can fail to see that he found Toledo, not in front of him, but in his genius as a painter? . . . It was in his atelier, with its black curtains drawn, that he finally crucified Toledo, but from that Toledo which first

appeared under the crucifix, he now succeeded in ex-
pelling Christ (CA, 191).

Whether represented or not this time, Christ is still
there. He has become the most powerful medium of
El Greco's painting: but He is as much at the service
of this painting as this painting is at His service. The
style, Christ, and the city are indissoluble: El Greco
has just painted the first Christian "landscape" (CA,
194).

If history influences both the artist and the man of
action (as we shall soon discover in Malraux's fiction)
in the early stages of their formation, it is they who make
history once they have found the sounds of their own
voices. Malraux's insistence on a link with the past—
immediate or remote—is, in the present writer's view, his
way of refuting Spengler's thesis of the isolation of civilizations, and, in his insistence on renewal and metamorphosis
rather than mere survival of past epochs (as was the case
in the Renaissance), Malraux also parts company with
Nietzsche's "eternal return." In other words, Malraux has
broken with his own masters; he has destroyed their
truths by wresting from them a new truth manifesting
his own vision of the world—a vision of creation in continuous progress, and of man working hand in hand with
God to renew the creation: "Oh dispersed, ephemeral,
and eternal world who, in order to be renewed rather
than simply reborn, stand in such constant need of men"
(VS, 464).

Malraux has not only broken out of the prison of
the world that formed him: he has also, as his fiction
reveals, revived the Augustinian one-cycle theory of history

—that one, grand cycle which began with the Fall and is prophesied to end with the Last Judgment, a cycle encompassing the period from man's expulsion from the Garden of Eden to the end of time. Man's life in time is envisaged as a continual struggle between the forces of good and evil, with the possible, ultimate victory of the former over the latter. Malraux has not only revived the Augustinian concept of history, he has revitalized it: his emphasis on man's active participation in the transformation of the scheme of things embodies the hope of the ultimate creation by man—in historical time—of an earthly society resembling St. Augustine's eternal City of God.

Notes

1. Vol. II of *La Psychologie de l'art.*
2. Malraux employs religious terminology throughout his study of the cyclic evolution of the artist.
3. VS, 419, 420, 421.

Part II
Contes Fantastiques

9.

The Birth of the Contemporary Hero

As we enter the fiction we shall meet Malraux's heroes all actively engaged in effecting a "transmutation of the scheme of things." They are introduced to us in Malraux's first fantastic tale, *Lunes en papier,* as the seven deadly sins whom we recognize as the direct descendants of Adam and Eve. The presentation of the heroes in this guise points to an analogy between Malraux's and St. Augustine's one-cycle visions of man's life in time as set forth in the introduction to this essay.

We are going to find that the twentieth-century progeny of Adam and Eve are by no means ordinary creatures interested in ordinary accomplishments. Like their forebears, they, too, are going to set out to rectify the creation as they find it. As we witness their birth, we are informed of the presence of spots—no doubt symbolizing original sin—on their otherwise white anatomies: "Seven of these personages were white, their chests and backs spotted with black baubles, insect shadows" (*Lunes,* 165).

Nine personages in all issued from the same fruit: the seven capital sins described above and two newcomers, red in color—a musician and a chemist, Hifili. The latter two, we soon find, are to replace Envy and Avarice, who die of weariness. Pride (*l'Orgueil*) introduces his colleagues to the newcomers: "Various sins: Anger, Lust, Gluttony, Sloth; I am Pride. Hardly a few minutes have passed since you witnessed the demise of Envy and Avarice who were excessively fatigued" (*Lunes,* 165).

The musician and the chemist accept Pride's invitation to join him and his colleagues as replacements for the deceased Envy and Avarice: "Immediately the two red men lost their color and became like the sins" (*Lunes,* 167). The implication of the replacements, of course, is that the seven deadly sins are subject to the cycle of renewal and from time to time must be refurbished with new blood, a possible explanation for the color *red* of the two newcomers and of their previous existences as a musician, suggesting "new spirit," and a chemist, suggesting "change" respectively. The regenerative power of music suggested symbolically here in *Lunes* is a theme which recurs intermittently in Malraux's novels, especially in *L'Espoir,* where Manuel begins to feel the pulse of a new life to the strains of Beethoven's music.

Ready to begin a new era, the twentieth-century versions of the seven deadly sins have been assigned the task of introducing the Malraux reader to contemporary man (in their own persons) and his world. It is a world in which God has been replaced by Satan. Fully cognizant of the state of affairs, the seven capital sins take counsel, and, after careful deliberation, decide that they in turn shall replace Satan, whom they deem their most formidable remaining adversary. They are of the opinion, however, that not until Death, Satan's number-one auxiliary, is out of the way, will the realization of their plan be possible. A dialogue ensues in the course of which Pride discusses with his colleagues both the state of the contemporary world and a possible course of action to alter the existing state of affairs. Pride opens the discussion:

Gentlemen, I presume that you are acquainted with God?
—I knew Him in the old days, replied Hifili; that old man is quite likeable.
—Likeable, yes, but somewhat vulgar, rectified the musician.
—And how could He be otherwise? He has associated with so many people, and so many people still associate with him today!
—He is no longer vulgar, resumed Pride. As a result of old age He has become completely unconscious. He has already changed His name and dress many times without attaching any importance to it; now, this time, Satan, who is no fool, has managed to take his place, and neither God nor anyone else has noticed it. Since Satan has replaced Him, we could replace Satan. What do you say?
—Our power would hardly be worth mentioning, declared Anger. Death, who is Satan's best auxiliary, will destroy us.
—I thought of that. It is extremely simple to disregard it; it suffices to kill Death (*Lunes,* 167–68)!

In *Lunes,* then, we encounter the twentieth-century descendants of Adam and Eve in a world being abandoned by God and overrun by Satan. We learn that God, after having undergone many metamorphoses ("he has already changed his name and dress many times") [1] in the hearts of men, is now in the declining phase of His cycle; and, even where He does linger on, He does so as an empty convention rather than as the source of spiritual regeneration.

In the following passage from *Lunes* we encounter our courageous, if vainglorious, heroes on their way to the Kingdom of Death—*Royaume farfelu*—where they intend to perform the extraordinary actions necessary to implement their plan:

> The sins did not at all like actions capable of being accomplished by just anybody; thus, they refused to use their feet, and thought it fit to advance, walking on their hands, toward the river, whose course was to lead them to the Kingdom of Death (*Lunes,* 171).

W. M. Frohock (*op. cit.,* 25–26) indicated that this voyage across a body of water already prefigures the action of Malraux's first three novels. It is also interesting to note that such journeys are traditionally symbolic of the beginning of a spiritual quest as evidenced by two entries on the subject in J. E. Cirlot's *A Dictionary of Symbols.* Under the entry "Night-Sea Crossing," we learn, "for Jung, this symbol is a kind of Journey into Hell comparable with the journeys described by Virgil and Dante. . . ." [2] Under "Journey" we discover that the voyage in general is symbolic of a quest "that starts in the darkness of the profane world . . . and gropes its way toward the light" [3] (Cirlot, 157).

    We know that the sins are begining a new epoch—and a new quest—for the author tells us that by walking on their hands the sins "were spotting the landscape with new asterisks or unknown punctuation marks" and that they are eagerly setting out to refashion the creation: "and they rejoiced inwardly, for they realized how badly the creation is in need of touch ups, and how much its harmony would have benefited had they been invited to participate in its establishment" (*Lunes,* 171-72).

    If one compares the immediately preceding quotation with the closing passage of Part II of *Les Voix du silence,* one is bound to be struck by the unity of Malraux's vision from *Lunes en papier,* his first fantastic tale, published in 1921, to *Les Voix du silence,* his last, fully completed volume on art: [4] "Oh dispersed, ephemeral and eternal world, who, in order to be renewed rather than simply reborn, stand in such constant need of men" (VS, 464)! In both of these passages Malraux envisages man as a creative being, proud of his capacity to rival the creation, and in both there is a vision of creation in continuous progress.

Once they have decided upon a course of action in order to defy a destiny imposed upon them at birth, the seven capital sins are transformed in appearance; the ex-chemist watches this transformation: "Hifili, now Avarice, watched them brighten. He was joyous. To see those spidery shadows change into imprisoned stars made him feel friendly toward them. Now, he could look at them during the day without suffering from that disgust which the sight of all objects similar in form to apterous insects caused him" (*Lunes,* 171).

What Hifili actually witnessed was the transformation of the sins from subjects of destiny into individuals ready to defy destiny. The "shadow-insect" metaphor is used recurrently by Malraux to designate the masses living on a subhuman level of existence—human creatures who have not yet experienced "the honor of being a man" by defying a destiny imposed upon them and forging one of their own. The "imprisoned star" (*étoiles prison- nières*) metaphor in this same passage is one of many used by Malraux to designate "the light in the darkness"— the divine spark within. What Hifili actually witnessed was the illumination of this divine spark in man—man's transformation from a passive into a creative being.

But alas! even before the heroes reach their destina- tion, the Kingdom of Death, we learn that their undertaking is to be in vain. Along the way they come upon their old friends, the serpents, with whom they engage in conversation. The following passage introduces not only the irony of this little tale but the essence of Malraux's tragic humanism:

> But the tallest of the serpents rose, and standing upright, poised on the tip of his tail, said:
> "You are fools. You mistake us for serpents! You yourselves are serpents! Those who know us regard us as respectable, proper, and dangerous. We are *bigotphones* [italics mine].
> And the sins suffered fright, for they understood that great things—tragic, though as yet uncertain things—were in store for them (*Lunes,* 174).

Ironically, the heroes are setting out to ultimately kill Satan (the serpent), unaware of the fact that the evil personified by Satan resides within their own persons and that the serpents, *bigotphones*,[5] are merely symbolic of the voices of the demons within man.

Finally we enter the Kingdom of Death where we make the acquaintance of one of the most interesting characters of this little tale, in the person of Death's valet, who is described as an old man resembling a foetus. This shrivelled up figure, whose appearance makes it difficult to determine whether he is beginning or ending life, is the symbol of the cycle of creation in which life and death play equally important roles—the one leading endlessly into the other. In the course of the action, the valet makes two entrances into her Majesty Death's apartments; during the first, his appearance is closer to that of an old man: "A valet entered. He seemed old and wrinkled; but he might well have been a foetus" (*Lunes,*

180). The second time he is designated simply as a foetus: "Death rang. The foetus returned" (*Lunes*, 183).

In order to facilitate the implementation of our heroes' plan to kill Death, Pride has disguised himself as the royal physician in order to gain access to her Majesty's chambers. In the following scene between Pride and Death, we learn that her Majesty, too, has undergone a series of metamorphoses from the Gothic to the present era. It is Pride who comments on the change in her appearance:

—Did your Highness not have at that time [on the occasion of his last visit] vertebrae of bone?
—Yes, yes; but I have replaced them with these, which are made of aluminum and are far more practical. . . . And all this [aluminum] is so light! Well, I must keep up with Progress. Everything was becoming mechanical, metallic, shiny; the character of my beauty remained Gothic: I was no longer in fashion (*Lunes*, 181–82).

As the dialogue continues, the irony of this little tale is deepened as an ailing Death, more than willing to abandon a life which disgusts her, transforms what was to be the "extraordinary accomplishment" of the sins into a meaningless gesture:

I should never have been able to commit suicide; what gratitude I owe those who were willing to spare me this pain? [*sic*] . . . The world is . . . tolerable only because we are accustomed to bearing it. It is imposed upon us when we are too young to defend ourselves and then . . . (*Lunes*, 185).

André Vandegans in his recent study dedicated to Malraux's early *contes fantastiques* interprets Death's willingness to depart this world as follows:

> The world is the kingdom of malice, of cruelty, of the absurd, of the ever-renewed struggle against hostile forces. It is ruled over by Death. The banality of the universe and the ennui that it engenders are so unbearable that one can imagine Death herself growing weary of it, to the point of happily agreeing to disappear. If, however, her subjects realize their supreme will to power, which is to destroy her, the meaning of their undertaking would immediately escape them. For the culmination of the absurd is that her annihilation would bring about the collapse of the only thing that gave life an aim: the will to conquer the absurd.[6]

The culmination of the irony comes at the end of the tale when the heroes—having expanded their energies and resources in the accomplishment of a task—have lost sight of their original aim: "Why had they killed Death? They had all forgotten" (*Lunes,* 186).

Our twentieth-century heroes, like their ancestors, have lost sight of the true purpose of human existence which is the destruction of Evil, the original cause of human mortality. Instead, they set out to kill Death, who is but the offspring of Evil, which resides in man.

The irony of this ending, where our heroes have forgotten their original aim, has another significance: it is Malraux's way of emphasizing the importance of continuity from one epoch to the other if any progress is to be made in human history; this idea of continuity was already stressed by St. Augustine in his discussion of the two ancient gods, Janus and Terminus, representing, respectively, the beginning and the end of the world:

> Would it not be a far more elegant way of interpret-
> ing the two-faced image, to say that Janus and Ter-
> minus are the same, and that the one face has
> reference to beginnings, the other to ends? For one
> who works ought to have respect for both. . . . For
> how shall one find how to finish anything, if he has
> forgotten what it was which he had begun? . . . Yet
> even now, when the beginnings and ends of temporal
> things are represented by these two gods, more
> honour ought to have been given to Terminus. For
> the greater joy is that which is felt when anything is
> finished; but things begun are always cause of much
> anxiety until they are brought to an end. . . .[7]

Malraux is going to awaken man, first, to an awareness of his original purpose, second, to the fact that Evil
dwells within his own being, and third, to the means
whereby his purpose may be accomplished—by concen-
trating on the betterment of human society rather than
wholly on himself, and by seeking the God within to
silence his demons.

But did our heroes actually kill Death? Not if we
ponder carefully her Majesty's last words, which obscurely
suggest that she is merely going to undergo another metamorphosis and reappear in a new guise: "My departure,
moreover, will be an honorable source of mystification.
They call me Death, but you well know that I am only
the Accident; slow deterioration itself is only one of my
disguises" (*Lunes*, 185).

What actually disappears from the earth at the end
of this little tale is man's outmoded concepts—not only

of Death, but of God and Satan as well. The new concepts, which issue from their demises in *Lunes* and of which the reader already has some intimation—will be further evolved in Malraux's subsequent works.

Notes

1. Who can fail to recognize this as a prelude to *La Métamorphose des dieux?*
2. Jack Sage trans. (New York: Philosophical Library, 1962), p. 218.
3. See *supra*, Introduction, p. 13.
4. *La Métamorphose des dieux*, which follows *Les Voix du silence* by order of date of publication, has not yet been completed: only the first of three proposed volumes has appeared.
5. The word *bigotphones,* of which the first part has been changed from "bigo-" to "bigot-" is a pun on the word *bigophone,* which denotes "a grotesque and noisy board-pipe." "Bigot," of course, means "bigoted."
6. *La Jeunesse littéraire d'André Malraux. Essai sur l'inspiration farfelue* (Paris: J.-J. Pauvert, 1964), p. 104.
7. *The City of God,* Marcus Dods, D.D., trans. (New York: The Modern Library, 1950), pp. 214–15.

IO.

A Fantastical Vision
of the Human Adventure

As we venture further into the Kingdom of Death or *Royaume farfelu,* the title of Malraux's next *conte fantastique,* we find ourselves in a sort of dreamland of history, where elements of civilizations far removed in time and space are fused and confused so as to create a historico-geographical "imaginary museum" of the human adventure from the beginning to the possible ending of time.[1]

As the action of the fable unfolds, it discloses a one-cycle vision of human history analogous to that of St. Augustine—a cycle that begins and ends in the Earthly Paradise.[2] In other words, this little tale sets forth, in rudimentary form, the world view that emerges from Malraux's entire literary creation.

The link with the beginning of time in *Royaume farfelu* is contained in the figure of Idekel, whose name has been traced back to the Old Testament: "Idekel is simply the transposition of Hiddeqel, one of the branches of the river flowing out of Eden" (Vandegans, 356). The identification of the two names, the historiographer's and the tributary's, evokes an image of man and history issuing together from the Garden of Eden to mark the beginning of the human adventure or man's terrestrial life in time.

As opposed to Eden, where man was immortal, the earth, which constitutes the setting of this fable, is the realm where men die: in other words, *Royaume farfelu* is the earth conceived as a Kingdom of Death; it is also a kingdom where mortals engage in bizarre (*farfelu*) adventures.

If the name of Idekel, the historiographer who is already an old man, takes us back to the beginning of the human adventure to lead us out of the Garden of Eden, the narrator, a somewhat younger historian, promises to lead us a stage further along the way to man's ultimate destination.

In an account to the narrator and the reader of his earlier experiences, Idekel suggests that history—the human adventure—is a series of spiritual journeys, each of which constitutes a cycle. Like his own, each cycle begins with a descent into "Hell," which engages man in a struggle against the demons of Evil. Also implicit in his account is the idea that each journey—or cycle—makes some progress in a struggle which is to continue until the end of time with a possible return to the Heavenly City. Viewed in this light, *Royaume farfelu* is an allegory, in a transfigured existential setting, of the spiritual journey of "everyman" from the expulsion from Eden to the contemporary period.

The cyclic structure of the fable corresponds to the cyclic vision of history it embodies. The outer structure is cyclic in that it begins as the narrator is completing one journey and ends as he is about to embark on another. The inner structure of the tale coincides with the Malraux-Augustinian one-cycle theory of history. It begins with Idekel's account of an earlier descent into Hell (*les îles Infernales*) and ends as the narrator, after accompanying

Idekel on a similar journey, is about to set out for Paradise (*les îles Fortunées*). This inner structure of *Royaume farfelu* prefigures that of the entire cycle of Malraux's novels, through which we accompany his contemporary hero on his journey from the Hell of an absurd world to an intimation of the Earthly Paradise.

Royaume farfelu also introduces the cyclic pattern of character development which continues through Malraux's novels right into his volumes on art, where we have already encountered it in "La Création artistique" of both *La Psychologie de l'art* and *Les Voix du silence* (*supra*, Ch. 8). This pattern is related to a master-disciple relationship which involves the cyclic evolution of the younger of the two heroes from a disciple, at the inception of the action, to a new master as the action draws to a close.[3] In *Royaume farfelu*, Idekel is the master and the narrator is the disciple who becomes a new master.

In the opening scene the latter is on a boat taking him from Europe to the Near East. As the boat approaches the shore, he sights an abandoned conqueror falling asleep under the trees. Some devils, who have been tormenting the passengers, take flight. No sooner do the passengers disembark than they are approached by merchants hawking exotic wares reminiscent of civilizations distant in time and place. One of the merchants burns a phoenix before the eyes of the spectators, who watch it rise from its own ashes and take flight. Immortal dragons are also for sale. Creatures such as the phoenix, the dragon, and the serpent, all of whom are allegedly endowed with the power to renew themselves at the ends of their cycles, recur intermittently in Malraux; fire, too, appears as a recurring cyclic symbol of destruction and re-creation.

Suddenly an official has the narrator and some of the other passengers thrown into a litter and whisked off to prison without any explanation. This incident, which introduces the theme of the absurd, to which the characters in *Royaume farfelu* submit without putting up a struggle, is followed by similar incidents as the action progresses.

Alone in his cell, the narrator indulges in reverie, during which he reveals the reasons for which he left his Mediterranean island to embark for a new land; his images suggest a civilization in the declining phase of its cycle: he speaks of "tarnished galleys," which like himself "were sinking . . . into a constellated mud, into a somber life. . . ."[4]

All of a sudden a jailor interrupts his reverie and leads him before the Prince of the land—*Le Petit Mogol*. The subsequent scene takes place at the palace where the Prince listens to his messengers' accounts of their recent journeys. The first to speak has just returned from Babylon. When the messenger describes Babylon as a deserted city, the Prince replies: "Very well, I will go farther, much farther. Have you heard of hell, hell—" (RF, 134). The allusion to Babylon brings to mind St. Augustine, in whose *City of God* Babylon, or the "City of the Earth," is the antithesis of the Heavenly Jerusalem, or the "City of God." Under the heading "Babylon" in Cirlot's *A Dictionary of Symbols,* we find the following:

> Babylon is an image of a fallen and corrupt existence—the opposite of the Heavenly Jerusalem and of Paradise. . . . In the esoteric sense, it symbolizes the solid or material world, in which the involution and evolution of the spirit takes place, or, in other words, the pervasion and desertion of matter by the spirit.[5]

The implication in the Prince's determination to penetrate

farther is that man's life begins on earth, Babylon, but his spiritual journey begins in Hell.

The next messenger to speak is Idekel himself. He has just accomplished the mission of conducting the Prince's Christian daughter to the land of a barbarian, fish-eating *Tsar* to whom, in compliance with the Prince's wishes, he (Idekel) has offered her in marriage. While Idekel was at the palace, a fire broke out leaving the *Tsarine* a widow. Left alone to rule, the *Tsarine* cast the old gods into the river of history—gods that we encounter again in *La Métamorphose des dieux.*

Without a hearing the narrator is led away to the army on the orders of the Prince—another instance of the "hero's" submitting to the absurd without resistance. In the army the narrator learns that both he and Idekel are to take part in an attack against Ispahan, a city in western Persia.

As the action continues, Idekel gives the narrator an account of his early life:

> I participated in the struggle against the demons which marked the reign of King Abbas. I went to the *isles of hell* [italics mine], with all the sages. . . . Legions of demons fled. . . . The inhabitants extended their snares and killed the demons with sword strokes. (Some, however, are still living . . .) (RF, 139–40).

Up to this point his expedition had not been a total failure, for some of the demons had been destroyed. Ultimately, however, Idekel and his colleagues were defeated. The following passage describes the transformation of the historiographer—as a consequence of the defeat—into a passive being no longer combating destiny but succumbing to it:

But all of the demons were not dead. I know how they finally conquered us. For several weeks I did not go out a single morning without finding illustrious sages strung up, one after the other, on the branches of the trees of the kings of Irkensie, the place where I lived upon my return from the *infernal isles* [italics mine]. . . . As for me, I defended myself for a long time against the evil deeds of the sorcerers; but in vain. Little by little I ceased to heed my conscience. I became indifferent to learning, to teaching, to everything. From then on, I found pleasure only in a strange kind of torpor . . . (RF, 140).

As Idekel continues his story he introduces us to the characters—the soldiers—who constitute the new army of men about to participate in the expedition which is to continue the history of mankind: "But it wasn't long before I knew misery, and I awakened, one day, in this army which is composed of nothing but violent sluggards among whom I represent a peaceful sluggard . . ." (RF, 140). This army, as described by Idekel, is made up of the negative counterparts of the heroes whom we encounter in Malraux's full-fledged novels; it is composed of men who submit to the absurd without putting up a struggle.

At about this point the narrator interrupts Idekel with a eulogy on the virtues of fire as the purifying element in the universe—an element already introduced in the scene of the marketplace, where the phoenix, set afire, rose anew from its own ashes: "You are old, but without doubt you have never seen a great incendiary. A great incendiary is one of the most perfect works of God. Fire infuses everything it touches with precious matter . . ." (RF, 140). The narrator finds that he is mistaken, for

Idekel responds by describing the burning of the palace of Ispahan that he witnessed during the course of his first expedition against that city:

> I saw it very clearly, because my nonchalant disposition had led me away from the gates; the fire advanced slowly along the roofs like an animal, with its crackling little purple and reddish-brown flames. The odor of burning things began to mingle with the scent which I had first believed to be that of roses and which was only that of those gardens stretched among mountains covered with snow . . . (RF, 141).

This great incendiary, the aging historiographer goes on to suggest, transformed the world into a phoenix which was to rise again from its own ashes; it marked the end of an old order out of which a new vision of the world would be created: "That night was one of the great nights of the world, one of those on which brutalized gods yield the earth to the untamed geniuses of poetry" (RF, 142).

And, in his judgment of a previous expedition conducted under Emperor Basil II, whose cruelty has been recorded by history, Idekel indicates that man can and should learn from history; he expresses the hope that the new expedition of which he and the narrator are now a part will attest to the evolution of man from a barbarous into a more human creature on the road back to the Heavenly City:

> Emperor Basil II, Idekel said to me, whom we historians call the Big Killer of Bulgarians ordered the blinding of innumerable Bulgarian combatants whom

he had taken prisoner. . . . We shall leave behind less barbarous testimony; *our road will become the road to Paradise* [italics mine] (RF, 143).

Immediately following is Idekel's fantastical parody of the biblical prophesy of the final coming of the Heavenly Jerusalem:

People will recognize the villages where we stopped by the familiar animals, who, having come from the Orient and the Occident,[6] are already meeting there, thanks to the negligence of our soldiers; by way of a thousand witty sayings, the little gray monkeys perched on all the walls will tell the travelers where we pitched camp. The parakeets, who are multiplying rapidly, will invade the region. The pippins and mongooses will docily follow the old men, and the children who play at the entrances to the villages will be surrounded by an attentive circle of learned rabbits . . . (RF, 143).

Unfortunately, given the nature of the soldiers who constitute the army, defeat is a foregone conclusion. The soldiers succumb to every messenger of Destiny; of these messengers, which include Hunger, Silence, Darkness, and Scorpions, the soldiers' own mediocrity is, perhaps, the most potent. The narrator himself compares this army, of which he forms a part, unfavorably with those of the past: "In former times, I had seen our armies: the men were dutiful and marched in good order. . . . We were advancing as we pleased, badly dressed and scarcely armed" (RF, 142).

The cycle from Idekel's past defeat to the present defeat is completed, but the fable ends on a note of hope:

a new cycle begins as the narrator (the young historian and the new master) sets out again, this time for Paradise —"les îles Fortunées" (RF, 152).

Now that we have some idea of man's original purpose —the destruction of the demons of Evil—and of the direction in which he is headed—"les îles Fortunées"—let us not disturb the conqueror left sleeping at the outset of *Royaume farfelu* (*supra*, p. 000) until the correspondents of *La Tentation de l'Occident* have set the stage for the role he is to play in the twentieth century as man continues his journey to the end of time.

Notes

1. This interpretation, minus the historico-geographical "imaginary museum" and the vision of the human adventure in its entirety, was inspired by André Vandegans, who saw in the same aspect of *Royaume farfelu* an attempt on the part of Malraux to find a common denominator for all civilizations and for the nocturnal part of man.
2. See *supra*, Introduction, pp. 7-8.
3. This relationship—minus its cyclic evolution—was pointed out by both W. M. Frohock and Gaëtan Picon in their pioneering studies on Malraux; it was further developed by Leon S. Roudiez in his article "Schème et vocabulaire chez Malraux," *French Review*, XLI, No. 3 (December, 1967), 304-18.
4. André Malraux, *Royaume farfelu* (Genève: Skira, 1945), p. 133. Henceforth cited as RF.
5. Jack Sage (trans.), (New York, 1962), p. 37.
6. This might be interpreted as a prefiguration of the eventual meeting of East and West, which is further developed both in *La Tentation de l'Occident* and in Malraux's first three novels set in the Orient.

Part III
A Cyclic Spiritual Journey
from Hell to Paradise

II.

The Crisis Facing East and West

La Tentation de l'Occident is, in essence, an essay written in the form of an epistolary novel comprising an exchange of philosophical letters between a Chinaman, Ling, traveling in Europe, and a Frenchman, A.D., traveling in China. These letters have been written for the specific purpose of providing the Malraux reader with some insight not only into the opposing world views of East and West and the germ of their possible fusion, but also into the contemporary crisis facing man in each civilization as the cycle of change continues its irreversible course.

Each of the travelers, in the course of the correspondence, gives his interpretations of the notions of man, life, and the universe embodied in the other's civilization as contrasted with his own. From these interpretations we learn that the crisis in both East and West involves a transformation of man and a consequent modification of man's view of the world and his role in it. Gradually it becomes apparent that the crisis is centered around the notion of man as an "individual." Whereas the individual is just beginning to emerge in a China about to awaken from centuries of torpor, we learn that in the West, where the pursuit of the self has reached its extreme limit— beyond which lies the absurd—he is in danger of disintegrating and succumbing to the absurd.

Through Ling, we discover that man in China conceives of his universe as an indissoluble whole, of which he himself is but a fragment. Governed by two opposing rhythms which maintain it in incessant motion, this universe, and everything in it, undergoes constant transformation. In rhythm with this flux, the soul of man "transmigrates" from one being, and hence from one life, to another, without any recollection of its previous existences. In its entirety, this incessantly changing universe, of which man is but a fragment, lies beyond the grasp of the rational human mind; yet, for the Chinese, knowledge of the totality is the only knowledge worth acquiring. Reality, which is transitory, and which, therefore, constitutes but a phase of life leading to an unknown future, is not worth knowing. Life in its entirety is viewed as a "series of possibilities."

According to the Chinese, knowledge of the "unknowable" universe may be obtained, not through any rational means proceeding from the known to the unknown, but through a method, practiced by Buddhists and Taoists, culminating in a loss of consciousness. Though experienced as a communion with the absolute ("the principle"), this is the very opposite of rational knowledge. Ling describes the method in one of his letters:

The images which had been attached to contemplation, the origin of the thinker's meditation, are blotted out; he now finds in these images only the idea of rhythms combined with a powerful exaltation. Idea and exaltation, now united, mount to the point of loss of consciousness which is communion with the principle, the only point at which the unity of the rhythms is experienced.[1]

This fusion of what had been opposing rhythms induces the "serenity" which is the ultimate goal of meditation in that it provides a temporary release from the incessant flux of life.

The Frenchman rejects Ling's equation of this experience with the attainment of the absolute: "While in the state of ecstasy, the thinker is not one with the absolute as your sages teach: what the thinker calls the absolute is actually the extreme point of his sensation" (TO, 99). A.D. views this "extreme point of sensation" as the greatest "intensity" of a man's capacity to feel, and it is in this intensity that he, A.D., will later discover a permanent, universal element in man.

Given the Oriental view of the universe, in which man as a separate entity is inconceivable, it is understandable that the concept of personality as it evolved in the West has remained, for more than 2500 years and right up to the contemporary period, but a latent possibility in the Orient.

As part of a creation over which he had no control, Oriental man looked upon himself as a passive being subject to transformation by time along with the rest of the universe. He therefore looked upon himself as a non-responsible being (nonresponsible in the Christian sense), whose ultimate aim was to flee the self, to offer the self up to the world. He envisaged life in its entirety as movement and continuity (with death as a part of that continuity) rather than as a series of fragments marked off, as in the West, by periods—or cycles—beginning with life and ending with death. All of Oriental man's values, with wisdom and serenity crowning the list, were related to an effort to merge the self with the totality: "to be" one with it, and then to retain consciousness of that oneness.

Western man's view of himself and his relation to his universe is radically different. Ling's reactions to the West reflect his awareness of having left the land of "being," where civilization is based upon refinement of sentiment, to enter the land of "action," where civilization is confused with order.

Ling's immediate impression of Europe is that it is "a land devoured by geometry" (TO, 25)—a land whose appearance bears the imprint of Western man's determination to "act" rather than to "be." Western man seeks to impose order on the chaotic multiplicity of his world, rather than to "be" part of it; his will is to leave behind some evidence of his pilgrimage on earth—to "conquer time" by imprisoning it in forms created by his own hands; in short, to give his world a meaning in human terms.

As opposed to the relatively stable world view which has dominated the East, where "constant transformation" is accepted as the law of the universe, the rapid and frequent transformations of the Western image of man and his world are, paradoxically enough, the direct consequence of Occidental man's perennial quest for permanence and stability. It was Western man's refusal to accept impermanence that impelled him to set up one system after another, one value after another, and one absolute after another, only to find them disintegrate, with time, into relative absolutes—into myths. The opposing world views of East and West stem from Western man's conception of himself as a being distinct from the universe on the one hand, and Eastern man's image of himself as a fragmentary part of the universe on the other. While the former seeks to "bring the world to man," the latter "offers himself up to the world."

The Occidental world view stems from Greece, the

cradle of Western civilization, where man declared himself a being distinct from the universe—a being who is
born and who dies, and who therefore seeks to explain
his universe in terms of his own life cycle. It is Ling
who makes this observation in a letter recording his
recollections of his impressions of a recent visit to a
museum in Athens:

> Some moments ago, when I evoked the humble mu-
> seum among the forms that I had seen across the
> world, the head of a young man with open eyes
> imposed itself upon me, as an allegory of the Greek
> genius, with its profound insinuation: to measure all
> things according to the duration and *intensity* [italics
> mine] of a human life (TO, 48).

The term "intensity" in the foregoing passage, combined with the implication of the same idea in the phrase
"the extreme point of sensation" (*supra,* p. 147) indicating
the point at which Oriental man loses consciousness to
merge with the absolute, is the basis for A. D.'s conclusion
that the notion of intensity is inseparable from the notion
of man. Whereas Ling rejects the idea of any permanent
element in human nature: "you believe that there is, in
what you call Man something permanent which does not
exist" (TO, 94), A. D. maintains the contrary: "I have
been observing China for almost two years. The first thing
that it transformed in me was the western notion of Man.
I can no longer conceive of Man without relation to his
intensity" (TO, 100).

    In another letter Ling distinguishes the Greek, Chris-
tion, and Oriental views of man's relation to his world:
"The Greek believes man to be distinct from the world
while the Christian believes him linked to God, and we

believe him linked to the world" (TO, 48). Aided by his book knowledge of the West, Ling reminds us that it was the Greeks who disrupted the continuity of life by dividing it into fragments—into cycles terminated by death: "The Greeks conceived of man as *a* man, a being who is born and who dies. The span of life became the principal element of the universe for them" (TO, 48).

As the evolution of Western man continued (our correspondents inform us), Christianity added to the Greek image of man as a being distinct from the universe the image of man as an individual distinct from his fellows, each of whom is caught in a conflict between the forces of good and evil in his own nature. And if the concept of finality associated with death originated in Greece, it was Christianity that gave death its tragic aspect in the West.

As both Ling and A.D. would have it, the Christian interiorization of destiny (whereby Western man became an individual conscious of, and responsible for, his own inner nature) contained the seed of what grew, after the passing of many centuries, into a frenzied pursuit of the individual to the exclusion of all else.[2] The result is that the Western now, abandoned by God and isolated from his fellows is thrown back on himself. Left to his own devices, he is on the verge of succumbing to the absurd which, according to A. D., is encountered at "the extreme point of the individual." The following "epigram" is a succinct summary, as Ling sees it, of the evolution of Western man from Ancient Greece—Christianity intervening—to the contemporary period: "After the death of the sphinx, Oedipus attacks himself" (TO, 49). Western man, who began his history as Oedipus attacking destiny as an external force, is now at grips with the forces of destiny which are threatening to destroy him from within.

What all of this amounts to is that, after destroying

one absolute after another—beginning with God and ending with Man—the Western individual, who has set himself up as the last incarnation of the absolute, is now faced with self-destruction. One failure after another to impose stability on flux has forced upon Occidental man an awareness and acceptance of "constant transformation" as the law of life. The last of a long line of absolutes, the individual himself is now being relativized. A.D. speaks of the crisis facing the West as "the disintegration of a Universe and of a notion of Man, to the structuring of which so many good minds contributed" (TO, 121). And he goes on, in the same letter, to discuss the dilemma facing European man, who is reaching out beyond his own borders for a solution:

More or less clearly, the idea of the impossibility of grasping any reality whatsoever is dominating Europe. . . . Whence the profound transformation of man, far less important in the cries that proclaim it than in its rupture of the barriers which, for a thousand years, had closed and fortified our world from the world outside itself. . . .

Reality, in its declining phase, allies itself with myths, and it prefers those which are born of the mind (TO, 121–22).

Ling is aware of the darkening twilight in the West, where a race dedicated to conquest through action and sacrifice has, for thousands of years, created and destroyed one absolute after the other, only to find itself severed from Being in a meaningless world where all action seems absurd: "the European evening is lamentable and empty, as empty as the soul of a conqueror" (TO, 71).

In the following passage, A. D. describes the emotional

state of his countrymen, confronted with an individualism in the declining phase of its cycle and conscious of the need to rechannel it lest the individual succumb to the absurd:

> Europeans are tired of themselves, tired of their individualism which is crumbling, tired of their exaltation. What sustains them is less an idea than a fine structure of negations. Capable of acting to the point of sacrifice, but full of disgust for the will to action which is twisting their race today, they would like to discover in the acts of men a more profound *raison d'être* (TO, 86).

Malraux is even more eloquent on the same subject in the closing lines of his "D'Une Jeunesse européenne" where he writes of Western man's awareness of the ephemeral nature of reality (following the decline of the individual as an "absolute") and the consequent emergence of a world view oriented toward the future:

> European youth is more concerned about what the world may be than by what it is. . . . It seeks to find in each man the interpreter of a provisional reality. . . . And the world is reduced to an immense play of relationships which no intellect endeavors to fix, since it is in the very nature of these relationships to change, to renew themselves incessantly. It seems that our civilization is moving in the direction of creating a metaphysics from which all fixed points are excluded, a metaphysics similar to its conception of matter. With Man and the Individual destroyed one after the other, what power has any such metaphysics over the needs of the soul? To try to make these needs

disappear and to erect, next to a conception of life in which everything that cannot be translated into acts and figures has become alien, a domain of the mind and of the sensibility—a domain endlessly moving, changing, built on ever-new relationships and an endless succession of new births. . . . Weak images, in the face of age-old human necessities. Toward what destiny is this violent youth headed, this youth marvellously armed against itself and liberated from the base vanity of naming "grandeur" its scorn for a life with which it cannot associate itself (JE, 151–53)?

The fusion of East and West has begun with the West's acceptance of the Oriental notion of life as an infinite series of possibilities, revealed by the cycle of constant transformation. As for the destiny of Western man—and his new *raison d'être*—we have to wait until his spiritual journey is completed in the novels before attempting to define his new image of himself and his world.

In counterdistinction to what has become the West's frenzied pursuit of the individual, the Orient, for thousands of years, has considered "an inattentive cultivation of the self" the supreme achievement of a truly refined civilization.

The different notions of man in East and West gave rise to two vastly different civilizations sustained by opposing values. Ling accuses Europeans of confusing social order with true civilization, which, from the Eastern point of view, is a matter of sentiment and is, therefore, psychological rather than social in nature. Ling claims that the true artist is not he who creates, as in the West, but he who *feels* as he contemplates a work of art. The acceptance of movement and flux as the law of life in the East, as contrasted with the longing for stability in the West, is manifested in the art of each: while the Chinese artist conceives of a cat in terms of the way it moves, the European sees its lines, its contours; in short, its form, which is static. If the Oriental passively submits to being transformed by time, the European seeks to conquer time by imprisoning it in forms. In contrast to the Chinese aspiration toward serenity, Ling sees his Western counterpart bent on action. If the Chinese's aim is "to be," the European's is "to do." A. D. fuses the two ideas into "to become," which is the essence of the existentialist notion of man. In the East, admiration is inspired by the attainment of wisdom and serenity, in the West it is the man of action—the man who sacrifices himself for a cause—who wins the admiration of his fellows. The Chinese aspiration is toward wisdom and understanding; the European's efforts are directed toward the acquisition of knowledge leading to the development of critical judgment. These attitudes extend into the domain of art: while the Oriental contemplates a work of art in order to feel and understand it, the European seeks to know and judge a work by comparing it with others. Whereas Eastern thought leads to a consciousness of "irreconcilable differences" in the universe, Western thought proceeds from evident analogies to hidden ones in the hope of ultimately attaining knowledge of the totality. If Oriental man aspires toward an ordered sensibility, Western man seeks an ordered mind. While thought and emotion are one in the East, they are separated in the West. Love in the Western sense is nonexistent in the Orient, where woman is not only devoid of personality but considered a separate species. Ling suggests that Westerners confuse love, as they seek to define it, with a desire to assimilate and identify with the opposite sex to the point of being able to experience simultaneously their own sensations and those of their partners. The theme of eroticism introduced here reappears in the novels. The opposing views of death in East and West are related to their respective world views: in the Orient, death is associated with the idea of continuity from generation to generation; the Oriental feels the presence of his ancestors and venerates them. By contrast, Ling is appalled by the European association of death with tragedy, and he also contrasts the impassive expressions on the faces of his countrymen with the faces marked by suffering which he encounters all about him in Europe.

"Unfortunately," the Oriental world vision, of which Ling is so proud, is about to crumble into ruins as "the temptation of the West"—the notion of man, not only as an individual, but also as an active, creative being capable of forging his own destiny—spreads to the Orient.

The figure who incarnates China in her death throes is the venerable old Chinaman Wang-loh, whom A. D. visits during his sojourn in China. Wang-loh describes the collapse of the system that has sustained the Orient for thousands of years:

The spectacle is extraordinarily powerful. A Theater of Anguish. It is the destruction, the collapse of one of the greatest human systems, a system which managed to live without the support of either gods or men. Collapse! China is vacillating like an edifice in ruins, and the source of her anguish is neither incertitude nor strife, but rather her trembling roof . . . (TO, 110).

Terms such as "destruction," "collapse," "is vacillating," "edifice in ruins," and "trembling roof," which vividly express the idea of disintegration in the foregoing quotation, continue to appear as Wang-loh continues his description of a dying China. In the following lines, he speaks of the passing into history of the philosophy which was the sustaining force of the Chinese system:

> Once Confucianism is reduced to crumbs, the whole country will be destroyed. All these men are dependent upon it. It has created their sensibility, their thought, and their will. It has given them the feeling of their race. It has fashioned the countenance of their happiness . . . (TO, 110).

He also speaks of the disintegration of the Chinese world view and notion of man:

> The beginning of the end sets in relief the character of what is still standing. What have they sought for 2500 years? A perfect assimilation of the world by man; for their life was a slow apprehension of the world, of which they wished to be the fragmentary consciousness . . . (TO, 110).

Wang-loh contrasts the foregoing world view, while at the same time pointing out its main weaknesses, with Western individualism:

> Opposed to what you call individualism is disintegration, or rather, the rejection of all structures of the mind. . . . A concept such as this bears within itself the seed of its own destruction—a contempt for force. China, which formerly used force as a vulgar auxiliary, is seeking it out again today, and is bringing to

it, like an offering to wicked gods, the intelligence of
its entire youth (TO, 110).

The "disintegration" of the soul in the bosom of the
universe was Oriental man's way of merging with the
eternal light of the universe.

Wang-loh expresses his regrets and nostalgia for the
"work of art" that was but is no more, and he speaks
of the forces effecting its destruction:

> The world will never rediscover the work of art that
> our sensibility once was. An aristocracy of culture—
> the search for wisdom and beauty, two faces of the
> same genius.. . . Watch their lamentable debris being
> dragged to the ground with the banners of propa-
> ganda, from the Anfou Club to the basest political
> meetings . . . (TO, 110).

The constellations of death begin to appear in the
sky as the last representatives of the old China disappear
one after the other. Wong-loh takes a dim view of the
meeting of East and West on the soil of China and an
even more pessimistic view of the future in store for
his countrymen:

> Unfortunately, we understand each other; and we
> shall never be able to harmonize our undetermined
> universe, concerned with the infinite, with your
> world of allegories. What is born of their confronta-
> tion, like a cruel genius full of indifference, is the
> supreme royalty of the arbitrary . . . (TO, 111).

And there remains in them [the young of China]

only a furious desire for destruction—just to see. . . .
To invent, to pile up money or unite territories, to
engage in useless psychology or construct allegories
to explain the world, all that is vain, absolutely vain
(TO, 112).

Wang-loh shows A. D. to the door; as he does, he is the
personification, in the trembling of his hands, of a crumbling China.

In his answer to A. D.'s letter apropos of his visit
to Wang-loh, Ling voices his accord with the old man's
views:

> . . . he believes that China is going to die. I think so,
> too. The China that surrounded his youth, with its
> art, its distinction, and its civilization whose entire
> interest was centered on the emotions, with its gar-
> dens and its abject misery, is almost dead today
> (TO, 115).

And Ling pinpoints the cause of China's death: "the
temptation of the West" [3] is giving birth to the Western
notion of man in China:

> The individual is being born in them, and with it
> that strange taste for passionless destruction and an-
> archy, which would seem the supreme diversion of
> incertitude if the need for escaping did not reign in
> all those imprisoned hearts, if the pallor of immense
> incendiaries did not light their way (TO, 117).

Ling regards the adoption and implementation of Western
ideas by the educated youth in his country as the conquest

of China's "soul" by the West, whose influence, up to this point, had been restricted to the political and economic spheres: "The new elite, composed of the men who have embraced Western culture, is so different from the former that we are obliged to think that the true conquest of the Empire by the West is beginning" (TO, 116).

In the following passage, Ling gives a vivid picture of the new China rising out of "the old vessel" or of death leading to new life, and he also envisages the rebirth of the old. Here, in a single passage, we have both movements of the unifying cyclic theme of Malraux's entire literary creation:

> The soul of the China that is being born, must doubtless be sought in the parts of this magnificent old vessel that are still alive enough to tempt youth. At least this culture that we see growing weaker will still retain, when it is almost extinguished, that supreme beauty of dead cultures which call forth and adorn renaissances . . . (TO, 116).

Ling also wonders whether the young Cantonese experiencing the anguish of Western individualism will some day find release in some great Chinese action. Succumbing to the West while at the same time hating it, these young men, newly born individuals, are thus far conscious only of injustice. The nature of the actions of these men, motivated by hate, is unpredictable. The following question, posed by Ling, indirectly introduces the terrorist Hong of Malraux's first novel, Les Conquérants: ". . . What then will be the gestures of those who will willingly risk death in the name of hatred alone" (TO, 118)?

And it is in Les Conquérants that the new China of which Ling speaks in the following passage begins to emerge: "A new China is being created, one which escapes even us. . . . the low voice of destruction is already heard in the most distant echoes of Asia . . ." (TO, 118).

In this same novel, the conqueror left sleeping on the shore in Malraux's *Royaume farfelu* is awakened in the person of Garine, who begins to acquire the "lucidity" for which A. D. expresses such an avid desire in the closing lines of *La Tentation de l'Occident.*

Notes

1. André Malraux, *La Tentation de l'Occident* (Genève: Skira, 1945), p. 95. Henceforth cited as TO.
2. This by no means implies that either of the correspondents holds Christianity responsible for this development.
3. Malraux's title, *La Tentation de l'Occident,* has a twofold significance: it refers not only to the spread of Western values in the Orient, but also to the invasion of Europe by the world through *le musée imaginaire.* The word *tentation,* meaning "trial" or "test," refers to the crisis facing both East and West as the two begin to meet. More will be said about the "trial" facing Europe in the section on the imaginary museum in Part IV of this essay.

12.

The Sensibility of the Absurd

If *La Tentation de l'Occident* and "D'Une Jeunesse européenne" disclosed the crisis centering around the notion of man as an individual in East and West as the twentieth century was reaching the quarter mark, *Les Conquérants*, Malraux's first full-fledged novel, whose central event is the Canton strike of 1925, plunges the reader into the thick of that crisis where both contemporary man and his civilization—European no less than Asian—are undergoing a radical metamorphosis. Man's age-old quest for identity is about to begin again as a struggle against absurdity and death in a world of crumbling values.

Like every metamorphosis, that effected by the action of *Les Conquérants* is destructive in its initial phase—destructive both of an image of man which represents an outmoded phase of the human spirit and of the phase of the civilization which sustained it. This destructive phase, which marks at once the end of the old cycle and the birth pangs of the new, coincides with the initial stage of the spiritual journey of the hero—with his descent into the metaphorical hell of an absurd world of invalidated values.

Engaged on either side of the struggle which forms the action of *Les Conquérants* are both Chinese and Europeans. The conflict is between those who would preserve the status quo and those who would destroy it; between those who would preserve the old China and European colonialism and those who would destroy them. On one side we have both Chinese and Europeans who benefit from a maintenance of the existing situation. On the other we have both the nascent Chinese individual, who is rejecting a world in which human dignity has been denied to all but the privileged few, and the European individual, who no longer finds any outlet for the expression of an individualism which has led him to the brink of the absurd in the West. The European is reaching out beyond his own borders, breaking out of the prison cycle of his own civilization, turning away from a world which has lost all significance, in a defiant gesture and a desperate quest for meaning.

What is at stake in *Les Conquérants* is the Old China and the Oriental notion of man as a fragment of the universe on the one hand, and European colonialism and a Western individualism at grips with the absurd on the other. By the end of the novel all four are in their death throes.

As the novel begins, the narrator of *Les Conquérants* is aboard ship somewhere in the middle of the Indian Ocean, en route from Europe to the Orient, or, more specifically, from France to China. Along the way he is to stop off at Singapore, Saigon, and Hong Kong before reaching Canton, his final destination and the scene of the great strike of 1925 which is destined not only to force another wedge into the already crumbling edifice of a 2500-year-old Chinese civilization but also to contribute to the ultimate destruction of the British interests in Hong Kong.

The opening line of *Les Conquérants* is a ship news bulletin announcing simultaneously the central event of the novel and the critical stage of the scene to which the anonymous narrator is journeying: "A general strike has been declared at Canton." [1] The restless, anxious mood which pervades the novel is thus set at the outset and is intensified as bulletin follows bulletin: "Each day the news gives a detailed account of the drama that is beginning, growing, becoming a direct threat, haunting everyone on the ship" (Conq, 15).

The world is changing: in a prophetic announcement the narrator declares: ". . . European domination is going to be destroyed" (Conq, 16). The Orient is changing, too: after stopping at Singapore, the narrator, aboard ship again, records his impressions of this world in ferment: ". . . another China is being born, the creature of a shapeless, tormented soul. It would be difficult to imagine a more exciting conflict: British and Chinese energies totally absorbed in the pursuit of money, and beneath the surface, amorphous yet active, the revolutionary mass, like an underground river" (Conq, 25).

The characters effecting these changes are introduced gradually, first indirectly, through flashbacks and documents while the narrator is still aboard ship, and then directly, as the narrator meets them either on his various stop-offs along the way, or at his final destination, Canton, the center of operations.

What unites the Western and Oriental heroes of *Les Conquérants* is their rejection of the world into which they were born—a world they are bent on destroying. All are more or less conscious of their uniqueness as individuals and of the fact that they have only one life, which must not be expended without leaving behind something that will survive their physical deaths.

Each of the leading characters is impelled to action by an obsession which has become an end in itself, an obsession independent of the ethical goal—the improvement of the lot of the Chinese masses—which might have initiated the action. Though their original purpose is being realized, the heroes are motivated primarily by self-interest—by a determination to defy physical death by leaving "a scar on the face of the map."

While still aboard ship, the narrator informs the reader that he is undertaking a journey made earlier by both Garine and their mutual friend, Lambert, before him. As the action progresses, a master-disciple relationship is discernible, first between Lambert and Garine, and then between Garine and the narrator. Lambert, the first to make the voyage from Europe to the Orient, had invited Garine to come at his (Lambert's) expense; Garine, in turn, does the same for the narrator. The master-disciple relationship in *Les Conquérants* is cyclic as it was in *La Création artistique* and *Royaume farfelu,* and as it will be in the novels that follow. Progress of some kind is always made as a cycle is completed by a disciple who becomes a new master. Shortly after the arrival of Garine, Lambert had returned to Europe and left his disciple to replace him as Director of Propaganda. By transforming his master's Propaganda Ministry from what had been a "comic opera" into an effective instrument of the revolution, Garine became a new master with the narrator as his disciple.

Intermittently throughout the course of the action it becomes apparent that Garine would convince his disciple, first, of the absurdity of life, and secondly, that "power for power's sake" is the only effective means of counteracting the absurd. In so doing, Garine introduces the dilemma of the absurd as the main theme of the novel, and himself as Malraux's first hero about to begin the cyclic spiritual journey of twentieth-century man. Garine is a hero who has broken with his past after several direct encounters with the absurd: first, in the guise of the unreal, theatrical nature of a trial which led to his imprisonment for complicity in an abortion affair, and more recently, in the form of the illnesses, malaria and dysentery, which are rapidly consuming him.

It was the critical situation in China which brought Garine to the Orient. A world in a state of eruption, and for which no new rational design appeared feasible in the immediate future, seemed the ideal setting for the exercise of power as a means of defying the absurd. For Garine, the revolution is a state of things, independent, for the most part, of any ethical goals.

As the action continues, it reveals a China that is rapidly adopting the values of the West. It is Gérard, the special envoy of the Kuomintang in Indochina, who makes this observation while briefing the narrator (during the latter's stop-off in Saigon) on some of the key figures with whom he will be associated in China:

> You know that China knew nothing of ideas that lead to action, ideas that are taking hold of her like a prey, just as the idea of equality took hold of the French in '89. China was unaware of even the simplest form of individualism. The coolies are busy discovering that they exist, simply that they exist . . . (Conq, 31–32).

Ironically enough, European colonialism is being destroyed by the spread of Western values in the Orient. Action and that individualism are gradually transforming what was the land of "being" into a land of "action." Oriental man, who once conceived of himself as a fragment of the universe, is rapidly becoming conscious of his existence as an independent entity. The propagation

of Western values among the entire population is destroying what had been a civilization for the elite few and
"hopefully" giving rise to one designed to serve all, including the coolies, whose untold miseries had made it impossible for them to experience fully human living.

And it is a Westerner, Garine, who is actively engaged in awakening these coolies; we are informed of this
as Gérard continues his briefing: "In giving them the possibility of believing in their own dignity or, if you prefer,
in their own importance, Garine's propaganda has acted
upon them in a disturbing, profound—one might say un-
foreseen—and extraordinarily violent manner" (Conq, 32).

Klein, the European organizer of the Canton strike
whom the narrator meets in Hong Kong, declares that a
point of no return has been reached in China: "Here,
things have changed! When the obstinate merchants wished
to restore the old state of affairs, their district burned for
three days" (Conq, 70).

Later, Garine himself comments on the westernization
of the Oriental world view: "The whole of modern Asia
is penetrated with the feeling of individual existence and
the discovery of death" (Conq, 119). These two concepts
—individualism and of death—born of Christianity and
Ancient Greece respectively, define man as an individual
who measures all things by the duration and intensity of
his own life.

Elaborating on the subject, Garine presents a picture
of the Chinese working class as an aggregate mass, whose
members, impelled by the growing intensity of their
consciousness of the Western image of man, are striving to
break out of this mass as distinct beings—". . . to attain
that personal, individual life that they confusedly consider
the most precious possession of the rich" (Conq, 120). By
breaking out of the collectivity, they hope to experience

what has thus far been denied them—". . . the feeling of
a more truly human existence. . ." (Conq, 120).

In the course of a discussion on the role of individualism in both the present revolution and that of '89, Garine,
in a rhetorical question, expresses the persuasion that
individualism, which was once a spiritual force, has become a temporal force in man's struggle for political and
economic freedom: "Was it not a similar feeling—that of
possessing a personal life, distinct in the eyes of God—that
constituted the strength of Christianity" (Conq, 120)? [2] At
one point, Klein emphasizes the difficulty of the task facing
the revolutionaries in their attempt to awaken the Chinese
masses: "Yes, to teach these people that something called
a human life exists! A human being—*ein Mensch*—is
indeed something rare" (Conq, 69)! Once aroused, however, these coolies make good revolutionaries: "They fear
seeing the end of the revolution and returning to the
humiliating state from which they hope to deliver themselves" (Conq, 32).

But the driving force of the revolutionaries, thus
far conscious solely of what has been denied them, is
hatred. It is the Oriental hero of the novel, the chief of
the terrorists, Hong, who incarnates this emergent Chinese
individual. Here is what Garine reports of Hong's attitude:
"Only action in the service of hatred is neither falsehood,
nor cowardice, nor weakness: it alone is a worthy opponent
of words" (Conq, 147). And here is Hong himself in
Garine's office: "And those who teach the wretched to
bear their misery—be they priests, Christians, or others
—must be punished" (Conq, 143). Later, during the
same scene, Garine quotes Hong on the composition of
mankind: "There are only two races, he said, the wretched
and the others" (Conq, 146). Hong is explicit about the
focus of his hatred: "he did not at all hate the happiness

of the rich, but rather their self-respect. 'A poor man, he added, can not esteem himself' " (Conq, 146).

After working under Garine for some time, Hong becomes impatient with what he considers the slow pace of Party measures and begins to take matters into his own hands. He orders the slaying of personages, one after another, on both sides; his victims include all those who, in his opinion, have in any way slowed down the efforts of the revolution. In some cases—particularly that of the Chinese banker whom Hong orders liquidated in spite of the fact that he rendered financial assistance to the party—his sole criterion is the wealth or dignity of the person singled out. According to Hong, this wealth or dignity had, in the past, been acquired at the expense of the masses.

Hong's hatred becomes an all-consuming passion; murder of his enemies becomes for him the only way of lending significance to a life that will be terminated for all time by death. Hong was made intensely conscious of having but "a single life, a single life . . ." (Conq, 146) in the Western sense—as opposed to the Oriental belief in the transmigration of the soul to another body—by his mentor Rebecci, a Westerner who also bequeathed to Hong the abandoned hopes of his own youth as a militant anarchist.

When Hong's independent actions become more dangerous than beneficial to the Party, he is captured and brought to the headquarters of Garine, whose rifle he grabs in an unsuccessful attempt to kill him. Garine's affinity for the young terrorist is expressed when he says that there are few enemies whom he understands better (Conq, 147), and orders Hong to be tried by a "special" tribunal.

What do these two men have in common—this

Oriental, Hong, who has just recently emerged from the depths of misery to experience life as an individual, and this European, Garine, at grips with an individualism which has led him to the brink of the absurd? It is their inability to exist in any organized society—their total rejection of society in any form whatsoever as absurd. Here is Hong's master, Rebecci, on the subject: ". . . when one has only one life, one does not try to change the social structure . . ." (Conq, 45). And here is Hong, the disciple, on the same subject: "All social structures are nothing but filth. A single life. Don't waste it. That's it" (Conq, 149). And finally, Garine himself: "I do not consider society bad, capable of being improved—I consider it absurd. . . . Absurd. I'm not interested in its being transformed" (Conq, 78).

So intense is Garine's sensibility of the absurd that he declares himself to be not only asocial, but amoral and atheistic as well. He openly admits that he has no love for his fellow men and that he prefers the poor only because they are the vanquished. But, and this is important, he is lucid—Garine is fully aware of his own motives and of the importance of his work in changing the lives of the Chinese masses who are just beginning to realize that they exist as individuals rather than as parts of an amorphous mass. He claims that he has awakened them: "I have created their hope. Their hope. I am not fond of set phrases but, in a word, a man's hope is his reason for living and dying. . ." (Conq, 159).

As for himself, Garine knows that he is incapable of adhering to any social order whatever. He cannot imagine himself as part of any organized society and therefore is not interested in its transformation. His life becomes an increasingly desperate effort to maintain and exercise power. It is in the use of force alone that he experiences existence and that he is able to pit himself against a world he has rejected. His focus becomes narrower and narrower as all other interests, including the goal to be achieved in the exercise of power, are forced out of the picture: "In power he sought neither money, nor consideration, nor respect—nothing but power itself" (Conq, 74). This observation, made by the narrator, is confirmed by Garine himself:

> My action makes me indifferent to everything but action itself, beginning with its results. If it was easy for me to join the revolution, it is because its results are far off and continuously changing. I am a gambler at heart. Like all gamblers, I think of nothing but the game, stubbornly and forcefully (Conq, 195).

As the action continues, we learn that other characters narrow their visions in much the same way; this includes Tcheng-Daü, whose initial "disinterestedness" gradually becomes an obsessive "self-interestedness":

> . . . he has imperceptibly become accustomed to his role, and found himself, one day, preferring this role to the triumph of those he is defending. . . .
> He has no children. . . . No one, after his death, will celebrate his birthday rites. . . .
> He cuts the noble figure of a victim who is concerned about his biography . . . (Conq, 103).

The disinterested Tcheng-Daü is intent upon not allowing a disinterestedness which is very rare in China to remain unknown. This disinterestedness, which seems to have been simply human at first, has become, by way of a subtle comedy, his *raison d'être:*

he seeks in it the proof of his superiority over other men (Conq, 104).

Hong, too, is interested in the transmission of an account of his deeds to the young who will follow him, and who, he hopes, will imitate him. The cycle of the Rebecci-Hong master-disciple relationship is, therefore, left for posterity—or for Tchen of *La Condition humaine* —to complete.

Garine's attitude is forcefully expressed toward the end of the novel. With victory for the revolutionaries in sight—with Hong Kong crippled and the Red Army advancing against the British-controlled forces—Garine, aware of his inability to exist anywhere but in a troubled world where the use of force is both possible and necessary, expresses, half in desperation and half in delirium from a mounting fever, his haste to abandon the scene for a new theater of action at the opposite end of the ideological spectrum. In the following dialogue it is the narrator who poses the question:

—Where the devil would you want to go?
—To England. Now I know the meaning of Empire. A tenacious, constant violence. To direct. To determine. To constrain. That is life . . . (Conq, 213).

It is at this point that the cyclic master-disciple relationship is completed; the narrator is ready to break with Garine when he realizes that Garine's *raison d'être*, "power for power's sake," is not the way out of the metaphorical hell of the absurd. Although Garine clings in desperation to his belief in the exercise of force as the only effective means of defying the absurdity of life, he, too, realizes, although his admission is indirect, that he is but a one-eyed (*borgne*) conqueror on the verge of becoming spiritually blind. His tragic perception is intensified by imminent physical death. The fever which is rapidly consuming him reinforces the absurdity of his life:

> What have I done, what have I accomplished! Ah, la la! It reminds me of the emperor who had the eyes of his prisoners put out, you know, and who then sent them back to their country, in clusters, led by one-eyed men. The leaders became blind little by little. One of those fine Epinal portrayals that expresses what the deuce we're doing here—finer than the little sketches of the Propaganda Ministry (Conq, 189).

Somewhat later, Garine's reaction to physical darkness translates his inner spiritual state: "I can't get used to this darkness; it always gives me the impression that I'm blind . . ." (Conq, 211).

Here is the narrator on the verge of breaking with his master:

> But everything in me tonight is on the defensive against him; I'm struggling against his truth which is surging within me—against that truth to which his imminent death is lending a sinister approbation. What I feel is less a form of protest than one of revolt. . . . He awaits my answer as if he were an enemy (Conq, 203).

The narrator explains the reason for his break: he is

unable to convince Garine that he should be able to live in the society he helped to create, even though it no longer provides an outlet for the wielding of "power for power's sake." "There is enough here to bind a man who has behind him the proofs of strength that you have given, enough. . . . Enough to bind him for his whole life . . ." (Conq, 203). In the following caustic retort, Garine identifies himself as the master: " 'I'm counting on *you* to instruct *me,* I suppose!' The irony in his answer was almost hateful. We both fell silent" (Conq, 203). The relationship is definitely dissolving, but not without sincere regret on the part of the narrator:

> Suddenly I would like to say something that might unite us. I am afraid—afraid, like a child, of a presentiment, to see this friendship end this way, to leave this man that I have loved and that I still love, in spite of what he says, in spite of what he thinks— this man who is going to die . . . (Conq, 203).

The narrator is aware that Garine himself has reached a point of perception:

> He himself does not believe what he is saying and yet he strains—his nerves tensed to the breaking point— to believe himself, to persuade himself. . . . Does he know that he is lost, does he fear it, does he know nothing? Now that his death is certain, his hopes and affirmations engender in me a sense of devastating exasperation. I have a mind to say to him: "Enough, enough! You are going to die" (Conq, 213)!

Malraux's first hero does not have the answer.

Although, in breaking with the past and contributing to the destruction of the powers that sustained it, Garine has completed the first stage of the journey, there can be no doubt that contemporary man's quest for a new identity is just beginning. Corresponding to Garine's physical state is the individualism which he incarnates—both are on their way out as *Les Conquérants* comes to an end.

Garine himself communicates to the reader the source of his individualism: "[My father] used to say . . . that one must be attached to oneself: he was not of Protestant origin for nothing.[3] Attached to oneself" (Conq, 190)! Nicolaieff, the police commissioner, predicts the end of the individual with special reference to Garine: "His time is over. Those men were necessary, yes; but now the Red Army is ready; Hong Kong will definitely be destroyed in a few days; we need people who can forget themselves better than he can" (Conq, 200). Nicolaieff also recalls Borodin's opinion on the subject: "there is no place in Communism for one who wants, first of all . . . to be himself, in short, to exist separated from others . . ." (Conq, 201).

The action of *Les Conquérants* represents the declining phase of the first movement of the Malraux cycle: from death to new life. Before the new can rise, the old must be destroyed, and Hong Kong is being destroyed as Garine remarks in exaltation: "To conquer a city. To destroy a city: a city is the most social thing in the world, the very emblem of society: there is at least one [Hong Kong] that the wretched Cantonese are busy reducing to a fine state (Conq, 213)! When the end of the struggle is in sight, Garine is no longer interested: "It is all the same to me. Now, it does not matter. . . . All this . . ." (Conq, 205).

The hero of *Les Conquérants* marks the beginning

of the destruction of an outmoded phase of the human spirit, that of the individual isolated from his fellow men, but it is not until *La Voie royale* that this individual meets final death in the combined persons of Grabot and Perken. After *La Voie royale,* the isolated individual will continue to appear, but as a minor character, not a hero.

Notes

1. André Malraux, *Les Conquérants* (Paris: Grasset, 1949), p. 15. Henceforth cited as Conq.
2. It will be recalled that the Protestant emphasis on the individual gave rise to the painting of portraits of individuals in the post-Renaissance period in northern Europe (*supra,* p. 83).
3. See note 2, *supra.*

13.

The Tragic Intensity of Death

Media vita in morte sumus.

An affinity between the two main characters, Claude and Perken, is discernible as the action commences; it is based upon attitudes shared by both: hostility toward established values, rejection of the world, a taste for action, and an obsession with death. Though this affinity establishes a master-disciple relationship, the reader is conscious of a radical difference between the two men from the outset—a difference which foreshadows the inevitable break in the relationship. Each has two obsessions, one of which—death—they have in common, but, while Claude is equally obsessed with the resurrective power of art and knows that he will make a contribution to the history of art in retrieving the Kmer statues, Perken's only release from his obsession with death is in the exercise of power —either over women (which introduces the theme of eroticism) or over defenseless, primitive natives. His reason for accompanying Claude on the treasure hunt for the Kmer statues is primarily motivated by a desire to procure sufficient funds, through the sale of the art treasures, for the purchase of machine guns which will enable him to prolong his suppression of the natives until his death. Perken is also activated by a determination to penetrate the mystery of the disappearance of a certain Grabot, who shares—but to the ultimate extreme—his own will to godhead.

Charles Blend cites the complete absence of any social purpose in Perken's wielding of power for power's sake, as sufficient reason for asserting the ethical superiority of Garine, who, though mainly indifferent to the outcome of his exercise of force, is at least lucidly aware of contributing to better the lot of those he is allegedly serving. Blend says: "Perken's goal, a personal mastery over the tribes in an area of Indo-China, is in fact, the type of action that makes it necessary to fight for human dignity." [1]

Perken, the master in *La Voie royale,* paints for Claude, his disciple, a moral portrait of Grabot as an utterly isolated, egocentric individual—the incarnation of an image of man that is destined to be destroyed by the end of the novel:

> . . . for him power is defined as the possibility of abusing it. . . . He has never thought of anything but himself, or rather of what isolates him. . . . Owing to his courage, he is much more separated from the world than you or I, because he hasn't any hope. . . . He is a man who is really alone, and, like all solitary men, obliged to fill his solitude, and he does this with courage.[2]

As the action unfolds, the admirable qualities of Claude's character, which ultimately sever the master-disciple relationship formed at the outset, are gradually disclosed. One such quality, which Perkens also possesses to a lesser degree, is initially revealed in Claude's conception of friendship: "Understand me. If I accept a man, I accept him totally, as I accept myself. Can I affirm that

I myself would not have committed any act committed by this man whom I have accepted as a friend" (VR, 58)? Later, the positive elements in Claude's makeup are set in sharp relief. They are revealed first by the tremendous joy he experiences upon retrieving the statues or, to paraphrase his own words, upon wresting his dreams free of the inert world in which they were imprisoned. Claude's qualities are further disclosed when, toward the end of the novel, he willingly risks losing the art treasures, which not only represented the realization of a dream but almost cost him his life, in order not to abandon his dying master, even though he, Claude, is already aware of the fact that they are "irremmediably different, of different races . . ." (VR, 150).

In *La Voie royale* both movements of the Malraux cycle are present. The second movement—the resurrection of a dead past after the passage of considerable time—constitutes the surface action of the novel. The first movement, present in the form of a death-in-life theme, constitutes the inner, tragic action of the novel, which brings to an end both a human life cycle—Perken's—and an outmoded image of man—that of the totally isolated, egocentric, blind conqueror of which Grabot is the supreme embodiment.

The surface action of the novel traces an adventure through the Cambodian jungle along the Royal Way, where the heroes, Claude and Perken, after several unsuccessful attempts finally locate and disengage, from the stone and the forest that threatened their ultimate total decomposition, two exquisite statues—representing dancing girls—of the Kmer civilization which had fallen to the Siamese invaders approximately a century prior to the commencement of the action. This rescue operation, which is a transfigured account of an archeological expedition undertaken by Malraux, his wife, and several companions in the early twenties, manifests the unpredictable life of the work of art and illustrates the continuation, in the present period, of the cyclic theme of resurrection elaborated in Malraux's volumes on art.

Continuing, too, in *La Voie royale,* is the cycle of change as it affects civilizations. The decline of European colonialism, according to a prophetic announcement voiced by Claude in the form of a rhetorical question, is destined to spread from the destruction of the British interests in the China of *Les Conquérants* to include the French interests in the Indo-China of *La Voie royale*: "Will his Institute [The French Institute of Colonial Administration] and the French still be here in Indo-China in thirty years" (VR, 48)? The course of subsequent history turned prophesy into reality in even less than thirty years.

The thematic focus, centered on absurdity in *Les Conquérants,* shifts to the omnipresence and tragic intensity of death in *La Voie royale* as the hero's sojourn in hell continues, and we move on from the first to the second stage of our hero's quest for a new identity. As either an external or an internal menace, or both, death is the constant companion of our heroes throughout the course of the action.

The theme of death is introduced at the outset in the disclosure of the destination of our heroes, whom we meet once again aboard ship en route from Europe to Asia. They are headed for "the dead cities of Cambodia" (VR, 34), which the narrator later refers to as "the deadest of all dead lands" (VR, 50).

It is the perpetual presence of Death in a variety of disguises, including *l'Accident,* to which specific reference is made in *Lunes,* that makes for the thematic coherence and dramatic intensity of *La Voie royale*—a coherence and intensity unequaled in Malraux's other novels. It is a common "obsession with death" (VR, 39) which initiates the master-disciple relationship between Perken and Claude while they are still aboard ship. And it was an intense awareness of death—death as the irrefutable proof of the absurdity of life—that led Claude and Perken to break with their world in an attempt to turn life to account in a defiant protest against the finality of existence. It is, therefore, death—and here is its positive aspect— which lends intensity to their lives, and impels them to reject the insignificant lives of ordinary men who submit to destiny in the form of the established order of the world into which they are born; death is the driving force behind their determination to leave a "scar on the face of the map"—to achieve immortality by lingering on in the memories of a great number of men after their own physical demises. Here are Claude's thoughts on the subject:

(Whence, if not from Death, arose that exigency, so heavily impregnated with the odor of mortal flesh, for things eternal?) What was this need for the un-known—this temporary destruction of the master-prisoner relationship, which the uninitiated call adventure—what was it, if not his defense against death (VR, 41)?

In *La Voie royale,* Death in the guise of an external menace is at once most tragic and most powerful in her role as the forest, for it is in this role that she excels not only as a constant menace in the present, but also as a prefiguration of her role—in *Les Voix du silence*— as the ultimate annihilator, at the end of the human adventure, of the traces of man's triumphal passage through history.

The forest in *La Voie royale* is a rich symbol. Viewed as a whole, it is a symbol of the world, but a world transformed into a realm of Death, and by extension into a prison, which is a metaphor of the human condition: *l'homme traqué* is one of the main themes of the novel.

The journey through the novel as a whole is a metaphor of a journey through life viewed as an escape from one prison to another: first, the prison of the world—and within the world, society; then, the ship—and aboard ship, the cabin; then, the forest—and within the forest, the decaying vegetation,[3] the overpowering heat, the infestuous insects, the gangrene, the stone, and the savages; and finally, especially in the case of Perken, the prison of the human body.

The forest is but a microcosm of the prison of Europe from which all three heroes—Perken, Claude, and Grabot —have broken free.

Death as an internal menace, or death-in-life, is almost inseparable from the theme of time in *La Voie royale,* in which Perken, already an old man when the action begins, is the living—or dying—embodiment of "Saturn devouring his children." Time is conceived of as a concrete physical presence within the body—a malignant presence which begins its destructive process from the moment of birth and gradually overturns and transforms the cradle of infancy into the coffin of old age: "What weighs upon me —how should I say it?—is my human condition: the fact that I am growing old, that this atrocious thing—time—is growing within me like a cancer, irrevocably. . . . Time, that's it" (VR, 106).

According to Perken, this death-in-life, which he refers

to as "gradual decline" (VR, 39), is the only real death
and is quite different from either being killed or a sudden,
accidental termination of life before decline has set in.
Death in this role of physical decline is introduced intermittently in several flashbacks, the most poignant and vivid
of which is Claude's recollection of his mother as the signs
of approaching age began to manifest themselves in her
outlook and physical appearance. He speaks first of the
effects of aging on her attitude toward life: "an abandoned
woman, obsessed by her age to the point of torture, certain
of her decline, and who looked upon life with desperate
indifference" (VR, 24). Claude continues with a description of his mother's attempts to hide the signs of her
decline:

> Rouged and powdered for solitude, for the portraits
> of former owners, for emblems of the sea—rouged
> especially for the mirrors against which she could not
> defend herself except by drawn curtains and the arti-
> fices of twilight, she died of a premature change of
> life, as if her anguish had been a premonition
> (VR, 24).

Later in the novel, an olfactory sensation evokes a related
image:

> The odor of decomposition from the pools enveloped
> Claude, who saw his mother again . . . looking with
> fright into the little mirror, adorned with a romantic
> galleon, at the sloping of the corners of her mouth
> and at the enlargement of her nose, and shading her
> eyelids with the gestures of a blind person . . .
> (VR, 59).

And Perken recalls his reaction as he witnessed the process of aging in the changing appearance of his wife, Sarah: "It was, above all, the end of something . . ." (VR, 61).

The concept of death as "the end of something" is developed by Perken into the existentialist theme of death's role in determining a man's destiny, or, as Sartre would say, the essence of his existence. Perken experiences approaching death most acutely as the force which terminates the possibility of further action, and thereby eliminates the hope of changing the significance of one's life. In the following lines, addressed to Claude, Perken anticipates the Sartrian theme of death—minus the aging—in *Huis-clos:*

> Growing old is so much more serious! Accepting your destiny, your function, a dog's kennel raised over the only life that you have. . . . You don't know what it is to experience destiny, confining and irrefutable, falling upon you like a regulation upon a prisoner: the certainty that you will be this and nothing more, that whatever you have not had, you will never have. And behind you, all those hopes that you harbor in your flesh as you will never harbor any human being . . . (VR, 59).

The death-in-life theme, which predominates during the hero's sojourn in hell, is reinforced and tragically intensified by the figure of Grabot, whose very name, as Albert Sonnenfeld has observed, is a compound of the German noun *Grab* (grave), and the French diminutive suffix, *-ot*.[4] The name "Grabot" in *La Voie royale* foreshadows not only the disaster and degradation of its bearer, as indicated by Sonnenfeld, but also the fate of the bearer's pursuer, Perken. "Grabot" is the "grave" to which

Perken's trek through the jungle is to lead him, for it is indeed in negotiating the purchase of Grabot's liberation from the native tribes that he, Perken, falls upon the war spike—death in the guise of *l'accident*—which is to cause his death. Finally, the name "Grabot" suggests the end, or the grave, of an obsolete image of man—of the completely isolated, totally egocentric, blind conqueror—of which its bearer is the embodiment. To the question: "What are you?" Grabot's response is "Nothing" (VR, 116-17): the blind conqueror, already present in Garine, has been reduced to "nothing" in the person of Grabot, the atavistic course of whose life (his reversion from a civilized to a primitive being) is diametrically opposed to the normal evolution of man. Grabot's will to godhead has reduced him to nothing. Claude and Perken refer to him as "a dead man," as "that cadaver" (VR, 117), and later, as "a cave man" and "a powerful ruin" (VR, 123).

Grabot's fate symbolizes the road down which Pride, the mostly deadly of the seven capital sins, leads its victim. After breaking out of the metaphorical prison of Europe, Grabot meets his nemesis in the concrete man-made variety at the hands of the very savages he had sought to conquer and subdue. In the visual image of the blind conqueror, Grabot, turning incessantly around the circular grindstone inside the native hut—an image which evokes the circular structure of Dante's "Inferno" in *The Divine Comedy*— Malraux has concretized the moral and spiritual degeneration of a conqueror whose initial, self-inflicted semiblindness has ended in total blindness, both physical and spiritual. Perken's reaction to Grabot's endless gyrating is the source of the foregoing interpretation: "An idiotic idea shook him: the pains of hell endured for the sake of pride . . ." (VR, 128).

All of this suggests that by 1930, the date of the

publication by Grasset of the first edition of *La Voie royale*, Malraux had already accomplished the demolition, in art, of a Western notion of man that had run its appointed course—that of the individual who had set himself up as an absolute to the exclusion of all other values. Malraux had already predicted the decline in "D'Une jeunesse européenne":

> But here we are at the point where triumphant individualism wants to acquire a more precise consciousness of itself. Laden with the successive passions of men, it has annihilated everything except itself; elevated by the finest minds of our era, preceded by the folly of Nietzsche and adorned with the spoils of the gods, here it is before us, and we no longer see in it anything but a blind victor. The idol is heavy with all the gifts of the world, but it no longer interests us, and our anxiety is all the greater because we see in this idol our own image . . . (JE, 145–46).

The entire last portion of the novel, beginning with the latter half of Part III where Perken realizes that he has been wounded in the knee as a result of having fallen on a war spike, is an account of Perken's death, and of his desperate struggle against it, alternating with his equally desperate drive toward it. Earlier in the novel, and as a reaction to Perken's definition of eroticism, Claude was already aware of the death wish in Perken: "What he wants, thought Claude, is to annihilate himself" (VR, 58). Later, Perken himself confirms his disciple's observation: "There is also something . . . satisfying in the crushing out of life . . ." (VR, 108).

This death wish also formed part of the makeup of Claude's grandfather who, for a substantial part of his life, was surrounded by more dead than living men: "the old man had taken the habit of going, each day, to the wall of the sailors lost at sea; he envied them their deaths and joyously welcomed his old age and the nothingness to which it would lead him" (VR, 29).

Once Perken's end is predicted by Dr. Blackhouse— "before two weeks are up, you are going to croak like an animal. There's nothing to be done, do you understand? Absolutely nothing" (VR, 145)—Perken finds it impossible to escape death's omnipresence. He encounters it in every look and gesture of those about him: "The imperious affirmation was expressed less in the words of the doctor than in the eyelids that Claude had just lowered instinctively" (VR, 149); a short time later he reads his fate in the face of the woman whom Xa, the native boy, has brought from the village. Perken's perception of his failure with this woman, whom he desperately sought to possess, is movingly expressed in the phrase: "One possesses only what one loves" (VR, 152). But as he prepares to leave her, he is moved by a violent desire to annihilate "that face that was driving him toward death" (VR, 153). Perken's response is extreme when the native chief assumes the role of death's messenger: "He [Perken] raised his head toward Savan. . . . For the second time, he encountered his death in the glance of a man; he felt a fierce desire to shoot him, as if murder alone would have made it possible for him to affirm his existence, to struggle against his own end" (VR, 170). A short time later, Perken satisfies this desire by killing two of Savan's men.

As the journey through the forest toward death is resumed, the sounds of the outer world, signaling the destruction of his hope, seem to act as an accompaniment to the pulse of death rising within him, ticking away the last minutes of his life. They are the sounds of the repressive column fighting the natives and felling the trees as it advances toward the territory over which Perken had once ruled—sounds which enforce upon the dying conqueror a sense of the absurdity of life in all its tragic intensity.

Slowly Perken sinks deeper and deeper into death; the sounds of the external world are reduced to a pulsating rhythm accentuating the throbbing pain severing him from the realm of men: "Each beam that fell without the slightest sound, as if in another world, resounded in his knee" (VR, 174). Crushing out life, and with it the hope that sustained life, time continues its relentless course in rhythm with the activity of the outer world and the mounting pain in Perken's body:

> From second to second he felt the no-longer audible thump of falling logs in the throbbing of his blood; he knew, at one and the same time, that in his own country he would recover and that here he was going to die; that on the cluster of hopes he once was, the world was closing in, a world encircled by that railroad as if by a prisoner's chain; that nothing in the universe would ever compensate for his past or present suffering: being a man was even more absurd than being a dying man (VR,174).

As the intolerable pain continues to mount, Perken yearns to be free of his body. He describes his experience as "a superhuman imprisonment, without hope" (VR, 175). And several lines later he sees himself as a "prisoner, still enclosed in the world of men: hateful. Alone. Alone with the fever that permeated him from his head to his knee, and the faithful thing resting on his thigh: his hand" (VR, 175). This last detail, we find, is important: "He returned to the surface for a second and remembered that the contraction of the hands occurs when the death struggle begins. He was sure of it" (VR, 175).

Malraux reaches the heights of mysticism when Perken is between this world and the next—he succeeds in communicating the ineffable experience of the separation of the soul from the body:

Perken opened his eyes; the heavens invaded his being, crushing yet full of joy. . . . He no longer knew anything of men, nor even of the earth . . . he now knew only the immensity, dazzling white by dint of light, that tragic joy into which he was vanishing, and which gradually filled the dull beating of his heart.

He no longer heard anything but its beating, as if it alone were able to respond to the furnace that was tearing his soul from the forest, as if it alone expressed the obsessive response of his wound to the sacred sky . . . this heart would cease to beat; it, too, would vanish into the implacable call of the light . . . (VR, 176).

The end is approaching rapidly, and as it does Perken realizes, ". . . nothing will ever lend significance to his life, not even this exaltation which is casting him, like a prey, to the sun" (VR, 176). In one of his last passages he identifies the earth as the realm of absurdity and death:

There were men on earth, and they believed in their passions, in their pain, and in their existence: mere insects under leaves, nothing but a multitude under the vault of death. The thought of it filled him with a profound joy that resounded in his chest and in his leg with each pulsation of his blood in his wrists, in his temples, and in his heart—a joy that was hammering out the folly of the universe vanishing into the sun (VR, 176).

With the increasing intensity of the soul-racking pain, Perken desperately seeks release from his last prison: "He gritted his teeth, intoxicated with a desire to flee his body, to become one with that incandescent sky that was drawing him up like a prey . . ." (VR, 177).

Finally, the contraction of his hand begins; Perken utters his last words, which define death as an ineffable, individual experience: "There is . . . no death. There is only . . . I. . . . One of his fingers contracted on his thigh. . . . I . . . who am going to die . . ." (VR, 178).

Perken dies as he lived—with a consciousness of the absurdity of his life; his hope dies with him. His passing coincides with the end of the death-in-life vision of the Malraux hero and the point at which the ascent from hell is about to begin as death becomes a meaningful part of life in *La Condition humaine,* the novel which brings the thematic wheel half-cycle.

As for Grabot, his final rescue and transportation to a hospital are ironic in the extreme: he is destined to linger on for what remains of his life as a living corpse, both physically and spiritually blind.

Of the three heroes only Claude has emerged from the forest—the realm of Death—with any true insight. For him alone the transformation of absurdity into significance has begun with a revelation of the importance in human terms of his resolution to accompany his dying "master" at the possible cost of losing the statues for which he had risked his life. The revelation occurs almost immediately after Claude discovers that he and Perken are "irremediably different" (VR, 150):

> The exercise of that power, which was something new, struck him as a revelation. It was above all such resolutions—they alone, that nourished the scorn that separated him from all the compromises of men. Victor or vanquished, he could not help but gain in virility from such an act, and, at the same time, gratify that need for courage and that consciousness of the futility of the world and of human suffering—a need and a consciousness that he had often seen, in rudimentary form, in his grandfather . . . (VR, 150).

Once again the cycle has been completed as Claude, the new master, has set the stage for the next novel, where Kyo, in *La Condition humaine,* begins the ascent from hell.

Notes

1. Blend, pp. 88–89.
2. André Malraux, *Les Puissances du désert: La Voie royale* (Genève: Skira, 1945), pp. 94–95. Henceforth cited as VR.
3. The role of nature as a symbol of death within this "realm of death," the forest, is the subject of an excellent article by Bertrand Logan Ball, Jr.: "Nature, Symbol of Death in *La Voie royale,*" *French Review,* XXXV, No. 4 (February, 1962), 390–95.
4. *Op. cit.,* p. 200.

14.

Death as a Meaningful Part of Life

Because he is constantly changing, never being but only becoming, man cannot know other things, which are also changing. Nor can he know unchanging God, for flux has no knowledge of being (Montaigne).

The structure of *La Condition humaine*, in terms of time, coincides with the annual cycle of nature. It is a cycle which begins in darkness on the first day of Spring and ends one year later in the bright Spring of Kobé. The first line of the novel reads, "March 21, 1927," and the second, "Half-past midnight." [1] The very last section of the novel opens with the phrase, "In the bright light of Springtime" (CH, 394), followed several pages later by a reference to "the dazzling splendor of Japanese Spring" (CH, 400).

The structure is also cyclic in that the novel is divided into seven parts, which, together with the tone —a progression from darkness and anguish at the beginning to light and a glimmer of hope at the end—suggest an analogy with the seven-day biblical cycle of creation.

Prophetic pronouncements in the opening section set the tone of darkness presaging the end of a world: ". . . an invisible crowd animated this night of final judgment" (CH, 30), "Victory or defeat, the destiny of the world, this night, lay in the balance" (CH, 56).

The hope that a new world will rise out of the destruction of the old is subtly suggested by the presence of a painting of a phoenix adorning one of the rooms in Gisors's house. Intermittent references[2] to the room and to the painting itself reinforce this hope. A fabulous bird, unique in its kind, the phoenix is a symbol of the endless cycle of destruction and re-creation. According to legend, when the phoenix senses the approach of death, it builds a fire in the desert, destroys itself in its flames, and then rises anew from its own ashes. It will be recalled that the resurrection of the phoenix was actually witnessed by the historiographer of *Royaume farfelu*.[3] Ironically enough, it is an old Chinaman—a staunch advocate of the status quo—who points to the painting of the phoenix as a fine example of the achievements of a culture whose existence is being threatened: "It is good that such things as the institution of courtesans, concubinage, and the absolute submission of women exist. . . . We can thank our ancestors, who thought that way, for these beautiful paintings (he indicates the blue phoenix with his glance . . .) of which we are both proud" (CH, 68–69). In reaction to this harangue, Gisors, the master theorist of the revolution, manifests his impatience: "Was he going to leave? This man clinging to his past. . . . The old man left, saying: 'Order, sir' " (CH, 69)!

In this novel whose structure combines the natural and biblical cycles of creation, the law of the cycle—change, itself—emerges as the new absolute. The paradox in the union of the terms "change" and "absolute" is resolved when we realize, along with Montaigne and Malraux, that in the world of time, change alone remains constant. Malraux progresses beyond his master, Montaigne, as this new absolute becomes, in *La Condition humaine,* not only a source of knowledge but also the measure of a man's worth. It is in relation to the theme of "constant transformation" that the realization of the hero's quest for a new identity takes a positive turn in the rapidly changing world of the twentieth century which is the setting of *La Condition humaine.* Awareness and acceptance of constant transformation as the law of life effects a change, not in man's fate, which remains constant, but in man's understanding of his fate.

It is the hero's growing awareness of his own power to act to change the world in which he lives that marked the beginning of his ascent from hell. "Effecting change" in an attempt to create a better world emerges as the only positive way of lending meaning to both life and death and, by extension of transforming absurdity into significance. The heroes of *La Condition humaine* who willingly die for their cause transform Perken's concept of death as a "confirmation of the absurdity of life" into a new concept of death, willingly accepted, as a "confirmation of the significance of life." The new concept of death brings the thematic wheel half-cycle in this, the third of Malraux's six full-fledged novels.

With the emergence of change as the new absolute, the emphasis is shifted from being to becoming. The knowledge that man can contribute not only to his own becoming but also to that of his fellow men is the positive solution to the dilemma of man's fate in *La Condition humaine.*

The surface action of the novel resumes that of *Les Conquérants,* with the center of the crisis shifting from the Canton strike of 1925 to the Shanghai uprising of 1927, and from the destruction of the British interests in Hong Kong to the destruction of the Franco-Asiatic Consortium in Shanghai.

The main characters, as seen within the framework of the changing world of *La Condition humaine,* may be divided not only into adherents of the world that is being destroyed and creators of the world that is coming into existence, but also into those who are able to live in the world they are instrumental in transforming and those who are not. Among those who represent the world that is receding into the past are: the old Chinaman who visits Gisors (*supra,* p. 196); Ferral and his associates, representatives (both in China and in Paris at the end) of French interests in a state of decline in China; and the Baron Clappique, a remnant of the disappearing European nobility.

Those working toward the creation of a new world include the theorist and master, Gisors, and the revolutionaries actively engaged in implementing his theories. Gisors's own son, Kyo, is the leader and organizer of the insurrection. His associates include Katov, Hemmelrich, Lou-Shu-Yen, and the three terrorists: Tchen, their leader, and his two disciples, Souen and Peï.

Directly related to the dominant theme of change is one of the major double themes of the novel—the pursuit of the absolute versus the relativity of all human powers. In this multihero novel there are those who continue to pursue an "unchanging absolute" and, whether this absolute be in the form of self-possession or dominion over others, its pursuers are doomed either to self-destruction or to a life devoid of meaning; they do not begin the ascent.

Tchen, ready to *die for* but not capable of *living in* a world he helps to create, is a transitional hero whose life ends in a realization of the death-wish—a frenzied pursuit of the absolute in self-destruction.

Three characters require special consideration. Clappique, who has no convictions of his own, acts as a go-between for both sides. He is the one character in *La Condition humaine* who, by his own admission, does not exist. He lives in the realm of the imagination—a creature who plays many roles in order to avoid any direct confrontation with "the human condition." For this reason, says Gisors, Clappique can neither change nor grow; he cannot become a man. Gisors, the master and theorist, is also a special figure. Never having translated his theories into action, he lives vicariously through his son and disciple, Kyo. When Kyo dies, Gisors's hope dies with him, and he is ready to abandon this life. Of all of Malraux's characters, he is the only one who, after having transmitted his hope to his son, seems to have succumbed to the "temptation of the Orient" by seeking release from the anguish of existence in opium. Kama, the artist, is the only one whose work is independent of the revolution. As an artist, he seeks to manifest the essence of the subjects he depicts—to transcend the world of appearances.

What all of the revolutionaries of *La Condition humaine*—including Tchen—have in common (as opposed to those of *Les Conquérants*) is the sincere and conscious desire to transform their world. They want to create a better world—a world unlike the one they rejected because it denied their dignity.

Each of these heroes began his work with the revolution as the result of a humiliating experience. Malraux uses the technique of the flashback to acquaint the reader with the nature of these experiences. Tchen was an orphan who lost his parents in the pillage of Kalgan; his uncle was executed in a political seizure. Tchen himself was left penniless with worthless diplomas, and, often on the verge of starvation, he was forced to work at menial jobs. The faith which the Protestant pastor Smithson unsuccessfully attempted to instill in him separated him from China; he became an individual who could no longer submit to the world in which he found himself. Tchen's hope, at least initially, is in the revolution, in the proletariat. Kyo suffered humiliation as a result of his mixed origin —half French and half Japanese—a humiliation which he recalls during his crisis with May, his wife. His work for the revolution is based upon "the will to dignity." Hemmelrich, deprived of love in an environment of abject poverty, suffered untold miseries as a child. As a young man, he was forced to serve in the Belgian Army even though he was a German by origin. Katow had faced a firing squad in Lithuania at the hands of the Whites under the most humiliating circumstances—hence, his work with the Reds in the revolution. Koenig, the counterrevolutionary, had been tortured by the Reds; he finds his *raison d'être* in vengeance.

In the intensely dramatic opening scene, "effecting change" becomes a creative act. Tchen's murder of Tang-Yen-Ta marks the breaking point between the old and the new. It is an act which alters the destiny not only of an individual, Tchen, but also of a city, of a nation, and, through the nation, of the world. Expressed in terms of birth, the murder is a creative act which not only marks Tchen's complete break with the established order, but also makes the initial victory of the insurrection possible. Here is Tchen, looking out on the balcony of the hotel after the murder:

There were millions of lives down there, and all of them, now, rejected his; but what was their miserable condemnation next to the death that was receding from him, that seemed to be flowing out of his body in long draughts, as the blood flowed from the other (CH, 16).

The new world is born in darkness—both physical and metaphysical. There is a correspondence between the darkness of the outer world and Tchen's inner world as he ventures out into the night after the murder:

Roused by his anguish, the night was bubbling like an enormous black pool of vapor full of stars. In rhythm with the gradual diminution of his panting it subsided, and, in the tear in the clouds, the stars resumed their eternal course . . . (CH, 16).

Once the insurrection is underway, the major themes, which serve not only to define *la condition humaine* but also to illuminate the hero's renewed understanding of it, are introduced by the major characters as they engage in both action and intellection. The themes are present in antithetical pairs. In addition to "the pursuit of the absolute versus the relativity of all human powers" (already mentioned above), they are: anguish and hope, life and death, humiliation and dignity, existence and essence, and, not to be neglected, eroticism and love.

Gisors the theorist provides many of the definitions for the major themes. In several passages he speaks of the human condition in terms of man's yearning for the absolute, of man's desire "to be more than a man in a world of men; to escape the human condition. . . . To be omnipotent rather than merely powerful. . . . Every man dreams of being god" (CH, 272). Man is actually a paranoid (CH, 82) who, in his aspiration toward a dual state, is not unlike the gods: "The ideal of a god, is it not true, is to become a man, knowing that he will regain his power; and the dream of man is to become god without losing his own personality" (CH, 273).

On the one hand, man conceives of himself as an eternal being, and on the other, he is acutely conscious of the finality of his existence. Awareness of the conflict between his aspirations and his limitations comes to him through thought, which is therefore the source of his suffering. Gisors expresses this concept in a modification of the Cartesian axiom: "All suffer, he thought, and each suffers because he thinks. In the main, the mind conceives man only in the eternal, and the consciousness of life can only result in anguish" (CH, 400–401).

But the negative aspect of the human condition does have a positive counterpart: the life of Malraux's Pascalian-Augustinian hero is defined in terms of an antithesis: "Gisors was *hope* no less than he was *anguish* [italics mine] . . ." (CH, 373); the definition is reinforced some pages later when Gisors speaks of his "hopes" and his "anguish" together constituting his destiny—his life (CH, 400).

Consciousness of man's limitations, especially the finality of his existence, leads to anguish: Kyo the disciple speaks of "the anguish of being only a man," and of "man who suffers and knows that he will die" (CH, 177).

The main characters of *La Condition humaine* have all experienced anguish; their escape from dread assumes a variety of forms: opium for Gisors, murder for Tchen, madness for Clappique, love for May, eroticism for Ferral, sadism for Katow (at least in the years prior to the commencement of the action), and vengeance for Koenig and Hemmelrich.

At the outset of the novel, only Kyo has learned to

conquer dread. He alone has found a hope—in the form of an idea worth living and dying for—an idea strong enough to counterbalance the anguish of man's estate. It is Gisors who informs the reader of this as he contrasts his son's heroic sense with that of Tchen, the terrorist:

> He [Kyo] was not anxious. His life had a meaning, and he knew what it was: to give each of these men, whom famine was killing off like the plague at this very moment, the possession of his own dignity (CH, 80).

Later Gisors reinforces this observation in a conversation with Ferral, during which he asserts that, in the absence of a hope as strong as Kyo's, *escape from* the intolerable anguish of the human condition is sought through a variety of means:

> It is always necessary to become intoxicated: this country has opium; Islam has hashish; and the West has women. . . . Perhaps love is, above all, the means employed by the Westerner to free himself of his human condition. . . . Tchen and murder, Clappique and his madness, Katow and the revolution, May and love, himself and opium . . . Kyo alone resisted these domains (CH, 271).

It is the terror of feeling separated, cut off, and alone, of feeling the abyss plunging between oneself and the rest, that causes anguish—"that fundamental suffering" (CH, 373)—to mount in man. Since anguish is also experienced in connection with the finality of existence, it is a means of communicating with the world beyond. At only one point in the novel does Gisors allow himself to reach this depth of suffering rather than escape from it through opium: it is when he desires to communicate with Kyo after his death:

> He felt that fundamental suffering trembling within him, not that which comes from beings or from things but that which wells up from the very depth of man's being and which strains to wrest his life from him; Gisors could avoid it, but only by ceasing to think about it; and he plunged into it more and more, as if that frightful contemplation had been the only voice that death could hear, as if that human suffering which permeated him to the bottom of his heart had been the only prayer that the body of his dead son could hear (CH, 373–74).

Anguish is also referred to as the experience that leads man to the point of his deepest solitude, and, in the following passage, Malraux succeeds in communicating the ineffable as he suggests this point to be the human soul:

> He [Gisors] felt himself penetrating, his consciousness intruding a domain which belonged to him more than any other; he felt himself, through his anguish, taking possession of a forbidden solitude where no one would ever reach him. For a second, he had the sensation that that was what was supposed to escape at the moment of death (CH, 83).

The deepest part of man, where he is utterly alone, and to which anguish leads him, is a point where the temporal meets the eternal. It is this point that Gisors reaches just as the effects of opium bring serenity and deliverance: "His eyes closed, and borne on great immobile wings, Gisors contemplated his solitude: a desolation which at once fused with the divine and expanded to the infinite the furrow of serenity that gently covered the profundity of death" (CH, 84).

In the course of the action, the sensation of the absolute as self-possession is experienced briefly by Tchen through murder and suicide, by Clappique in the gambling scene, and it is sought by Ferral through eroticism and power over others. In all three cases the pursuer is doomed.

Tchen is convinced that men who have rejected the world cannot live without a "certainty" of some kind. His conviction is voiced by way of a comparison between his own "certainty" or absolute and that of Vologuine, the secretary of the International Delegation in Hankow:

> For this Vologuine, it is the same, I think; but for him it is obedience rather than murder. When one lives as we do, some kind of certitude is a necessity. For him, carrying out orders is sure, I think, as killing is for me. Something must be sure. It must (CH, 177).

It is not long before Tchen becomes the slave of his own "absolute"—or, as Gisors analyzes the situation—before the roles of pursuer and pursued, of possessor and possessed, are reversed:

> Tchen had plunged into the world of murder and would never leave it: fierce desperation was driving him into the domain of terrorism as into a prison. . . . The ideas which had sustained his life were now going to kill him (CH, 75–76).

There can be no doubt that Tchen's initial commitment to the revolution was not born of total despair: "Everything rushed him into political action: the hope for a different world, the possibility of eating, even miserably (he was naturally austere, perhaps through pride), the chance to satisfy his hatred, to implement his ideas, to give full expression to his character. The revolution gave a meaning to his solitude" (CH, 79).

Unfortunately, Tchen loses sight of his initial goal; terrorism becomes an end in itself. Unconsciously he realizes that only in a suicidal drive toward death will he capture the sensation of complete self-possession, the craving for which becomes increasingly intense with every murder he commits. It is Kyo who realizes the strength of the death wish to which Tchen's pursuit of the absolute has led him:

> "He will kill himself," thought Kyo. He had listened to his father enough to know that one who pursues the absolute so violently finds it only in sensation. Thirst for the absolute, thirst for immortality, therefore fear of death: perhaps Tchen ought to have been a coward, but he felt, as all mystics do, that his absolute could only be seized instantaneously. Whence, without doubt, his scorn for everything that did not lead to the instant that would unite him with himself in a vertigo of self-possession (CH, 180).

The absolute as self-possession and mastery over the fate of others—Kyo's in particular—is experienced by Clappique in the gambling scene, where, through a frenzied sensation of identification with the spinning ball on the roulette wheel [4] he becomes, at least for a brief spell, destiny's master. It will be recalled that Clappique entered the gambling house instead of keeping his appointment to inform Kyo of the danger besetting him in the persons of Chang Kai-Shek's officers:

> What had money to do with that ball, hesitating at the rim of muzzle-like holes—with that ball that enabled him to embrace his own destiny, the only means he had ever found of possessing himself (CH, 288)!

> Now, now, he was gambling his last coppers, his life, and that of another, especially that of another. He knew that he was betraying Kyo; it was Kyo who was chained to that ball, to that table, and it was he, Clappique, who was that ball, master of all and of himself—of himself, who, nevertheless, was watching it, living as he had never lived, outside of himself, exhausted by a vertigo of shame (CH, 290).

Ultimately, however, the roulette wheel emerges as the real victor: it becomes a metaphor of the cycle of destiny, a wheel of fate spinning out both the end of Kyo's life and the gambler's own nemesis.

Ferral, on the other hand, seeks both self-possession and dominion over his partner in eroticism: "His pleasure sprang from the fact that he put himself in the place of the other, constrained—constrained by him. In short, he never went to bed with anyone but himself, but his success was contingent upon his not being alone" (CH, 275–76). He is completely insensitive to his mistress Valérie's existence as an independent human being: "she was nothing but the other pole of his own pleasure. Never had she lived: she had never been a little girl" (CH, 145). Ferral's utter disregard for others is not limited to women; it includes his associates at the Consortium as well: "he had a unique talent for denying their existence" (CH, 100). His method for achieving this is summed up as follows: "he forced or paid" (CH, 100). Ferral's ultimate objective is to return to France to resume the political game, and his reason is: "That is where the power is" (CH, 106). To Gisors's request for his definition of intelligence, Ferral's reply is: "the possession of the means for coercing men or things" (CH, 268).

The futility of the pursuit of the absolute, even in terms of self-knowledge, is illustrated from the outset of the novel in Kyo's inability to recognize his own voice on the language recordings in Hemmelrich's shop. To Kyo's question: "Well, why did they change it" (CH, 25)? Lou, Hemmelrich's partner, answers: ". . . everyone easily recognizes the voices of others. But we are not accustomed to hearing ourselves . . ." (CH, 25). Later, Kyo's recollection of "that record, *his* voice, that he had not recognized a little while ago," arouses a "complex anxiety" (CH, 37) which grows until, even later, "the obsession of the record invades him" (CH, 54). Gisors explains to Kyo that while others hear our voices with their ears, we hear our own with our throats, and then he cites an analogous experience of his own: "I have had the experience of suddenly finding myself before a mirror without recognizing myself . . ." (CH, 55).

Reinforcing the theme of the relativity of all human powers is man's inability to attain anything but a relative knowledge of others. Gisors wonders whether Kyo would be able to imprison himself in the terrorism of Tchen's universe, but then realizes that such understanding would be beyond his powers: "At that depth, what did he know of his son" (CH, 75)? On the next page the father's aware-

ness of his inability to know his own son is poignantly
accentuated: "For the first time, the phrase that he
[Gisors] had so often repeated: 'It is impossible to know
human beings,' was associated in his mind with the face
of his son" (CH, 76).

One can, however, know what one has changed.
"Effecting change" as a source of knowledge is first expressed by Gisors with regard to Tchen: "Why do I have
the impression that I know him [Tchen] better than my
son? It was because he understood much better in what
respects he had changed him; that capital modification,
his work, was precise, limitable, and, in human beings, he
knew nothing better than what he himself had brought
to them" (CH, 78).

In *La Condition humaine,* the theme of change as a
source of knowledge is also related to that of love and,
by extension, to that of essence. Love, which invariably
changes the persons sharing it, is a source of knowledge in
the form of an intuition of the essence of the loved one.
Kyo poignantly expresses his awareness of this during his
crisis with May, when, as a result of her infidelity, he feels
the abyss plunging between them:

> I do not know her. I know her only to the extent that
> I love her, only in the way in which I love her. One
> possesses only what one changes in a person, said my
> father . . . (CH, 66).
>
> "To the others I am what I have done." To May
> alone he was not what he had done; to him alone,
> she was something quite different from her biography
> (CH, 67).

Kyo expands the foregoing into a definition of love:

Men are not my kind, they are those who watch me and judge me; my kind are those who love me and do not watch me, who love me in spite of everything— though I be base or guilty of treason—who love *me* and not what I have done or will do, who would love me as I would love myself—as far as, and even including, suicide. With her alone I have in common that love—lacerated or not. . . . It certainly was not happiness—it was something primitive . . .—the only thing as strong as death in him (CH, 67–68).

The definition is completed when Kyo finally agrees to allow May to accompany him to the rendezvous which is to lead to his death: "He now understood that the willingness to lead the being one loves to death is perhaps the most complete form of love, that which cannot be surpassed" (CH, 244).

The theme of love is reinforced by the painter Kama who, when asked by Clappique why he paints, responds: ". . . first of all for my wife, because I love her . . ." (CH, 226). Gisors, too, loved his Japanese wife. How different the eroticism of Ferral and Perken, who experience only irremediable separation!

The theme of essence, as opposed to existence, also finds expression through the conflicting views of Ferral and his mistress, Valérie. While Ferral asserts what Sartre reaffirms in *Huis-clos,* "A man is the sum of his acts, of what he has done, of what he can do. Nothing else . . ." (CH, 271), Valérie maintains that "no human being can be explained by his life" (CH, 139).

The appropriateness of the title of the novel appears in its full light as we realize that *La Condition humaine* reveals not only the negative but also the positive aspects of man's estate—not only man's limitations, which constitute his anguish and his *misère,* but also his powers, which constitute his hope and begin to reveal his *grandeur.*

What distinguishes this from Malraux's first two novels is that all of its revolutionaries choose not only their lives but also their deaths. Even though the initial victory of the insurrection is turned into defeat when Chang Kai-Shek breaks with the Communists, neither the lives nor the deaths (Tchen's death excepted) of the heroes have been in vain. All have contributed to the transformation of their world; they have transformed humiliation into dignity—both those who die and those who survive.

Tragic though some of their fates might be, they have all (with the exception of Tchen) begun the ascent from hell. These heroes mark the beginning of the reintegration of the solitary hero, who has found an idea worth living and dying for, into the world of men. Toward the end of the novel Tchen, the transitional hero who is also the master of the terrorists, finds one of his disciples, Souen, breaking away from him when he tries to instill in both of them his (Tchen's) own death wish by saying to them: ". . . we must throw ourselves under the car with it [the bomb]" (CH, 219). This, of course, is a reference to his determination to liquidate Chang Kai-Shek—a determination which imperceptibly changes into a frenzied desire to kill himself instead. In reply, Souen says: "I prefer to make . . .—to make several attempts than to decide that I will make only one because afterwards I will be dead" (CH, 220). When Tchen insists that the meaning of life is found in terrorism through "the complete possession of oneself" (CH, 221), Souen becomes frightened and, in his reply, we discern that his break with his master is imminent: "I am less intelligent than you, Tchen, but for me . . . for me, no. . . . It is for our people that I am fighting, not for myself" (CH,

222). As the scene continues, Souen, who does not share Tchen's craving for the absolute through complete self-possession, reveals the reason for his break, which once again completes the cyclic master-disciple relationship:

> —You [Tchen], you, perhaps, need that. I do not know. . . . He was struggling. "If I agreed, you understand, it would seem to me that I am not having myself killed for all, but. . . .
> —But? . . .
> —For you (CH, 222).

When Souen refuses to follow him Tchen decides to act alone, but, concerned about his biography, he orders Peï, the disciple who is willing to accompany him, to remain behind and serve as a witness to his, Tchen's martyrdom: "—You who write, he said to Peï, you will explain" (CH, 223). Tchen does throw himself, with the bomb, under the car but, still alive after the bomb explodes, he is forced to give himself the *coup de grâce* with his own revolver: "he pulled the trigger without realizing it" (CH, 280).

If Tchen's murder in the opening scene of the novel contributed to the cause, his frenzied suicidal pursuit of the absolute did not; Tchen chose his own death, but did not accomplish his alleged purpose—Chang Kai-Shek was not in the car. As for his disciples, one, Souen, becomes a new master as he dies in prison a martyr for the cause; he receives the gift of death from Katow who relinquishes his own cyanide, divided in two, to him (Souen) and a companion sitting beside him. Katow's act or, as critics have called it, his "sublime gesture," brings us to the midway point of the thematic cycle—the point at which death becomes not only a meaningful part of life but, when freely chosen or freely given, as in the case of Katow, "that gift of more than . . . life" (CH, 366). When Souen in the darkness of the prison fails to grasp the cyanide —which is momentarily lost—Katow's first reaction is one of anger, which soon turns to desolation as he thinks of the cyanide as "the greatest gift that he had ever made, and which was perhaps made in vain" (CH, 367). The concepts of life and death are totally fused, and even reversed, in Katow's poetic apostrophe when the "gift" of death is found and he exclaims: "Oh resurrection" (CH, 367)!

In relinquishing the cyanide to his two comrades, Katow becomes the master, not only of his own fate, but of theirs as well; he is doubly a martyr as he is led away to be burned alive in the locomotive. Lou Shu-Yen, Hemmelrich's partner, preceded Katow to the same death.

Kyo, who is foiled by Clappique, the buffon, makes the final decision in taking his own life. It is through a death resembling his life, both of which were freely chosen and freely given, that Kyo emerges as *the* hero who begins the ascent from Hell. When his hour comes, Kyo has no regrets; the following thoughts pass through his mind as he prepares to take his cyanide: ". . . he would die among those with whom he would have wanted to live; he would die like each of those men lying there, for having given a meaning to his life. What would a life for which he had not been willing to die have been worth" (CH, 362)?

With Kyo, Gisors's hope died, and for him, too, life and death have been fused: "there is almost no anguish left in me, May; since Kyo has died, I am indifferent to death. I am, at the same time, delivered (delivered . . .) of death and of life" (CH, 398). If Kyo the disciple was

indebted to his father, Gisors, for the hope which transformed the humiliation he suffered as a half-caste into
the dignity he found in revolutionary activity, he progressed beyond his master—and thus completed the cycle
—by translating theory into action.

As for Peï, Tchen's second disciple, he becomes a
master who will, though no longer as a terrorist, carry on
as an agitator for the revolutionary cause. He conveys his
intentions in a letter to May in which he also informs
her that Hemmelrich, for the first time in his life, has
found a hope in his work; he is living in the kind of
world he helped to create. May, too, will carry on her work
for the revolution, even though her main hope, Kyo, is
dead.

Though Kyo and the insurgents have been defeated,
May believes that there is no reason to abandon hope:
"The Revolution had just passed through a terrible malady, but it was not dead" (CH, 395). When Ferral tries
to convince his associates in Paris, at the end of the novel,
of the contrary, they reinforce May's persuasion:

> The Communists have been crushed everywhere,
> answered Ferral. . . .—The Communists, without
> doubt, but by no means Communism. China will
> never again be what she was, and, after the triumph
> of Chang Kai-Shek, new Communist waves are to be
> feared . . . (CH, 383).

As for Ferral himself, he meets the same fate as do
all Malraux heroes whose lives are egocentrically motivated: "But he was beaten: having made efficacity his
highest value, nothing compensated for the fact that he
found himself in this humiliating position opposite these

men whose persons and methods he had always scorned"
(CH, 390). He is confronted with the absurdity of his life
when the Minister of Finance in Paris predicts the end
of the Franco-Asiatic Consortium: "All the events of
Shanghai were going to disolve into total nonsense" (CH,
392).

As for the go-between, Clappique (who does not exist),
he is finally forced—after a close call with madness, and
for fear of death at the hands of Chang Kai-Shek's men—
to return to Europe and face reality for the first time in
his life. But, true to character, he returns to Europe "disguised" as a sailor.

With the return of Spring which completes the cycle
of the year, our heroes have transformed the world they
rejected into one they are not only able to *live in* but
are still ready to *die for*. The world *of La Condition
humaine,* like that of Malraux's earlier novels, is a changing world. What is new about this last of Malraux's novels
set in the Orient is that its heroes have found—in their
roles as active participants in the perpetuation of change
—a new identity and the meaning of both life and death.
They have found that they can transform humility into
dignity, anguish into hope, and absurdity into significance.

If *La Condition humaine* ends with the political
defeat of its heroes, their moral victory is a certainty,
because they have changed their world, and "without
doubt a man's worth is determined by what he has transformed" (CH, 395). Foremost among the heroes is, of
course, Kyo, followed by Katow, Lou Shu-Yen, and Souen,
all of whose deaths prevented their living in a world they
helped to change. The survivors, who are able to live in
the world which they are transforming and for which
they are still ready to die, are Hemmelrich, Peï, and May.
What these heroes have bequeathed to Kassner, who

follows them, is their readiness to sacrifice their lives. Ferral is the last of the conquerors.

Notes

1. André Malraux, *La Condition humaine* (Pairs: Gallimard, 1933), p. 20. Henceforth cited as CH.
2. Such references may be found on pp. 51, 68, 73, 74, 232, and 244.
3. *Supra,* p. 137.
4. For a more extensive analysis of Clappique in this role, see Gerda Blumenthal, *André Malraux: The Conquest of Dread* (Baltimore: The Johns Hopkins Press, 1960), pp. 26–28; see also Sonnenfeld, *op. cit.,* p. 202.

15.

The Rediscovery of Life

As the second half of the cycle of six novels is about to commence with the hero's return to the West in *Le Temps du mépris*, the thematic cycle, which began with "the discovery of death" in the early novels, winds slightly beyond the halfway mark as Kassner, upon his release from prison, begins "the rediscovery of life."

Significantly, it is after a confinement of nine days— a metaphor of the nine-month cycle from conception to birth—that Kassner is reborn to the world and to life.

Shortly after the opening of the novel the reader is plunged, with the hero, into the concrete, man-made hell of a Nazi prison camp; into a circular cell which once again suggests not only a metaphor of the cycle of destiny, but also of the circles of Dante's "Inferno." [1] The shape of the cell confronts the hero, isolated from all human contact, with Destiny in one of her most formidable guises: "The condemned incarcerated in round cells, where nothing fixes their gaze, always go insane." [2] The prisoner's terror of oncoming madness absorbs his consciousness to the point where it diminishes, if it does not blot out, his fear of Destiny in the guise of torture and death.

Valiantly Kassner struggles to ward off the madness with which he is threatened by a tremendous effort of the mind—"controlled madness" (TM, 72)—and of the will.

The secret, he knows, is not to remain passive. Kassner begins his struggle first, by re-creating scenes from his past life with the help of images evoked by musical strains which pass through his mind's ear; then, by establishing contact with a fellow prisoner by responding to the tapping—in which he later discovers a codified message—on the wall of his cell; and, just before his release from prison, by preparing a speech which he delivers to an imaginary audience of comrades.

The hero's *sense of life*—one of the two main characters according to Malraux in his preface—is gradually revealed in the dominant themes. First and foremost is the theme of sacrifice, which is cyclic in that the novel begins and ends with Kassner's readiness to sacrifice his life for his cause. Kassner's initial sacrifice (he is apprehended as a consequence of having prevented a list of comrades' names from falling into the hands of the police) is followed by that of the comrade who makes his release possible; then by that of the pilot who risks his life in flying him from Germany to Czechoslovakia; and finally by Kassner's own disclosure, at the end of the novel, of his readiness to return to Germany where he will once again sacrifice his life for his *raison de vivre et de mourir*.

The theme is reinforced by Kassner's visions of a vulture attacking him. These visions identify the hero with Aeschylus' Prometheus, who defied the gods to come to the aid of man. The tragedy of the novel lies in the fact that the sacrifice is necessary. Charles Blend notes the parallel between the two heroes in his book on Malraux, where, speaking of *Le Temps du mépris*, he says:

An apparently simple story that shows us a hero who is dragged away to isolation and imprisonment by two shadowy figures, and who in his delirium three times imagines a vulture descending upon him, it obviously recalls *Prometheus Bound*. The parallel is supported by the author's reference to Aeschylus in the preface.[3]

Second, the hero's *sense of life* is revealed in the theme of fraternity. This theme, already introduced in the relationships between Garine and his narrator, between Claude and Perken, and between Kyo and his fellow revolutionaries, is intensified in *Le Temps du mépris* by virtue of the hero's solitary confinement at the beginning of the novel. Indeed, Malraux informs us in his preface that the revitalization of this theme is to be one of the main objectives of his work. His hope is that fraternity will displace individualism at the top of the prevailing hierarchy of values. Malraux deplores the fact that individualism, which he views as but one aspect of the human personality, has tended to exaggerate the uniqueness of each person to the point where it has severed him not only from the totality of his own being but from what unites him to his fellow beings as well.

For Kassner the focus definitely shifts from the differences that separate men to the shared experiences that unite them. The shift in focus is most dramatic in the prison episode where Kassner realizes that only by maintaining contact with another human being can he escape the dread of becoming insane—of succumbing to the power of his own imagination [4] in the isolation of his cell. His prolonged, persistent effort to reassure himself of the continued presence of the comrade in the cell adjoining his is not in vain: both men benefit from the reestablishment of communication, even though it is only that of alternately tapping and listening (TM, 92).

The theme of fraternity is emphasized again when Kassner and the pilot who has volunteered to fly him out of Germany risk their lives together (TM, 128); and still again, when, in the meeting hall in Prague, Kassner re-encounters that fraternity which only men in large gatherings—and sharing the same passions and truths—are privileged to experience (TM, 163–64).

Third, the hero's *sense of life* is revealed in the theme of "human grandeur" which moves into a position of increasing importance as the hero's quest for identity continues. Already manifested in the themes of sacrifice and fraternity, the theme of human grandeur is expanded by the hero's awakening to an awareness of the agelessness of human pity, heroism, and sainthood, and of the courage and dignity of man's relentless assault on the earth. In his preface, Malraux relates the theme to the true purpose of art, which, in his view, is to awaken men to a consciousness of the grandeur which is part of their nature (TM, 9). Malraux repeatedly communicates his awareness of the fact that the vast multitude of men are not yet conscious of their *grandeur;* they have not yet learned to respond to their inner voices (TM, 153).

The most positive theme of *Le Temps du mépris*—the one which links this novel most significantly with the Malraux hero's cyclic spiritual journey—is the hero's "rediscovery of life." As Kassner emerges from the darkness of his nine-day confinement to rejoin the world of the living, he brings us just beyond the midway point of the journey—and the thematic cycle—that began with Malraux's early heroes' "discovery of death" in the hell of an absurd world. Kassner's experience prefigures the ultimate victory of life over death at the end of the quest. As the novel draws to a close, life becomes a positive force that gradually overshadows death in the hero's vision of human destiny.

It will be recalled that the correspondents of Malraux's epistolary novel, *La Tentation de l'Occident,* had sparked the sensibility of the absurd by exposing a world in a state of ferment, a world of crumbling values in both East and West. A determination to escape that meaningless world had impelled the protagonists of Malraux's full-fledged novels to embark on their quest for a new identity. The first three of those novels, all of which were set in the Orient, engaged the heroes in a desperate struggle against the absurd—against a life whose futility was accentuated by the finality of death.

For the protagonists of both *Les Conquérants* and *La Voie royale,* Death represented destiny's most formidable auxiliary, the archenemy that had to be defeated, the foe that had to be conquered whatever the cost. It was death that rendered their predicament intolerable by snuffing out all hope of altering it. Both the conquerers and the adventurers were on the losing side of the struggle: death emerged victorious over both Garine and Perken. The turning point of the combat occurred when death, freely chosen for a cause, was tranformed into "a meaningful part of life" in *La Condition humaine,* the last of the three novels set in the Orient.

In *Le Temps du mépris,* Kassner, who is aware from the start that death in the service of his cause will heighten the significance of his life, goes beyond the revolutionaries of *La Condition humaine.* Upon his release from prison, he begins "the rediscovery of life" itself. In a passage which, in harmony with the rest of the novel, is a masterwork of style, Malraux enables the reader to share with Kassner the experience of his ascent from the hell of prison to the surface of life: first the simple life of every day, and then the miracle of procreation which leads to a revelation of the eternity, not of the dead, but of the living.

The rediscovery of life begins in the opening section of Part Seven [5] with Kassner's arrival in Prague, marking the end of his flight from Germany—and prison—to freedom. From the window of the car taking him, at considerable speed, from the airport to the center of town, Kassner the experience of his ascent from the hell of which would lead to a German prison. The sight of the dazzling city lights arouses in him a desire "to walk on the unreal sidewalk," *unreal* because the speed of the car and the profusion of lights fuse and confuse the separate images into a host of undistinguishable contours which at once concretize and harmonize with the blurred perceptions of the hero as he resumes contact with reality. Kassner's reaction to the scene, as he perceives it, situates him in a sort of "twilight zone" between the inhuman experience of prison or nothingness and the world of concrete reality or life.

The myriad objects on display in the windows— "pineapples," "pâtés," and exotic "Chinese objects"— evoke in Kassner's imagination scenes reminiscent of the fairy tales of childhood, with a resulting fusion of past and present in his mind. The scene also awakens memories of the mythological underworld: these streets might have been those on which "a devil had decided to unite all the commerce of Hell. . . ." But Kassner remembers, "it is he who is returning from Hell and [that] all of this is simply life. . . ." The car stops in the center of town, and Kassner is able to realize his desire to walk on "that unreal sidewalk" and to catch a glimpse, at closer range, of the shop windows whose lights and multiform objects had captivated his imagination even when he saw them only as a confused mass from the windows of the automobile.

Kassner's reorientation to life is by no means effortless or uninterrupted; the danger of his sinking back into the prison of darkness where he was continually confronted with the threat of madness, torture, and death remains constant. During the entire course of his walk this danger is periodically communicated by phrases that put him in an in-between realm, that compare his mental state to that of a drunkard, and convey his inability to rediscover either himself or the world. The earth and everything on it seems strange to him; he has difficulty recognizing the most familiar objects on display in the shop windows: ties, suitcases, candies, first-aid kits, and gloves.

Of the windows that attract Kassner's gaze, that of the glover is perhaps the most significant, for its contents evoke images of the human hands that fill them: "hands that could do everything," the authors of all the other objects to which Kassner's numbed senses are beginning to react. Such is his surprise at the accomplishment of these hands —the inhabitants of the gloves—that he sees the whole earth populated with them; he even envisages the possibility of their existing independently of the beings— "men"—of which they are but a part.

From the shop windows displaying inanimate objects, Kassner's promenade leads him to a furrier's window where he catches sight of a living creature—a little puppy whose whole being is painted in such lively images that he seems to leap before our eyes. There is an impulse to reach out for and caress the little white furry creature whose playful but "awkward" movements indicate that he is just beginning life. Ironically, the puppy is beginning life in the midst of death in this window, with its display of the "dead skins" of other animals who seem to prefigure his own destiny. This close association of the two ends of the cycle—life and death—is a constant in Malraux.

Kassner's glance and thoughts are next directed on "that flesh destined for prisons and cemeteries, passersby," making their way "tranquilly" toward the square. Again there is a note of irony, for these "passersby" (*passants*) seem to be *passing* not only through the city but also through life to the ultimate destiny—death—which they share with the puppy.

Upon his arrival at the square, Kassner's whole being, at least momentarily, responds to the scene. He comes upon a series of shops whose merchants are selling the very essentials of life: "food" and "clothing" (*victuailles* and *vêtements*). Finally, he comes to a fruit vendor's stall, whose image inspires the lyrical outpouring of the poetic apostrophe: "Oh magnificent fruits, full of all the respiration of the earth!" This is perhaps the first time in Malraux that we encounter a poetic apostrophe to the fruits of the earth. For the first time nature appears as a beneficent force which sustains life. Up to this novel, and especially in *La Voie royale,* nature was a symbol of crushing destiny, a negative force against which man had to struggle to remain alive. This brief hymn to life is expanded from *L'Espoir* to *Les Noyers de l'Altenburg,* where it culminates with the hero's mystical revelation of the resurrection at the end of time.

Kassner wants to live; he thinks of his wife: "To find Anna first of all." The desire expressed at this point becomes a reality by the end of the novel. Kassner begins to participate in the life that surrounds him: he enters a tobacco shop, buys some cigarettes, and lights one. But, upon leaving the tobacco shop, the world seen through the smoke of his cigarette once again (or still) seems unreal to him. The smoke subtly suggests his still foggy intellectual state.

Kassner's walk leads him past another series of tradesmen: a hat-maker, a dealer in Moroccan leather goods, and a watchmaker. The clocks and watches on display in the latter's shop surprise Kassner: "time" is being sold—a "prisonless" time. The implication is that time stops in prison while it continues in life. And this *time* of life finally leads him to a cafe where he no longer sees only inanimate objects made by the hands of men, but men themselves: "People."

Kassner is almost startled by the realization that "they [people] still existed;" "that they had continued to live" while he was in prison—"the blind realm," where both *time* and *life* had stopped; where darkness had prevailed in contrast to the lights and multifarious forms which are now reawakening his senses. Kassner wonders what his own relation to these people might be: would they be friends, enemies, or merely indifferent? He observes them; he guesses their sentiments: there were superficial ones who were satisfied with "half-friendship" (*demi-amitié*) and with "lukewarmness" (*demi-chaleur*) and those who sought a deeper communication with their partners. Finally an image of "some hands with interlocked fingers" suggests that communication with one's fellow begins in the true essence of the last fragment of the entire passage: "Life."

Upon leaving the cafe Kassner goes beyond the surface of life to begin Malraux's hero's discovery of the secret of life. The revelation of this secret is prefigured in the image of an apple tree—a symbol of the beginning and continuity of man's life in time—which Kassner envisages, in his mind's eye, as forming part of the scene in the countryside which lies just beyond the city: "Down there, in the night, lay the whole sleeping countryside and the tall apple trees standing upright in the centers of their rings of dead apples" (TM, 152). The image of the ring of dead apples around the living tree suggests the endless cycle of destruction and re-creation, of death and rebirth.

The second movement of the Malraux cycle is introduced as Kassner sees in his rediscovery of life a prefiguration of possible resurrection after death: "Oh peace of prisonless evenings, evenings where no one dies beside one! Could he not come back, on an evening like this, after he had really been killed" (TM, 152)?

The significance of the image of the apple trees is heightened when we realize that Kassner is the first Malraux hero who has a child in whom he sees *not,* as did Hemmelrich in *La Condition humaine,* a form of destiny limiting the man by preventing him from releasing in action the pent-up hatred destroying him, but the positive aspect of man's fate. Kassner sees in his child a source of renewed *hope;* he views procreation as a means of achieving immortality here on earth.[6] His hope is reinforced by that of his wife, Anna, who looks upon their son as a symbol of the miracle of birth that has never ceased since the beginning of time. The narrator communicates Anna's thoughts on the anguish of the expectant mother in labor—an anguish which is overpowered by its ineffable antithesis, joy (TM, 178–79). The hope associated with procreation is further developed when Kassner, upon gazing out of the window of his home with his wife at the end of the novel, catches a fleeting glimpse of a young boy who quickly disappears into the shadows. Kassner closes his eyes after this glimpse of the boy, and when he reopens them, the sense of life is revealed to him as "the eternity of the living and not the eternity of the dead . . ." (TM, 183). In the same passage Kassner speaks of "the gift of virility" as "the only thing in man that might be greater than man" (TM, 183).

The positive aspect of *Le Temps du mépris* appears in its full light when we realize that Kassner is the first of Malraux's heroes for whom the outside world represents life and freedom as contrasted with the realm of death from which he has just escaped.

The tragedy of the novel lies in the fact, already mentioned above, that the cycle of human sacrifice is about to begin again as the action draws to a close: in rejoining the revolutionary effort, Kassner knows that he will meet his death.

Notes

1. The first instance of this parallel was cited (*supra,* p. 187) in connection with the circular grindstone around which Grabot endlessly gyrated in VR. See also Geoffrey H. Hartman, *André Malraux* (London: Bowes & Bowes, 1960), p. 53.
2. André Malraux, *Le Temps du mépris* (Paris: Gallimard, 1935), p. 46. Henceforth cited as TM.
3. Blend, p. 32.
4. Brian T. Fitch designates the imagination as one of Malraux's universes in his book, *Les deux univers romanesque d'André Malraux* (Paris: Minard, 1964).
5. The quotations on pp. 221–25 are from TM, 147–51.
6. See also Sonnenfeld, *op. cit.,* p. 208.

16.

The Infinite Possibilities
of Human Destiny

The Malraux hero's rediscovery of life, already under-way in *Le Temps du mépris,* continues in *L'Espoir* with Manuel's revelation of the infinite possibilities of human destiny. This revelation not only constitutes the hope which justifies the title of the novel, but also offsets the tragic aspect of life—the incessant conflict between "being" and "doing" (*être* and *faire*) within both man and the world—disclosed by the action of the novel, which engages the hero, during this next stage of his spiritual journey, in the turbulent conflict of the Spanish Civil War.

Man's hope is revealed in the cyclic evolution of Manuel, who is reborn to a new life at the beginning and at end of the novel. The period of his evolution coincides with the time structure of the novel. Manuel is about to be reborn after a metaphor of the nine-month, conception-to-birth cycle ending as a new cycle of nature is about to begin in the Spring of the year: the action of the novel begins in July and ends in March. The full significance of the hope embodied in Manuel's evolution is disclosed in the last section of the novel where it is extended to man, as he continues to evolve in time.

In *L'Espoir* there is an individual hero, Manuel,

whose development constitutes the unifying element of the novel by revealing both the hope and the tragedy of man's terrestial life, and a collective hero. The latter is a composite of all the characters—including Manuel—whose multifarious and conflicting views and attitudes translate, for contemporary man, as his quest for a new identity continues, the complexity of all life, and consequently, the impossibility of either/or solutions in a changing world which is not amenable to them.

The action of the novel engages the characters in the tragic conflict between the ideal and the possible, between illusion and reality, between what man would "be" and what he can and must "do"—between *être* and *faire*.

The vision of life as an incessant conflict and interaction of opposing forces that emerges from *L'Espoir* is related to St. Augustine's concept of history as an endless interplay of good and evil—of the City of God and the City of the Earth—both within man and in the world as a consequence of the Fall. The word "interaction" is the key to the anti-Manichean view of life which emerges from *L'Espoir,* and which Malraux shares with St. Augustine. The concept is that of an intellectual for whom it is difficult to draw a clear dividing line between absolutely right and absolutely wrong action in human affairs. Malraux's anti-Manichean world view is revealed indirectly in his grasp of and sympathy for the opposing attitudes, divergent views, and conflicting ideologies of the numerous characters who populate *L'Espoir;* it is expressed directly by one of them, Garcia, who distinguishes the intellectual from other men: "The great intellectual is the man of nuances, degrees, quality, in essence, anti-Manichean. Now, the means of action are Manichean, because *all action is Manichean. . . .* Every great revolutionary is a born Manichean. And every politician." [1] The parallel between Malraux and St. Augustine is subtly reinforced by the reappearance, at least twice in *L'Espoir*, of the image of the apple tree (already encountered in *Le Temps du mépris*) which traces the origin of their vision back to the expulsion from Eden when man, who was created immortal, began his existence in time with a movement from unity to ever greater diversity. The tree is at once a symbol of the source of knowledge and of the origin of death, of the incessant opposition and interaction of the forces of good and evil, and of the continuous cycle of destruction and re-creation; it is a symbol of man's temporal existence.

Both Malraux and St. Augustine see in the unending cycle of destruction and re-creation the possibility of progress which may eventually diminish the conflict arising from the moral ambiguity of human nature. But, unlike St. Augustine, who envisages the final transformation of the "two cities" into Heaven and Hell for all eternity, Malraux the agnostic is at once more tragic and more hopeful: he is more tragic in that he sees time flowing certainly toward death and only "perhaps" toward eternity; he is more hopeful in that he envisages the ultimate purpose of human history as the redemption of *all* men through the creation, by man, of a human society modeled on St. Augustine's City of God.

If there is tragedy in the incessant conflict, there is hope in the constant change. This spark of hope illuminates what would otherwise be a totally tragic vision of the human adventure on earth. If the individual hero, Manuel, embodies the hope that *change* can bring progress in the course of a single lifetime, the collective hero of *L'Espoir*—a composite of men from all over the world, united in a common cause on the soil of Spain—incarnates Malraux's hope that progress, through constant change, will lead to the eventual reunification of mankind—the ultimate goal of human history. The tragic action of the novel almost belies its title when it becomes evident that the hope which it discloses cannot be realized without constant sacrifice: "it takes many dead men for humanity to advance one centimeter" (E, 205).

The very first page of the novel thrusts the reader into the thick of the Spanish Civil War, into the complexity and chaos of a country in upheaval, into the midst of an ill-trained, ill-equipped nascent revolutionary force struggling for existence. Coinciding with the birth of the revolution is the rebirth of Manuel: from a life absorbed by a passion for skiing he is reborn to a life dedicated to combat:

> And suddenly Manuel noticed that this car (the ski car) was of no concern to him. There no longer was any car; there was this night laden with a dim and boundless hope, this night when every man had something *to do* [italics mine] on earth (E, 19).

In the opening chapter we encounter Manuel feverishly gathering, by telephone, information on the progress of the revolution from all parts of Spain.

Through an alternation of action and intellection the dilemma facing the unorganized revolutionary forces is disclosed as one involving a choice between individual revolutionary fervor on the one hand and the necessity for discipline and organization on the other. The word "illusion" in the title of Part I, "The Lyrical Illusion," presages the fate of the individual revolutionary fervor —it is doomed to death. The necessity for discipline and organization arises from the nature of modern warfare

where man struggles not against man, but against organized machines. The choice is between change or death;
this applies not only to the fervor of individual combat
but also to the "apocalypse of fraternity" which it engenders. The problem is posed and explained at the
outset by Garcia:

> The Apocalypse wants everything immediately; the
> revolution obtains little—slowly and with difficulty.
> The danger is that every man bears within himself
> the desire for an Apocalypse, and that, in the struggle,
> this desire, after a rather short time, means certain
> defeat, for a very simple reason: by its very nature,
> the Apocalypse has no future (E, 110).

Somewhat later, Ximénès, the master who is preparing
Manuel for his new role in life as a leader and organizer
of the revolutionary forces, reaffirms Garcia's views:

> Courage is a thing that is organized, that lives and
> dies, that must be kept in repair as guns must. . . .
> Individual courage is no more than good raw material
> for the courage of the troops . . . (E, 154).

Under penalty of death, the "lyrical illusion" and the
"Apocalypse of fraternity" must be transformed into the
reality of an organized fighting army. The tragedy is that
man must temporarily abandon his ideal in order to
achieve it. He must become less a man in order to create
conditions which will enable all men to come closer to
the ideal of fully human living.

This conflict between what man would be and what
he can do constitutes the dominant theme of *L'Espoir,*

a theme which is the source of the unending conflict both within the individual and in human society. The conflict is manifested in the evolution of Manuel, who gradually ceases "to be" what he is "acting" to achieve as he learns to command. The interaction of these opposing forces is also apparent at the outset of any struggle in that the weaker side is forced to adopt the techniques and acquire the equipment of the stronger, and in the outcome of the struggle when the victor, in order to survive, is forced to implement at least some of the hopes of the vanquished.

As the War of Spain gains momentum, Manuel learns how to command; as a symbol of his new role, he carries a pine branch which he does not abandon until the end, when he is about to be reborn a second time. Manuel learns prudence and organization, obstinacy and rigor, but as he does he becomes the first Malraux hero for whom the Communist Party represents the danger of becoming a fatality rather than, as for Kyo and Kassner, a means for the exercise of the will: "Manuel is an honest man, but he is blind to everything except his party" (E, 190), observes Hernandez. It is significant that Hernandez, the uncompromising proponent of "being" in this first part of the novel, should notice the change in Manuel, the chief exponent of "doing." In the course of a dialogue with a Fascist leader, Alba, who defects to his company, Manuel unequivocally states his position with respect to the opposite poles of the "be-do" antithesis: "—I am not interested in what people *are,* I am interested in what they *do* [italics mine]" (E, 151). Garcia, who performs somewhat the same role in *L'Espoir* as Gisors did in *La Condition humaine,* takes a middle position: he is sympathetic to both attitudes but leans in the direction of the possible. His grasp of the antithesis which must be reconciled, at

least to the point where the transformation of the Apocalypse into an army will be possible, is set forth in the
following passage addressed to Hernandez, the anarchist:

> —The Communists want *to do* something. You, and
> the anarchists, for different reasons, want *to be* some-
> thing. . . . This constitutes the drama of every revolu-
> tion like this one. The myths according to which we
> live are contradictory: pacifism and the need for
> defense, organization and Christian myths, efficacity
> and justice, and so on. We must organize them, trans-
> form our Apocalypse into an army, or croak (E, 191).

Most of the main characters, along with the hopes
linking them to the revolution, are introduced in this
first part of the novel. While all of them would agree
that the hope of the revolution might best be defined as
the creation of conditions which would lead to the improvement of the quality of man, not all accept the need
for a compromise between being and doing as a *sine qua
non* for the realization of this hope.

The action of Part I ends, as its title predicts, with
the temporary defeat of the as yet unorganized, undis-
ciplined revolutionary forces. Defeated in the battle of
Toledo, they have no alternative but to evacuate the city
and proceed to Madrid. The tragic fate of the "lyrical
illusion," which demands all or nothing, is reinforced
by the death of Hernandez; he rejects any expedient which
would even temporarily threaten to diminish the quality
of man. In vain Garcia seeks to persuade him of the need
to compromise between being and doing in order to
implement the possible:

—Hernandez, to think of what should be instead of what one can do, even if what one can do is shoddy, is poisonous. Moral perfection and nobility of character are individual problems, in which the revolution is far from being directly engaged. The only bridge between the two, for you, alas—is the idea of your sacrifice (E, 192).

Condemned to die as an indirect result of a noble gesture testifying to his quality as a man, (he acceded to the wishes of the Fascist General Moscardo, by having the General's letters to his wife delivered), Hernandez chooses death even when, at the last minute, he has the opportunity to escape. The basis for his choice is the "all-or-nothing" philosophy later demolished by Camus in *La Chute*: "Hernandez was waiting to be executed. He had had enough of it. More than he could take. The men with whom he might have wanted to live were only good for dying, and, with the others, he no longer wanted to live" (E, 222).

A concrete image of the Pascalian metaphor of men as prisoners awaiting their final destinies terminates the first part—the "lyrical illusion"—of *Man's Hope,* as Hernandez is about to die:

. . . until the end of time, three men, endlessly replaced will stand here waiting to be killed.
—You wanted the earth! cries one of the fascists. You have it!

Three others, Hernandez among them, mount, in the odor of hot steel and upturned earth (E, 231).

With the opening of Part II the exodus from Toledo proceeds. It is autumn; the leaves are falling and the church bells are ringing; the "wreckage of the revolutionary dream" is on its way to the railway station to board trains for Madrid where the moribund dream is destined for resurrection into the reality of a Republican army born of a compromise between "being" and "doing."

Part II, whose title is the name of the river—the Manzanares—to be crossed by the revolutionary forces in the course of the action, is subdivided into two main sections: "Being and Doing" (*Être et faire*), which, as indicated above, is the dominant theme of the novel, and "Blood of the Left" (*Sang de gauche*), which vividly communicates the theme of sacrifice.

During the first of these subdivisions, "Being and Doing," the ground and air forces of the Republican Army are converted, in spite of their outmoded equipment, into effective combat units. The two outstanding leaders are Manuel, who transforms his troops into a disciplined, organized fighting regiment, and Magnin, who does the same for the pilots under his command. The International Brigade becomes a reality; men from all nations of the world, and a host of different persuasions, are united and fighting together for a common objective in the War of Spain. Anarchists, Socialists, pacifists, Christians, atheists, and agnostics rally round the Communists who possess the virtues—but only those—of action, which is indispensable to victory. As representatives of the various groups acting through the Communist Party propound their divergent persuasions, they disclose the complexity arising from the interplay of "being" and "doing" in the rapidly changing world of the twentieth century.

Manuel, his pine branch under his arm, learns how

to act—and how to command. Even before his troops reach Madrid, he experiences his first success. By keeping his promise to locate food and bedding for his men when they are temporarily unable to continue on to Madrid due to a mechanical breakdown of the train, he wins their confidence:

> Now, they all wanted *to do* [italics mine] something; they jostled to spring into order as they had wanted to rush into the train (E, 241).
>
> For the first time, he was opposite a fraternity that was assuming the form of action (E, 243).

Manuel's efficacy as a commander is consolidated when, upon returning to his regiment after a visit to the officers of the Popular Front, he finds, at the gate of the convent where his troops are stationed, "the first spontaneous guard of the War of Spain" (E, 244).

As the conflict continues, vividly described scenes of tank warfare and bombing missions engage the Revolutionary Army in battle after battle against the Fascists.

During the latter portion of "Being and Doing" Madrid prepares for the approach of the Moors. All through the last chapter of this first subdivision of Part II, the advance of the Moors continues; finally, a battle ensues —the first battle of the International Brigade. The chapter ends with the Moors in full retreat as the victorious Republican troops reach the Manzanares.

In "Blood of the Left," the second subdivision of Part II, the bombing and burning of Madrid begins: "A sinister twilight rose over the Age of Fire. The three greatest hospitals were burning, museums were burning, the National Library was burning . . ." (E, 340). Upon witnessing the scene, the American journalist Shade re-introduces the theme of resurrection: he envisages a new Madrid rising, like a phoenix out of the ashes of the old: "It is the first day . . . thought Shade" (E, 340)—the first day of the new world.

In this section the hero, Manuel, becomes increasingly efficient in his new role, but as he does, he also becomes, by his own admission, harder and harder, and less and less human. The turning point in his development occurs when he is faced with a crucial decision involving the death punishment of five deserters who were planning to defect to the enemy's side. His task is rendered all the more difficult because the men are volunteers. In one of the most poignant scenes of the novel, Manuel makes his choice by remaining silent when two of the condemned men, crawling in the mud on their knees, grab hold of his legs and plead for mercy:

> Never had he felt to this extent that it was necessary to choose between victory and pity. . . . Suddenly, the man allowed his arms to fall and looked at Manuel. . . . He was beyond resignation. . . . And, with the indifferent bitterness of those who already speak from the other side of life:
> —Then, you have no more voices for us, now (E, 343)?

From this point on the conflict in Manuel between being and doing—between his image of himself as a man on the one hand, and what he is forced *to do* in order to remain a leader of men on the other—grows in intensity. When, as a result of excessive shouting, Manuel actually does lose his speaking voice, the physical condition is but an outward manifestation of the loss of his inner voice

—the soul of the man he once was. The words of the condemned man resound in his conscience: "he could not forget those faces upturned and covered with mud, or the question: 'You have no more voice for us' " (E, 356)?

As time passes, Manuel comes to look upon the day of the executions as the most important day of his life. He realizes that, contrary to what his master Ximénès had once said, leadership involves more than being loved without seducing: "it had been necessary to kill, not enemies but men who had been volunteers . . ." (E, 356). The emotional impact of the episode on Manuel is evidenced as he becomes "sadder and sadder and harder and harder . . ." (E, 356).

The extent of his transformation is noted by Ximénès, who is confronted with Manuel some time after the executions: "The change in Manuel's face, his cropped hair, his air of authority, had surprised Ximénès right away. Of the young man he had known, he recognized only the dampened pine branch that Manuel held in his hand" (E, 357). In the course of the ensuing discussion with Ximénès, Manuel justifies—or perhaps "rationalizes" would be more exact—his decision, first, on one basis:

> —I knew what had to be done, and I did it. I am determined to serve *my party* [italics mine], and I will not allow myself to be stopped by psychological reactions. I am not a man to have remorse (E, 357).

and then on another: "I assume full responsibility for these executions: they were carried out in order to save the others, *our men*" (E, 357). Ultimately, however, he discloses a tragic awareness of his own dehumanization as the triumph of doing over being in his own person becomes more assured with each promotion in rank: "Only listen: not one of the echelons that I have reached in the name of greater efficacity, of better leadership, has failed to separate me more from the men. Each day *I am less and less human*" (E, 357).

In rebuttal to Ximénès, who proposes that man (except perhaps through Christ) is too small to maintain a balance between being and doing or between fraternity and leadership, Manuel reveals the germ of a forthcoming break both with his master and with himself—a break paralleling that of the mature artist with his own creation. Manuel wills not only to *do* something for his party, but also to *be* close to his men: "—To have drawn closer to the Party is worth nothing if it means being separated from those for whom the Party works. Whatever the effort of the Party may be, that bond, perhaps, can live only through the effort of each of us . . ." (E, 358). When Manuel repeats to Ximénès the haunting phrase of the executed man, the latter replies: "—Eh! what do you expect then, son? To condemn tranquilly? . . . You will become accustomed even to that . . ." (E, 358).

Somewhat later Manuel revives the subject, which has become an obsession, in a confrontation with Heinrich, whose words not only define the tragedy of leadership, but also confirm, by indicating a correspondence between the inner and outer man, the tragic change in Manuel:

—We are in the process of changing the fate of the war. You don't think we can change things without changing ourselves? From the day that you accept a command in the army of the proletariat, your soul is no longer yours. . . .

—You can keep your heart: that is something else.
But you must lose your soul. You have already lost
your long hair. And the sound of your voice (E, 360).

Manuel loses not only his voice and his soul but also
his regiment; upon learning the news from the Chief of
Staff, he exclaims:

—But my regiment? My regiment!
—I think that they are going to incorporate it into
another division.
—But I know it man for man! Who can possibly . . .
(E,359).

As Part II ends, the enemy is once again retreating; the
Republicans are victorious for the time being.

Of special interest is the reappearance of the title of
the whole novel as that of its third and last part. Significant, too, is the fact that unlike Parts I and II, each of
which contains two major subdivisions which seemingly
reinforce a vision of conflict and division—of the incessant
opposition between being and doing not only within man
but in human society as a whole—Part III is a unity
containing, like the first two, numerous chapters, but no
major subdivisions. Part III is also unique in that it introduces a new hero—human grandeur—incarnate in the
people. For the first time in Malraux the people play not
only an active but also a leading role in what is perhaps
the most stirring and compelling scene in Malraux's fiction
—the descent of the wounded aviators, borne on stretchers
by the Spanisher peasants, from the mountains of Valdeli-
nares to the town of Liarens after the battle of Teruel.
This scene situates the source of man's hope in the funda-

mental grandeur of all men—manifested by the peasants
in the Battle of Spain.

The combination of the title and the structure—im-
plying an identification of hope and unity—communicates
the eventual reunification of mankind as the essence of
Malraux's hope for man. This reunification is to be
achieved by the hero—the fundamental grandeur of all
men—of this third and final portion of *L'Espoir*. Reinforcing the identification of hope and unity as the essence
of the novel is the emergence into view, in the course of
the descent, of the already familiar image of the apple
tree. Though evocative, particularly in this scene, of the
tragic indifference of nature to man's plight in time, the
tree is also symbolic of the organic unity of mankind,
the tragedy of the Fall, and the hope leading from unity
back to unity via the continuous cycle of destruction and
re-creation symbolized by the ring of dead apples sinking
back into the earth:

> From the new plunge, the path descended directly
> over Linares: Magnin recognized the apple tree. . . .
> Magnin, an equestrian statue sitting sideways on his
> saddleless mule, was looking at *the apple tree standing
> in the center of its dead apples* [italics mine] . . . and
> that rotting ring, impregnated with seeds, seemed to
> be, beyond the life and death of men, the rhythm of
> the life and death of the earth (E, 421).

Of some consequence, too, is the fact that the tree is
sighted several times in the course of the descent by
Magnin, the commander of the air battle over Teruel,
with whom we might identify Malraux, who took part
in the mission himself. The importance of the scene is

heightened by the author's dedication of *L'Espoir:* "To my comrades in the battle of Teruel."

The peasants figure prominently all through the concluding portion of *Man's Hope,* where they seem to speak with a voice that echoes across the centuries—that of fundamental man. Their grandeur is set in relief more than once. Particularly impressive is the scene in which a peasant accompanies Magnin in the hope of locating for him, from the air, the Fascist airfield at Teruel—the target which is to engage Magnin and his pilots in the most dramatic bombing mission of the novel. Tears come to the peasant's eyes when he almost despairs of being able to locate the site of the airfield; his eagerness to be of assistance is conveyed in the following phrase: "If one could have died of looking and searching, the peasant might be dead" (E, 404). Finally, he sights the airfield: "The peasant pushed him [Magnin] toward the left with all his might, as if Magnin had been the airplane, and indicated to their left a poster advertising vermouth" (E, 404). And when he had accomplished his task, "the peasant, curled up near the mechanic, tried not to bother anyone . . ." (E, 405).

A detail about the peasant's inability to read assumes significance when, some pages later, we encounter one who can. The scene in which a little girl is reading a newspaper to her illiterate father prompts Garcia to propose to Magnin that even if Franco is victorious, he will have to implement, to some degree, the hope of the Republicans, that is, the amelioration of the lot of the peasants, lest he be subjected to incessant guerrilla warfare: "in every war, each takes from the enemy, whether he wants to or not . . ." (E, 441).

The nobility of the single peasant who assisted Magnin is duplicated by the group of peasants who, as indicated above, bear the wounded aviators over the mountains to Linares. The will of these peasants is symbolic of man's will through the ages:

> But it was not death, at this moment, that harmonized with the mountains: it was the will of men. . . . And that whole march of dark peasants, of women, whose hair was hidden under epochless scarves, seemed less to be following the wounded than to be descending in an austere triumph (E, 423).

Not only assisting, but also actively engaged in the conflict, the peasants are fighting to possess the land that they have been cultivating for centuries: "The angry peasants who fought under him [Magnin] were fighting to erect those little walls, the first condition of their dignity" (E, 431). After the battle of Teruel, Magnin could not forget the grandeur displayed by the peasants from the outset to the termination of the mission:

> Magnin was thinking about the peasants. . . . The peasants obsessed him: the one that Garcia had sent him, those whom he asked for automobiles in the villages; those of the whole descent from the mountains, those whom he had seen fight under him the night before (E, 441).

The part played by the Spanish peasants in *L'Espoir* no doubt is the clue to the meaning of the prophetic statement made by the old Alvear: "The age of the fundamental is beginning . . ." (E, 287), a statement that prefigures the theme of "permanence" in Malraux's last novel, *Les Noyers de l'Altenburg*.

Though transformation of the social structure by the revolution cannot contribute directly to the realization of the hope embodied in the novel—the elevation of the quality of man—it can play a role. Garcia says, "No state, no social structure creates either nobility of character or quality of mind; at the very most we can expect propitious conditions. And that is a great deal . . ." (E, 348).

Though man has a long way to go before he will accomplish the purpose of history, the hope that he will ultimately succeed is contained in a prophetic vision introduced early in the novel by a former monk, Collado, to a group of peasants. Beginning with an original account of the temporary failure of Christ's mission—a failure ending with the assemblage of all the poor of the earth on the soil of Spain—the monk, by changing the tense of the verb to the preterit perfect, projects the eventual success of that mission into the far distant future in a vision of the ultimate completion of the redemption of man by man. Collado's account ends with a vision of the Second Coming of Christ—"the star" in the following passage:

—And when all men had done too much killing and when the last file of the poor had set out . . . a star that one had never seen rose above them . . . (E, 163).

While *L'Espoir* is primarily concerned with man's hope for the creation of a better world in the present, the vision which it discloses extends beyond the present to a distant epoch when the purpose of history—the destruction of Satan or of man's hatred for man—will be realized. In the novel, this hope, reiterating that of Collado, is voiced by Ximénès, a fervent Catholic: "The

hatred of men also wears out . . . God has time to wait
. . ." (E, 165).

The constant change by means of which the goal of
human history will be realized is experienced by the
individual in the course of his own lifetime as demonstrated by the cyclic evolution of Manuel in *L'Espoir*.
The first indication we have that Manuel's cycle is about
to be completed is that, in Part III, the symbol of his
authority—the pine branch—has disappeared: "Manuel
. . . no longer held anything in his right hand" (E, 434).
The cycle leading to Manuel's rebirth is completed in the
Spring of the year: "The melting of the snow had begun;
the water was flowing . . ." (E, 443). As Manuel listens
to Beethoven's *Adieux,* he seems to be saying farewell to
the phase of his life which is ending and welcoming the
new one taking form within him. The idea of the termination of one phase and the initiation of another is suggested
in the following passage containing a summary of Manuel's
cyclic evolution:

> One day there would be peace. And Manuel would
> become another man, unknown to himself, as the
> combatant of today had been unknown to the man
> who had bought a little ski car to go skiing in the
> Sierra (E, 445).

The experience leads Manuel to an awareness of the
infinite possibilities of a single human destiny: "One discovers war only once, but one discovers life several
times" (E, 445).

From the music, the Spring, and the new life rising
within him, Manuel has a revelation, in harmony with
his own experience, of the infinite possibilities of man's
destiny as his cyclic evolution continues:

Manuel heard, for the first time, the voice of that which is graver than the blood of men, more disquieting than their pressence on earth: the infinite possibilities of their destiny—and he felt within him that presence mingled with the sound of the brooks and the steps of the prisoners, permanent and profound like the beating of his heart (E, 445).

Man's hope cannot be realized without constant sacrifice.

Note

1. André Malraux, *L'Espoir* (Paris: Gallimard, 1937), p. 345. Henceforth cited as E.

17.

The Mystical Intimation
of the Earthly Paradise

The omnipresence of the cycle is perhaps the most notable feature of *Les Noyers de l'Altenburg*, where the thematic wheel, coinciding with the end of the hero's journey, comes full cycle. If the second half of the circle of the contemporary hero's quest for identity began with Kassner's rediscovery of the simple life of every day and continued with Manuel's revelation of the infinite possibilities of his own and of man's destiny in *L'Espoir*, young Berger, in *Les Noyers de l'Altenburg*, completes the circle and the hero's ascent from hell with a fleeting glimpse of "the Earthly Paradise" as the ultimate end of the one great cycle that began in Eden. His mystical vision transports him to the end of the human adventure and even beyond: through the half-open doors of "barns of Paradise" (NA, 194), he envisages man, resurrected from the dead, passing with time into eternity.

Like that of Kassner and Manuel before him, young Berger's rebirth and revelation occur after a metaphor of the nine-month cycle from conception to birth—a cycle coinciding, in the case of Berger, with the period from September, 1939 to June, 1940, or from the date of mobilization to his first combat experience in World War

II. As the latter is about to begin, the hero, who is also the narrator, informs the reader of the metaphorical significance of the period in question:

> . . . we are mounting toward the front lines.
>   In the infinite, the Flemish night. Behind us *nine months* of barracks and cantonment; *the time that it takes to make a man* [italics mine] (NA, 170).

Following a close confrontation with death in a tank upturned in a dark ditch, young Berger envisages his rediscovery of life as a prefiguration of the realization of the biblical prophesy for the end of time.

But the cyclic structure of Malraux's last novel indicates that the human adventure is by no means over, and that the actualization of the hero's vision is projected into a far-distant future. It is not until we reach the last section of the novel that the cyclic narrative winds back to the beginning,[1] where we learn the ultimate fate of Malraux's last hero, who, having ended one quest with a mystical intimation of the secret of life and of man's terrestrial adventure, is about to initiate a new cycle: he is a prisoner—the starting point of all of Malraux's heroes—quartered, and significantly so, in the "vessel" of Chartres "under construction" (NA, 16). The phrase "under construction" suggests a correspondence between the history of Chartres Cathedral, which dates back to the pre-Christian era of the Druids, and man's history, neither of which is yet completed.

As the novel opens, with the termination rather than the commencement of the action, Malraux's hero is back not only in France, the point of his departure, but also in a Christian setting. Young Berger, a prisoner of war, is in Chartres Cathedral, where he is writing an account of two spiritual journeys: the entire cycle of his father's within the final phase of his own, which has already been completed. In the course of the narrative, we learn that the end of the father's cycle served as both an inspiration and a starting point for that of the son and disciple who, as inevitably happens in Malraux, eventually progresses beyond his master. The cyclic structure of the novel might be designed as follows:

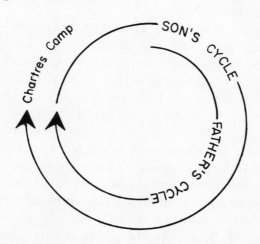

Malraux's twofold conception of the cycle represents both continuity and progress rather than isolation (Spengler) or eternal recurrence (Nietzsche).

In terms of time, the cycle, from the decisive experience of the father to that of the son, winds from World War I to World War II:

> How near I have felt to my father since certain instants in his life have seemed to prefigure my own! I was wounded the fourteenth, taken prisoner the eighteenth; his fate in the other war—on the other

side . . . was decided on June 12, 1915. Twenty-five
years ago, almost to the day . . . (NA, 25).

But the entire novel involves four generations—from great-
grandfather to great-grandson, or from Dietrich Berger,
a fictionalized representation of Malraux's grandfather,
to Malraux's own son, Pierre-Gauthier, to whom the novel
is dedicated. Implicit in the novel is the affirmation that
progress is made as the cycle of time winds from generation to generation.

The more deeply one penetrates *Les Noyers de l'Altenburg,* the more one is persuaded of the predominant
role played by the cycle in Malraux's vision of life. If
young Berger's revelation occurs after nine months of
training, his father's, which prefigures his own, occurs
at the end of the ninth subsection of the account of his
life which constitutes the cyclic nucleus of the novel. The
number nine, as we have seen, recurs repeatedly in association with Malraux's heroes' rediscovery of life. We encounter it first in Kassner's nine days in prison, then in
Manuel's nine months of Civil War, and finally in young
Berger's nine months of training for active combat in
World War II. Invariably, the completed cycle introduces
the theme of resurrection or rebirth—the second movement of the Malraux's cycle.

According to Cirlot in *A Dictionary of Symbols,* the
number nine is "the end-limit of a series before its return
to unity" (189), which in Malraux would correspond to the
completion of a cycle; Cirlot goes on to state that the
number nine "is the number *par excellence,* for it represents triple synthesis" (189) and a "triplication of the
triple" (189). And the structure of the center portion of
Les Noyers de l'Altenburg, which recounts the cycle of
Vincent Berger's life, is precisely this—a triple synthesis.

It comprises three main parts, each of which contains three subsections, making a total of nine. Each of the major divisions ends with the disclosure of a truth, culminating with that revealed in the ninth and last subsection, where, upon returning from "the valley of the dead" or "the infernal forest" of poison gas, Vincent Berger views the living fields which he espies in the distance as a prefiguration of "the Promised Land."

The son's mystical intimation, following his close call with death in World War II, recalls that of his father in World War I. The parallel (not to be confused with equivalence) of the two visions no doubt inspires young Berger to record both, including the events leading up to them, for posterity. Writing, he informs the reader, is the only means of remaining alive in the prison, Chartres Camp, where he eagerly awaits news of the cessation of hostilities—of peace.

As was the case with *La Condition humaine,* the opening date of Malraux's last novel is symbolically related to the cycle.[2] The date—June 21, 1940—which appears on the first page of *Les Noyers de l'Altenburg* does more than designate the initiation of a new season. According to Cirlot, "The key to knowledge corresponds, within the cycle of the year, to the month of June" (159). And there can be no doubt that young Berger's vision of time flowing into eternity—of man returning to the Earthly Paradise as prophesied in the Bible—is spiritual knowledge of the highest order.

From Chartres Camp, where the novel is being written, the narrator transports the reader back in time to the first significant events in his father's life.

The first panel of the triptych or triple synthesis of Vincent Berger's cycle is a cyclic narrative opening and closing with his return to Europe following an account of his adventures in the East. Graphically, his three-part cycle might resemble the following:

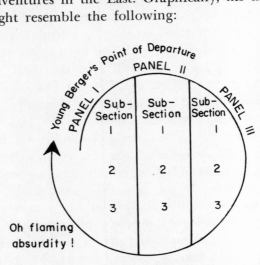

In the first of the three subsections of Panel I, the reader is introduced, by way of biographical details provided by the narrator, to the Berger family, particularly its three dominant figures: Vincent Berger (the only one present on the scene for the time being), Dietrich Berger, the narrator's grandfather, and Walter Berger, his uncle.

Upon his return to Reichbach, Vincent Berger, the narrator's father, is informed that his own father, Dietrich Berger, is critically ill. The Berger family, which had drifted apart over the years, has been convoked to present at the passing of the old man, whose character—though the particulars of his life which disclose it differ vastly—recalls Claude's grandfather in *La Voix royale*. Like old Vannec, Dietrich Berger rebelled against the established order on more than one occasion. After a pilgrimage to Rome ending in an unsuccessful attempt to consult with the Holy Father about his differences with the Church authorities in

Reichbach, Dietrich Berger broke with the Church. Refusing to enter the church building, but still faithful, he continued to listen to mass from outside, even in the most inclement weather. When, on another occasion, the municipal authorities refused to extend the lease of a synagogue in Reichbach, Dietrich Berger, himself the mayor of the town, provided quarters for it. (For a time, he also harbored a traveling circus on his estate.)

Walter Berger, the narrator's uncle, is introduced as the organizer of the Altenburg Colloquia, one of which is set for the following day. His character, we are informed, bears much in common with that of Dietrich Berger.

As for Vincent Berger, the reader is provided with some particulars connected with a legend surrounding his adventures in the East—a legend that preceded his own return to Reichbach but did not yet include an account of his discovery of the myth upon which his adventure was based.

The second subsection of the first panel recounts, in a flashback, Vincent Berger's adventures in the East, beginning in Constantinople where, as a professor of philosophy, he quickly won the esteem of the young intellectuals. This esteem was attributable, according to young Berger, to the following factors:

> He owed it [his prestige] as much to his passion for the subject as to his teaching: when he spoke of Nietzsche (his first *cycle of courses* [italics mine], in 1908, was called *The Philosophy of Action*), the echo of the still almost secret voice of Zarathustra always amplified the moving eloquence of Professor Vincent Berger . . . (NA, 39).

The word "action" proved to be more important than the word "philosophy" in the title of Professor Berger's course. It was not long before he became actively involved in politics, both as director of propaganda for the German Embassy in Constantinople and as an assistant to Enver Pasha, a Turkish general whose goal, which became the *raison d'être* of both men, was the realization of Turkish unity. Though the hope for Turkish unity—*le touranisme*—was ultimately dispelled for Vincent Berger, Enver Pasha refused to accept any evidence which might destroy his *raison d'être*. As a result of his travels throughout the regions inhabited by the peoples directly concerned, and who manifested utter indifference to the whole idea, Vincent Berger began to realize that the hope of Turkish unity which had oriented his life was nothing but a myth. It was not, however, until his humiliating experience at Ghazni, where he was stoned by a madman, that his disenchantment was complete. After the incident at Ghazni, which is recounted in the third and final subsection of Panel I, Vincent Berger, ill with fever, decided to return to Europe. In so doing, he completed the cycle from Europe to Europe. From Marseilles, where he had the impression of reentering the world of time—the second millennium of the Christian era—as contrasted with the "timeless" world of the Arabs, he left for Germany, but not before feasting his eyes on the displays in the shop windows on the streets of Marseilles.[3]

Panel I ends with an announcement of the death of Dietrich Berger, by suicide, five days after Vincent's return to Reichbach.

Panel II is set at Altenburg, where Vincent Berger meets his brother, Walter. Although the latter was not present at his father's death, he informs Vincent that

shortly before the fatal incident, the old man had declared that, in spite of what might happen, he would, if
he had to again, choose no other life than his own.

Their father's death engages the two brothers in a
discussion on the notion of man that anticipates the subject
of the colloquium scheduled for the following day. Neither
Walter, who asserts, "man is what he hides" (NA, 67), nor
Vincent, who avers, "man is what he does" (NA, 67),
expresses Malraux's complete notion of man as a combination of "what he is" and "what he does." The passing of
his father gives rise in Vincent's mind to the whole question of the human adventure, whereupon he reintroduces
one of the major themes of *L'Espoir*—the infinite possibilities of destiny, both human and natural. Viewing the
exterior scene from one of the windows of the library
at Altenburg, he declares:

> The human adventure, the earth. And all this, like
> the completed destiny of his father, could have been
> different . . . (NA, 68).
> Like a single human destiny, life in its entirety was
> an adventure. He was looking at the infinite multi-
> plicity of the landscape . . . (NA, 69).

The idea that all might have been different embodies the
concept of free will, that is, of the creative will, both
of nature and of man.

In an analogy between the people and the leaves,
both of which form part of the landscape he is viewing,
Vincent seems to arrive at the ratio, leaves : trees :: individuals : man, in which he discovers the secret of life:
while individuals and leaves die, man and the tree continue
to bear new fruit:

> And from the simple presence of the people who
> were passing there, hurrying by in the morning sun-
> shine, similar and different like leaves, there seemed
> to gush forth a secret which came not only from
> death lying in wait in his back, a secret which was far
> less that of death than that of life—a secret which
> might not have been less poignant if man had been
> immortal (NA, 69).

The theme of the immortality of man introduced
in the foregoing passage is subsequently developed and
extended to the individual in Walter's account of Nietzsche's sublime song rising out of the darkness both of
the tunnel and of his mind (he was already insane). The
song is a metaphor of the creative powers that enable
man to defy the destiny of ordinary mortals and achieve
immortality in time. In describing his reaction to Nietzsche's song, Walter begins what Vincent later completes,
Malraux's progression beyond his master, Pascal:

> I had just discovered something. Something impor-
> tant. In the prison of which Pascal speaks, men have
> succeeded in drawing from themselves a response
> which fills, if I dare say so, with immortality, those
> who are worthy of it. . . . And in this wagon . . . the
> millennia of the starry sky have seemed to me just as
> effaced by man as our individual destinies are effaced
> by the starry sky . . . (NA, 71).

Continuing on the same subject—man's capacity to defy
destiny—Walter, in one of Malraux's most striking and
memorable metaphors, identifies the Greek sculptor of the
head of the young man in the Acropolis Museum with the

first creation of man by man: "The first sculpture which represents a human face, simply a human face—liberated from monsters . . . from death . . . from the gods. On that day, man also drew man from clay . . ." (NA, 72). For Malraux, this first creation of man by man marked the beginning of Western civilization.

The first subsection of Panel II ends with a continuation of the theme of art's power to release man from Pascal's "prison." The following oft-quoted passage represents the point where Vincent Berger announces Malraux's break with, or progression beyond, his master:

—The greatest mystery is not that we are thrown by chance between the profusion of matter and that of the stars; it is that, in this prison, we draw from ourselves images powerful enough to deny our nothingness . . . (NA, 72).

At the outset of the second subsection of Panel II, Vincent, having taken leave of Walter, meets his cousin, Hermann Mueller, with whom he continues the discussion of man. The statues of grotesques adorning Hermann's room introduce Vincent, indirectly and prior to his entry, to Moellberg, their creator, who is to be one of the principal speakers at the colloquium. These grotesques, which Moellberg refers to as his monsters, actually reintroduce the Malraux-Augustinian image of man as a compound of good and evil.[4] The statues bear names corresponding to the aspects of human nature which they represent: "Some were beneficent, others maleficent" (NA, 76). These grotesques foreshadow the dramatic conflict between the opposing forces of good and evil to be experienced directly by Vincent in World War I. But the symbolic significance of these monsters is not limited to the moral duality of human nature; it also attests to their creator's life interest in "a coherent evolution of history":

> But the grotesque in itself, as a form and as a system, emphasizes the close bond between continuity and discontinuity—of ambivalence, that is to say, as expressed, for instance, in the myth of Gemini. Hence, the grotesque is a general symbol for the world of phenomena and of a coherent unfolding of existence (Cirlot, 128).

Presently, Moellberg himself enters the room; he has just returned to Europe after a trip through Africa, where he had unsuccessfully sought evidence to substantiate his concept of an ordered, progressive structure of human history. Vincent, who had followed reports of Moellberg's findings, comments on the man and his work. In Berger's opinion on the reasons for Moellberg's failure, we discern the way in which Malraux's own study on the same subject, "the human adventure," differs:

> And it was precisely in the epoch when the pluralism of civilizations was already drawing the attention of a number of minds (and in particular my father, who had lived in Islam) that Moellberg, obsessed with order and unity, began to extract from ethnology, the domain that is the most fertile in differences, the notion of a rigorous continuity of man, a structure of the human adventure (NA, 79).

The key to the essential difference in the two studies lies, of course, in "rigorous continuity,"—a phrase which does not take into account the numerous civilizations existing simultaneously on different cultural levels. Malraux's solution to the problem of "the pluralism of civilizations" lies in the "fundamental."

Subsequent to Moellberg's announcement of the fate of his manuscript which has been, figuratively speaking, "burned" (NA, 79), after fifteen years of research, the topic, dropped for the moment, is to be resumed at the colloquium, whose title has been changed from "The Eternal Elements in Art" (NA, 77) to "The Permanence and Metamorphosis of Man" (NA, 77).[5] The reason for the change is attributed to the fact that "eternity is the wrong word" (NA, 77).

The last subsection of Panel II is dedicated to the colloquium itself. In the course of the discussion, each of the participants propounds certain concepts which, when completed by the mystical visions of Berger-father and Berger-son, compose Malraux's vision of man and human history as revealed in his complete *oeuvre*.

The colloquium, "The Permanence and Metamorphosis of Man," raises two essential questions: first, whether human history—on the level of thought and will—manifests a permanent element in man or simply endless metamorphosis; and second, whether this history, were it to be written, would be meaningful or absurd. The question as to whether or not there is a basis for writing a history of the human adventure is posed by Moellberg, and though he himself has renounced the attempt, there can be no doubt that he is still grappling with the problem and, hence, still deems it possible: "can one isolate a permanent idea, valid everywhere, valid through history, on which the notion of man may be founded" (NA, 91)? Moellberg's impasse centers around the problem of metamorphosis, as the following passage attests:

> . . . if the human adventure subsists only at the price
> of implacable metamorphosis, it matters little that
> men transmit to one another, for a few centuries,
> their techniques and concepts: for man is an accident,
> and, in the essential, the world is made of oblivion
> (NA, 99).

Moellberg is the most interesting participant at the
colloquium. What critics have failed to note, in their comments on whether Malraux accepts or rejects his ideas, is
the fact that Moellberg often though unknowingly, voices
the solutions to his own problems and that his solutions
have become the basis for Malraux's history of the human
adventure. This is particularly true with regard to Moellberg's pronouncement on the question of metamorphosis,
which, at first glance, seems diametrically opposed to the
notion of permanence, the two constituting an irreconcilable paradox:

> The successive psychic states of humanity are irre-
> ducibly different, because they do not affect, do not
> cultivate, and do not engage the same *part* of man
> (NA, 103).

Upon closer examination the reader discerns, though
Moellberg does not, that his statement contains, in the
word *part,* italicized by Malraux, the key to the resolution of the paradox: the "successive psychic states" are
manifestations of "different parts" of the "same Man"—
fundamental Man; each "part" represents one of the "infinite possibilities of human destiny" manifested as civilization follows civilization in Malraux's cyclic view of history.

Confirming my interpretation of Moellberg's pronouncement is an opinion voiced by Stieglitz, who, in the following passage, affirms that he not only deems it possible to reconcile the paradox in a history of the human adventure (he speaks of "seemingly heterogeneous" elements) but also proposes the reconciliation as a task for the Germans—a task that Malraux has accomplished in his volumes on art:

> . . . I do not at all see why what you call the human adventure could not become a history, although formed of elements which at first seem heterogeneous. I affirm that we Germans, free of the prejudice of classicism, are particularly qualified to succeed in the writing of such a history (NA, 103)!

Count Rabaud further substantiates the notion of "permanence" in spite of "metamorphosis" when he speaks of the artist's power to conquer time and death, to speak to men across the ages, and to establish in his creations "the eternal identity of man with himself" (NA, 81). Continuing in the same passage, Rabaud defines the source of this power as the human soul—"that divine part":

> Thus certain men have that great privilege—that divine part—of finding in the depths of themselves, in order to make us a present of it, that which delivers us from space, from time, and from death (NA, 81).

And finally here is Malraux himself, in La Métamorphose des dieux, where, in a passage distinguishing Egyptian art from Greek art, the former manifesting the "eternal" and the latter the "immortal," he suggests that both are expressions of the "same soul," that of fundamental Man:

> The eternal and the immortals are not born of the same part of the soul; but the immortals and the heroes that vie with them, can be born only of a soul forgetful of the Eternal (MD, 57).

Moellberg begins what indeed has become Malraux's history of the human soul in his volumes on art—a history which, according to Moellberg-Malraux, is one of man's struggle against the angel of death (hence the title, *La lutte avec l'ange*).[6] This struggle began in Ancient Egypt where the Egyptian counterpart of what later became the immortal soul in the Christian era appeared in the form of basalt images of the dead. These images, which served as doubles for the mummies, were intended to survive even the mummies. The notion struck Moellberg-Malraux when viewing these images in cases in the Cairo Museum:

> These cases contain souls.
>
> The first representations that humanity made of of the soul.
>
> When man had ceased being a prisoner of the cosmos, he had necessarily encountered death: to conceive of himself was to conceive of himself as mortal. He had therefore begun *to struggle against death* [italics mine]. Whatever the duration of the mummy may be, basalt is certainly more durable! The sculpted image is therefore added to the mummy. It acts as a spare body for the double (NA, 96).

Moellberg-Malraux analyzes what happened when Christianity invented the immortal soul—a soul that is responsible and judged:

> The images of doubles disappeared from the tombs.
> In their places appeared little winged statues which no longer resembled the dead person, the statues in the Cairo case. Survival became immortality. Eternity was substituted for time. After a thousand years of stammering, humanity succeeded in inventing the human soul (NA, 96).

Additional evidence that Malraux by no means totally rejects Moellberg is contained in the latter's suggestion about the role of history in disclosing the "sense" (though he himself denies that it has any) of the human adventure. It is the "sense" or "significance," voiced by Moellberg in the following passage, that Malraux discloses in the thematic cycle of his novels—a cycle winding from a "death-in-life" to a "life-in-death" vision; the final vision is one in which both life and death have meaning in a continuous process of creation:

> —It is history's task to give a meaning to the human adventure . . .—to link man with the infinite. . . .
> —We are men only through thought; we think only what history allows us to think, and without doubt, it has no meaning. If the world has a meaning, death must find its place in it, as in the Christian world; if the destiny of humanity is a History, death is a part of life, but if it is not, life is a part of death (NA, 99).

It becomes apparent that Malraux has succeeded in demonstrating what Moellberg deemed impossible, and, contrary to what critics—notably Frohock and Hoffman—have said, Moellberg's ideas are more often seized upon, corrected, completed, and implemented, than rejected outright. Another interesting case in point is Moellberg's position on the problem of the existence or non-existence of a permanent element in man—on the level of thought— throughout the ages. Insisting that thought, which elevates man from the animal state, differentiates one man from another, Moellberg's stand is negative. He further rejects the notion of "permanence" by asserting that, even in terms of animality, men have little in common. Then, almost as an afterthought—witness the following quotation—he adds what in fact belies the assertion he has just made by including, as an element of permanence, man's perennial striving *(l'acharnement),* on the level of thought, to transcend his human condition:

> Except for thought . . . you . . . always have an animal.
> . . . Men hardly have in common anything but sleep
> —when they sleep without dreams—and the state of
> death. . . .
>   What does it matter to us whether there is a
> permanence in nothingness, if precisely what consti-
> tutes the dignity of man is condemned forever! If the
> striving of the best attains only what is most perish-
> able . . . (NA, 102).

This afterthought, which is immediately grasped and positively restated by Count Rabaud, constitutes the core of Malraux's humanism: man's power to question the scheme of things is the source of his greatest dignity—his grandeur in the Pascalian sense:

—This striving, at least, is durable, dear Moellberg, said Count Rabaud. Something eternal dwells in man —in thinking man . . . something that I call his divine part: it is his aptitude for calling the world into question . . . (NA, 102).

Moellberg's counterreply to Rabaud—"Sisyphus is eternal, too"—raises the whole question of the absurd which is the starting point of Malraux's hero's spiritual journey, and, incidentally, the point at which Vincent Berger leaves his son, who begins the cycle of the contemporary hero that is now reaching completion. The problem of the absurdity or significance of the human adventure is finally resolved by the two Bergers, not at the colloquium, but, as might be expected, through direct involvement in the concrete reality of history—World War I and World War II.

Also discussed in connection with the question of permanence are two closely related problems: man versus the individual, and human nature itself. The solution to the first lies in determining which is more important: that which links each man to his fellows or that which distinguishes each man as an individual. The answer is given, first, by Vincent Berger: "Man begins with the other" (NA, 87), and then by Thirard, in whose reply we discern a parallel between the spiritual journey of Malraux's hero in his cycle of fiction and that of the heroes of three famous novels of world literature: *Robinson Crusoe, Don Quixote,* and *The Idiot.* In all four cases, the theme, which answers the question in favor of man, is the same: the reintegration of the solitary hero (the isolated individual) into the community of men. The journey ends with the return of the "isolated prisoner" to the world:

In the three cases [four, with Malraux's cycle of
novels] . . . a man is initially presented as separated
from his fellow men! Robinson by shipwreck, Don
Quixote by madness, and Prince Muichkine by his
own nature, by . . . you see what it is a question of
. . . let us say: by innocence. The three solitary figures
of world fiction! And what are these three stories?—
the confrontation of each of these three solitary figures
with life, the account of his struggle to destroy his
solitude, to be reunited with men. The first struggles
through work, the second through dreaming, and the
third through sainthood (NA, 85).

And Thirard continues on the next page where he explains
the figurative meaning of "prisoner":

As if humanity lacked deserted islands, as if they did
not exist on every corner! But the streets are paved
with deserted islands! And everywhere there is a way
of being cut off from the community of men: through
humiliation, through shame (NA, 86).

The second question related to the problem of "permanence" is also answered, by Vincent Berger, in the
affirmative: the history of the human adventure does
manifest a permanent element in human nature:—"But
because of Adam, or rather Eve, the fatality of the Christian has become human nature itself" (NA, 89). Vincent's
reply, which has taken us back to the dawn of the human
adventure—to the Fall—offers additional evidence in support of a Malraux one-grand-cycle theory of history paralleling that of St. Augustine.

Walter Berger, who continues the discussion, further

strengthens this parallel by pointing out that Christian fatality—as opposed to Greek—was relativized by the second of the three capital events—the Fall, the Redemption, and the resurrection at the Last Judgment—in St. Augustine's cycle. "Then, said Walter, Christian fatality, experienced individually, is not absolute. The Redemption . . ." (NA, 89).

The mystical revelation of the third event—the resurrection—which occurs at the end of both Bergers' cycles, is foreshadowed by Vincent's intimation of the secret underlying the "permanence-metamorphosis" paradox as he contemplates the natural scene outside the Altenburg Priory after the colloquium. Emerging into the fields, Vincent comes upon a scene reminiscent of that which marked the beginning of the Malraux hero's rediscovery of life in *Le Temps du mépris* and *L'Espoir*. Once again it is the apple tree that symbolizes and reveals the rhythm and tension—the endless rebirth and incessant interaction of pairs of opposites—sustaining all life, both human and natural. Reinforcing the moral duality of human nature evoked by the image of the apples are not only the words "anguish" and "sunshine" but also the light of day illuminating the fruits: it is twilight, a symbol of dichotomy, and it is the twilight of a half-sunny, half-rainy day. In a simile of ineffable beauty, the description winds, like the cycle from death to rebirth, from twilight to dawn:

> The sun was setting, illuminating the red apples on the trees. An idle thought—orchards of endless rebirths—always lit up by the same anguish as if it were the same sun! This rainy and sunny day, so accidental, so unusual, like . . . the overwhelming and banal mystery of life in the anxious light of dawn (NA, 105).

As the sun slowly sinks under the horizon, and we move through the fields with Vincent Berger, the walnut trees of Altenburg, embodying the mystery of the "permanence-metamorphosis" paradox, come into view. Looking at the trees, Vincent perceives a parallel between the "endless will and metamorphosis" manifested in the "convulsed wood and twisted branches" of the walnut trees and the creative will of man. This parallel suggests a correspondence between the natural and the human adventures, both of which are perpetuated by the cycle of constant death and rebirth suggested by the "wide ring of dead nuts and young shoots" surrounding the trunks of the trees. The walnut trees thus emerge as symbols at once of the tree of life and the tree of man—fundamental man or Adam. The two trees represent the common source (the permanence) from which all diversity (metamorphosis) emanates. The mystery of life is thus revealed to Vincent as "the metamorphosis of the fundamental" by the cycle of incessant destruction and re-creation.

The double symbolism of the walnut trees is elaborated in a triple analogy: between the logs of the trees and the human animal; between the statues carved out of the logs and civilized man; and between the statues and the different civilizations they represent. The revelation comes to Vincent when he perceives an analogy between the statues of Atlas and two Christian saints, carved out of walnut logs, and the history of the human adventure from Ancient Greece to the Christian era—the two civilizations whose images of man combine to form Malraux's notion of Western man.

If the walnut trees reveal the secret of the permanence-metamorphosis paradox, they also suggest the possibility of eternal life as the direction toward which the endless "will" and "metamorphosis" will lead man at the end of the human adventure. Unlike the statues of Atlas (head bent down) and the saints, all three of which manifest human suffering and striving, the walnut trees—raising their twisted branches toward the heavens—suggest the future direction of the tree of man:

> My father thought of the two saints and of Atlas; the convulsed wood of these walnut trees, instead of shouldering the burden of the world, opened on to an eternal life through their polished leaves silhouetted against the heavens and their almost ripe nuts —through their whole solemn mass standing erect over the broad rings of young shoots and the dead nuts of winter (NA, 105–106).

The possibility of time flowing to eternity suggested by the identification of the tree of life and the tree of man in the walnut trees is borne out by the mystical revelation of both father and son, following their direct encounters with death in World War I and World War II respectively. The concluding sentence of Panel II indirectly announces the outbreak of World War I, in which the father, Vincent Berger, is to play an active role: "Europe had not known war for forty years" (NA, 106).

Panel III of the triptych of Vincent Berger's cycle contains a fictional, but intensely vivid account of a direct confrontation between the forces of good and evil—a confrontation in which the ultimate triumph of good over evil emerges as a symbolic prefiguration of what may come to pass at the end of the human adventure.

The action of this last panel begins June 11, 1915, on the front of the Vistula, where Vincent Berger is serving as secretary to Captain Wurtz, chief of the German Secret Service. The theme of evil is introduced at the

outset in an attempt on the part of Captain Wurtz to use
a child as an instrument of treason—as a means of un-
covering the identity of a Russian spy, Rosnova, believed
to be his mother. Appalled by the scene, Vincent Berger
requests a transfer to another division and is surprised
when, some time later, he is summoned, with Captain
Wurtz, to participate in an experimental attack of chemical
warfare. The chemical to be used is poison gas, invented
by a certain Professor Hoffman who, as the incarnation
of evil present on the scene, is unique in Malraux's fiction.
Nothing dulls Hoffman's enthusiasm for the lethal weapon
that is the product of his own mind. This is evident from
one of his first statements: "But we are in the prehistoric
period of chemical warfare" (NA, 121)! to one of his last:
"You see! you see! Absolutely decisive" (NA, 160)!

It is not long before the living earth is transformed,
by the gas, into an "infernal wood." But, even in this
hell, where "the gases had not left a centimeter of life"
(NA, 147), and where the apple trees reappeared "deader
than the others because of their greater fertility" (NA,
147), there was a light in the darkness: "the sun was
shining" (NA, 147).

It is at this point that the "straw" in the sunshine
emerges as the source of the regeneration of life; it is the
same straw which Vincent's son looks upon with wonder-
ment, first, when he issues from the ditch in World War
II, and again, in the prison of Chartres Camp:

> In the same way that the gases had mingled every-
> thing in the same purulence, life seemed to be bur-
> geoning again from a single form of matter, from
> that *straw* [italics mine] whose tension, like that of
> a watch spring, animated, all at once, the tenderest
> blades of grass and the most delicate leap of the

grasshopper, already hidden in the dust rendered misty by the sun (NA, 162–63).

Corresponding to the light of the sun is the light of the human spirit. In one of the most stirring scenes of Malraux's fiction, human pity, rising from the depths of the human spirit, transforms enemies into brothers. In a dramatic triumph of good over evil, orders are disregarded and war is abandoned. Seen issuing from "the valley of the dead" (NA, 148), and the "infernal woods" (NA, 150) of poison gas, is a German soldier carrying a dying Russian, his enemy—an enemy upon whose chest Vincent catches a glimpse of the Huguenot cross and dove, an image he warmly welcomes: "that little image seemed that of a friend to him" (NA, 153).

The symbolism of the cross—sacrifice—and of the dove—the soul and eternal life—combine to suggest "endless sacrifice leading to eternal life" as the "incomprehensible significance" of the human adventure. The cross is a recurrent image in the novel; it reappears during the son's encounter with death in World War II. The dove symbolism confirms Malraux's belief in the eternity of the human soul, which he refers to as "the eternal part" of man in *La Métamorphose des dieux* (35), and as "the victorious part of the only animal who knows he must die" (NA, 169).

The passage in Cirlot on dove symbolism seems both pertinent and illuminating:

The Slavs [it is a Russian who is dying in the novel] believe that at death, the soul turns into a dove. The bird partakes of the general symbolism of all winged animals, that is, of spirituality and the power of sub-

limation. It is also symbolic of souls, a motif which
is common in Visigothic and Romanesque art. Christianity, inspired in the Scriptures, depicts the third
person of the Trinity—The Holy Ghost—in the shape
of a dove . . . (81).

The symbol of sacrifice reappears as the dying Russian
borne on the shoulders of the German issuing from "the
valley of the dead" evokes in Vincent's mind the image
of the descent from the Cross: "At closer range, a body
pushed from beneath, still in shirt sleeves, surged into
view with the hanging arms of descent from the cross.
Then the one who was carrying it" (NA, 150). The symbolism of the "white" shirt of the dying man over the "black-
ened" uniform of his bearer suggests the ultimate triumph
of good over evil.

Christian symbolism becomes increasingly important
as this dramatic episode draws to a close with the ascent
of the living from "the valley of the dead." As Vincent
emerges from the fields of poison gas—the valley of the
dead—he spies in the distance "lines of sunflowers"—
symbols of the ascending spirit—"swaying in the wind"
(NA, 154–55). The ascent is complete when, accompanied
by two other Germans and the Russian they are carrying,
Vincent identifies the scene—the flowers and colors, the
trees and waters of the living earth—which they glimpse
in the distance through the line of sunflowers:

. . . in the distance, colors still existed, flowers, tawny
and green patches of earth, the singing of the wind
over the glistening river and over the immensity. The
Russian, stretched out on his back among them, made
an effort to turn over on his stomach, and finally
succeeded. The two Germans slowly straightened up

again, their knees still half bent, as stupefied as my father, to behold this valley of *The Promised Land* [italics mine] (NA, 155).

The ascent is complete, but the human adventure is not. Indeed, the revelation of the Promised Land, which occurred in a mystical flash, is immediately dimmed by the picture of human suffering witnessed by Vincent Berger as he himself, wounded in the knee and gassed, is carried unconscious to an ambulance. His last two cries are an expression of revolt: first, against the human condition —"What the devil was man doing on earth anyway! Oh flaming absurdity" (NA, 164)! and second, against human sacrifice—in his delirium, he feels that his life has been lived in vain: "the meaning of life was happiness, and he had occupied himself, fool! with something other than being happy" (NA, 164)!

The father's cry of absurdity marked the starting point of his son's spiritual adventure [7] which, in this last of seven novels, is about to be completed with a mystical intimation of the Earthly Paradise.

The indication that our hero's ascent is about to be completed is evident on the very first page of the last section of the novel, where he writes: "I am eager to reach the point where writing, finally, will be something other than changing hells" (NA, 169).

In a flashback the narrator takes us to September, 1939—to a notice of mobilization announcing the outbreak of World War II. Significantly, the notice is posted on the Church of Beaulieu. Forming part of the scene and reinforcing the theme of sacrifice introduced by the poster are the tympanum of the church, "the only one on which the sculptor represented, behind the arms of Christ opened over the world, those of the crucifix like a menac-

ing shadow" (NA, 170), and a statue of the Virgin holding
the Christ Child, in whose hands the vine growers had
placed one of the most beautiful bunches of grapes. Cirlot
has two entries that elucidate the symbolism associated
with the scene: one under "Grapes":

> Grapes, frequently depicted in bunches, symbolize at
> once fertility (from their character as a fruit) and
> sacrifice (because they give wine—particularly when
> the wine is the colour of blood) (116),

and the other under "Bunch":

> In Christian art, a bunch or cluster always symbolizes
> Christ and sacrifice. So, in the book of Numbers
> (XIII, 23), one reads: "and (they) cut down from
> thence a branch with one cluster of grapes" (33).

What makes the symbolism of the grapes all the more
poignant in the narrator's description are the rain drops
falling from them like tears:

> On the deserted square, on the posters, and on the
> pity of the unknown sculptor, the drops of water on
> the bunch of grapes trickled from grape to grape, one
> after the other in the silence (NA, 170).

Nine months after the declaration of war, young
Berger finds himself in a tank with three companions en
route across the fields to meet the enemy. Like his father
before him, Berger is now in direct contact with the raw
material of mankind—with soldiers, who, for the most

part, belong to the peasantry, and in whom he discovers
both the "misery" and the "grandeur," both the good
and the evil, of fundamental man. What obsesses him is
the human soul which links him to these men and which
he refers to as "the formless part of my companions," and
"the nobility which men are unaware of in themselves"
(NA, 169). These two definitions communicate Malraux's
hope and constant concern with making all men aware
of the soul which links them with the divine.

The cyclic theme of sacrifice winding from generation to generation or from Berger-father to Berger-son
is duplicated by one of young Berger's tank corps companions, a young peasant named Pradé, and his son, who,
like his father in the last war, is being deprived of an
education because of this one. Pradé speaks to Berger
about it in the following passage:

> He is eleven years old, the chap; about the same age
> I was in the other war. That is what kept me from
> educating myself. . . . He is a smart lad, a smart lad.
> . . . In order for him to continue studying, it would
> be necessary for me to work, and all I'm doing is
> acting like an imbecile with a gun. . . . He was the
> first one in the family who could have been educated
> (NA, 179)!

In the tank with Berger, in addition to Pradé, are
·two other companions, Bonneau and Léonard, making a
total of four; the number is significant because it later
reintroduces the symbolism of the cross.

When the tank moves into the fields, the narrator
announces, "The war is beginning at this moment" (NA,
180). As they advance toward the enemy, mention is made

for the first time in Malraux of something existing "beyond
the human adventure":

> . . . there is no longer anything but an earth of
> ditches, an earth of mines; and it seems that the tank
> is crawling by itself toward some burrowed ambush,
> and that future races are beginning this night their
> own combat, beyond the human adventure . . .
> (NA, 181).

But it is not long before the tank, turned from its course,
descends into the hell of a dark ditch; the lights in the
tank go out, and the narrator says, "We are thrown
against the wall of our common ditch: Berger, Léonard,
Bonneau, and Pradé—a single cross" (NA, 189).

After an interminably long, anguished struggle in
this dark *fosse* (the word's triple denotation—ditch, pit,
and grave—translates not only the literal experience but
also the metaphysical journey of the four men—their descent into the "pit" of hell and the realm of death), they
finally succeed in returning the tank, which had been
turned upright in the ditch, to its normal position. Cries
of joy are heard as the lights go on again and the tank
proceeds across the fields. As the tank gropes its way out
slowly into the night, young Berger catches a glimpse,
though not directly, of life in the distance: "in the mirror,
the free plain extended to infinity . . ." (NA, 190). There
is an implied parallel between the image in the mirror reflecting life, and life as a mirror reflecting eternity—a
parallel which the subsequent mystical vision of the hero
confirms.

When they reach the village, they find it evacuated.
In the darkness of the night, they come upon a barn; they

enter it and sink to the straw-covered ground—that same straw (a cyclic image of life in the novel) which had announced Vincent Berger's return from "the valley of the dead" and was now to announce theirs. A light shines in the darkness; the narrator describes the scene: "Before my electric lamp, lit for an instant, I see Pradé, bent over, grasping the straw and pressing it, as if he were hugging life" (NA, 191). Just before he closes his eyes, Pradé utters a hope which prefigures what actually comes to pass: "Perhaps we shall come back alive tomorrow" (NA, 191).

During the cycle winding from night to day, they sleep. It is daybreak when the mystical intimation of the resurrection at the end of time begins: "The morning is as pure as if there were no war" (NA, 191). As he returns to life, young Berger reacts much as Kassner had before him: "There is nothing in this morning that I do not look upon, I, too, with the eyes of a stranger" (NA, 192).

Reinforcing my interpretation of this entire last section as a temporal experience prefiguring the resurrection at the end of time is young Berger's impression of having returned after the lapse of many centuries. The sight of living animals "on this strange earth" (NA, 192) brings to mind the animal fables of the Middle Ages—"the time when animals used to speak, the ambiguous poetry of the old fables, we bring them back with us from the other side of life" (NA, 192–93). Not only the animals but the whole scene takes young Berger far back in time, perhaps to the dawn of the human adventure: ". . . these are the barns of Gothic times; our tanks at the end of the street are filling up with water, monsters kneeling before the wells of the Bible. . . . Oh life, so old! And so persistent" (NA, 193)! Man, no less than nature, has been persistent, for "there is nothing here that does not bear the mark of man" (NA, 193). Even the peasants (fundamental man) who have been forced to flee their homes seem to young Berger to belong to a race "that has come, through the millennia, from the darkness encountered last night . . ." (NA, 193).

As young Berger thinks of all those who left their mark upon the earth before descending into the realm of death, he recalls a familiar image:

> Once again Pascal comes to mind: "Let us imagine a great number of men in chains, and all condemned to death, some of them being slaughtered each day in the presence of others: those who remain see their own fate prefigured in that of their fellows. . . . That is the image of man's condition (NA, 194).

But death is not the final answer! What critics have failed to point out is that Pascal's metaphor of the human condition reintroduces and accentuates the theme of resurrection in the passage almost immediately following it:

> But, this morning, I am all birth. I bear within me the eruption of the terrestrial night upon issuing from the ditch . . . and just as I saw the night, roaring and full, surge from the ditch, so I behold, now, rising from the night, the miraculous revelations of the day (NA, 194).

And "the miraculous revelation of the day" transforms the barns of this abandoned village into "these barns of Paradise" (NA, 194). Everything in this Paradise—the simplest objects, the animals, the trees, and the houses— reveals to young Berger that life as "an infinite series of possibles" remains a mystery: "All this might not have been, might not have been this way" (NA, 194). What made it so was the "will" and "metamorphosis" manifested in the walnut trees of Altenburg, symbols at once of the tree of life and the tree of man—and of creation in continuous progress—a creation whose mystery will be revealed only at the end of time. If the road to the end remains a mystery in terms of the metamorphoses yet to be wrought by the force of human and natural will acting upon the incomplete series of cycles, the end itself is disclosed to young Berger who has a mystical illumination—first, of the mystery of the Redemption, and then, of the mystery of the resurrection.

Two images which form part of the scene of the Paradise in which he finds himself spark the illuminations: the half-open door of a deserted farmhouse and an old peasant couple seated on a bench in the sunshine. The first affords him a glimpse of a scene that evokes the Nativity, and in a flash its mystery is revealed: the gifts of the Magi were the keys with which Christ opened the doors of eternal life to mankind:

> The door of the farm that I am passing has been left open by the fleeing farmers: I catch a glimpse of a semi-pillaged room. Ah! the Magi Kings did not bring gifts to the Child, they simply told him that, on this night of his arrival, half-open doors were swinging on miserable lights—doors half-opened on to the life that is revealed to me this morning for the first time—on to a life as strong as the darkness and as strong as death . . . (NA, 195).

The half-open door is a symbol of the gateway to the other world.

The peasant couple—alone in this entirely deserted village—symbolize the last couple: Adam and Eve at the end of time. They also symbolize the secret connection between the cyclic resurrection of the earth and the resurrection of man at the end of the one, grand cycle that began the human adventure. These peasants, who seem to blend in with the natural scene, and who know the secret of the annual regeneration of the earth, await death fearlessly and patiently; they await it as if they knew that death meant not the end, but the passing to a new life. The old peasant woman responds to the younger peasant Pradé's greeting with an intriguing smile on her lips as she continues "to gaze into the distance at death with indulgence, and even—oh mysterious blinking, piercing shadow at the corner of her eyelids—even with irony . . ." (NA, 195).

To young Berger, who has just returned from "the grave" (*la fosse*), the entire scene represents a temporal image of the end of time, when the last couple—the old peasants—will complete the adventure begun by the first —Adam and Eve—as the final cycle winds not from death to new life, but from death to the resurrection of the dead—from time to eternity:

> Half-open doors, linen, barns, marks of men, Biblical dawn into which the centuries hustle, how the whole dazzling mystery of the morning is deepened by the one that appears on those aged lips! Let the mystery of man reappear with a vague smile, and *the resurrection of the earth is no more than a quivering backdrop* [italics mine].
>
> I know now what the ancient myths about beings snatched from the dead signify. I hardly remember terror; what I bear within me is the discovery of a simple and sacred secret.

Thus, perhaps, God looked upon the first man . . . (NA, 195).

With this last passage the hero's spiritual journey and Malraux's fiction have come to an end.

Young Berger, whom we next encounter in the prison of Chartres Camp as the narrative winds back to the opening portion of the novel, is a new hero who has attained the lucidity for which A.D. in *La Tentation de l'Occident* expressed a burning desire. He has an obscure intimation that the creation of man by man must be completed—that all men must be made aware of the *grandeur* which links them to the eternal—before his vision terminating the one, grand cycle of the human adventure can become a reality.

Notes

1. W. M. Frohock, Rima Drell Reck, and Albert Sonnenfeld also pointed out the circular structure of the narrative in their studies on Malraux.
2. *Supra,* p. 195.
3. *Supra,* p. 222.
4. Both Malraux and St. Augustine consider evil to be *not* a positive force but "the absence of good."
5. Critics have stressed the word "permanence" of this title and have not resolved the paradox created by the conjunction linking "permanence" with "metamorphosis." For a resolution of the paradox, see *supra,* pp. 5–6.
6. This was the original title of three volumes, of which *Les Noyers de l'Altenburg* was the last; the other two were destroyed by the Gestapo. Malraux is said to have revised this last volume to incorporate, in condensed form, the essence of the original three, with profound modifications (Gabriel d'Aubarède, "Rencontre avec Malraux," *Les Nouvelles Littéraires*, No. 1283 [April 3, 1952], p. 4).
7. See diagram (*supra,* p. 254).

Part IV
Man's Open Future

18.

Toward a Universal Artistic Culture

The new hero is, of course, André Malraux himself, whose history of the human adventure is about to be brought up-to-date as we reenter "the imaginary museum," where we find him exploring the cultural heritage of the world—past and present—for an intimation of the future course of mankind, for an intimation of the next stage in the long history which began in Eden and which will hopefully end—lest time flow to death rather than to eternity—with the realization of his last fictional hero's vision.

Unlike the nineteenth-century museum, whose store of treasures was limited not only by what it could contain but also by what it could acquire, "the imaginary museum," made possible by the invention of the camera —"the printing press of the plastic arts"—is at once gathering, metamorphosing, and disseminating all that can be photographed of man's art from prehistoric times to the present: "The successive waves of the worldwide resurrection that is filling the first imaginary museum are being classified, still confusedly, according to a world order" (VS, 125).

The wheel of the present study—from the art of the past to that of the present—comes full cycle as we penetrate this "Apparition of the Twentieth Century" (Malraux's designation for the imaginary museum), for a glimpse of the possible future of mankind.

Once inside we find the contemporary artist grappling with the same permanence-metamorphosis paradox resolved by Malraux's fictional hero in the course of his spiritual journey through many of the major existential crises of the first half of this century. The artist is in the process of discovering, in the imaginary museum whose masterpieces reveal the creative power in all art, the presence of a permanent divine faculty in man—a faculty which echoes his defiance of destiny across the centuries. The artist is also discovering that time not only brings forth ever new forms from this faculty but also metamorphoses those of the past. In other words, the concept of metamorphosis is not limited to a continually changing present; it also involves a continually changing past viewed from the perspective of an ever-changing present.

Corroborating the foregoing is the reappearance, in *Les Voix du silence,* of the "tree-man" metaphor which had resolved the permanence-metamorphosis paradox for young Berger in *Les Noyers de l'Altenburg.* The metaphor is expanded to suggest the ratio—divine faculty: tree of man :: seed : tree of nature; the picture is one of both trees constantly changing and constantly growing:

> Time involves all the forms of the past in the metamorphosis which it imposes on man's entire world, and our consciousness of this metamorphosis coincides with our awareness of duration itself. And this awareness is no longer like the perception of a voyager, who sees man ever similar to himself before the changing landscapes of time—it is the perception symbolized by the grain that becomes a tree (VS, 625).

But the dilemma of the isolated individual [1]—a dilemma which Malraux has solved in his fiction—remains as yet unsolved for the contemporary artist, whose forms primarily express a forceful rejection of his world.

The history of Western art from the Renaissance onward reveals that the cycle of profane art has wound upward in time and outward in space, through the imaginary museum, into a spiral embracing the globe. The cycle of profane art that began with the artist's determination to conquer the "real" world in the Renaissance has reached the extreme limit of its expression with the rejection of that same world and the creation, by each individual artist, of his own autonomous world subservient to no other value than that of art itself. The result is a highly individualistic and, therefore, heterogenous art which has become even more specific with the invasion of Europe by the whole world's art through the imaginary museum. The advent of the imaginary museum has given rise to an unprecedented phenomenon in the history of art: a confrontation of the world's masterpieces.

Time and place are being obliterated within this "temple" which houses the most divergent expressions of the human soul. While Western art reaches out, through the imaginary museum, like an octopus to conquer the globe, it is in turn being influenced by the whole world's art which continues to pour into this treasure house of photographic reproductions and metamorphoses.

While the Western artist regresses in time to resuscitate the primitive and savage arts of man's earliest beginnings, artists the world over are imitating the painters of Montparnasse. From this confrontation of metamorphoses within the museum, Western art is emerging the victor. While it is embracing, rather than succumbing to, the savage arts, the latter are being destroyed by the power of Western art which is lulling to sleep the parts of the human soul which gave them expression.

> The masks, the ancestors that we look at, are no longer being sculpted, and while they are entering our museums, our most ordinary figures are sufficing to kill them in Africa. We evoke with pity the frescoes of Nara . . . but Japanese painters, in third-rate cities, are imitating painters of Montparnasse that are unknown in Lyons. . . . It is time to realize that the world has not produced, in three hundred years, a single work of art comparable to the greatest of the West (VS, 589).

In the midst of what Malraux refers to as "our barbarian Renaissance" (VS, 541), the contemporary Western artist, not content with the mysterious regions of man he is discovering in the primitive and savage arts, is also plumbing the most distant domains of popular art; he is studying the art of children, and even that of the insane. We find that the artist is, in all probability, seeking what his fictional counterpart has already discovered: "If the contemporary artist is vulnerable to the elementary to this degree . . . it is perhaps because he vaguely hopes to find *the fundamental* [italics mine] in it" (VS, 535).

Malraux makes particular mention of Henri Rousseau (*Le Douanier*) as the artist who escaped the wheel of history—the cycle of impressionist art—to usher in the contemporary period by reviving and renewing the innocence and fantasy of the art of man's earliest beginnings:

> In the miserable atelier of Plaisance, the primitive melody that [Rousseau's] *The Charmer* . . . plays,

summons up the fetishes and the oldest dreams of the world . . . (VS, 512).

Like the eternal song [of the poet], Rousseau expresses the cycle of the seasons, the fine silhouette of branches against the sky and the piling up of russet leaves on the earth, with the same apparently calm efficacity as the primitives express religious sentiment (VS, 508–10).

The dilemma of the contemporary Western artist, who is resuscitating the arts of the primitives and savages —all of which were created in the service of a supreme value linking man to the cosmos—is that his own art continues to serve no other god than art itself. He paints pictures the way his predecessors created gods, says Malraux. Our receptivity to arts far removed in time and space from our own is explained in terms of the unprecedented nature of our quest:

Our art is not, and does not pretend to be, the expression of a capital *notion* of man in a civilization founded on that notion (it is because our epoch wants a heterogeneous notion, whose meaning it has not yet grasped, that it so willingly admires what it does not understand) (VS, 596).

Contemporary Western art is more desirous of transforming the world than of harmonizing with it or choosing from among its elements. It is an individualistic art which has *not* renounced its conquest of an autonomous world even though it has ceased to find in it a *raison d'être*. Our art is that of a splintered culture uncertain of its destination:

For a tradition, that is to say, a culture which, in all domains, had a conception of itself, our art substituted a culture which has no conception of itself. For a system of affirmations our culture has substituted a domain of seeking—a domain in which the artist—and perhaps man—knows only his point of departure, his methods, his will and his direction. An Art of Great Navigators. . . . But can a culture of Great Navigators have a conception of itself (VS, 602)?

The forms of our contemporary art, however, which express nothing other than the artist's break with his world and, of course, his rejection of it (this does not mean that it is not a great art), are combative forms, which seem to be groping their way to a new truth. It is this groping which perhaps explains why a painting which recognizes no other value than itself is resuscitating so many values foreign to itself.

Obscurely and gradually the results of this groping are beginning to appear. The imaginary museum, whose birthplace is the West, has already revealed that all arts are branches of the same tree—the divine faculty in the human soul—and that all art is an "anti-destiny" (VS, 637), that is, a manifestation of "the victorious part of the only animal who knows he must die" (NA, 169).

Aware that it cannot survive intact without undergoing a metamorphosis, our twentieth-century art continues to explore the imaginary museum for a unifying element, for a truth: "as if its searching were bringing us all at once the past of the world and our future" (VS, 125). Elsewhere Malraux voices the same idea with regard to our obsession with history, which he refers to as "the anxious interrogation of the past to discover the destiny of the world" (VS, 539).

What we have learned thus far from our study of the world's masterpieces is that our art bears much in common with the sacred arts of the past (including those of the primitives and the savages), at least insofar as "it, no less than they, considers valid only those forms which are heterogeneous to the world of appearances" (VS, 593–94); ". . . we refuse to submit to appearances with as much force as Byzantium did" (VS, 601).

But Malraux is careful to point out that if our art has rejected the world, it has not yet discovered a truth which would link man to the Other World—a link which is the *sine qua non* of all sacred art: "Related to all the sacred styles and a stranger to all others, our art seems to be that of a religion of which it is unaware" (VS, 591). And Malraux continues: ". . . our art is the creation or summons for a world separated from the real world, [but] it is not the expression of it. . . . Now, the sacred requires not only an absolute, it also requires that the life of the society in which it appears be oriented by that absolute" (VS, 596).

The struggle continues, but perhaps the glimmer of an unknown light is beginning to shine through the myriad forms which already populate and continue to invade the imaginary museum,. Malraux says, "the great resurrection of our time required our art, but . . . it cannot survive its victory intact" (VS, 638). The past is being resurrected, and out of the past is beginning to emerge "the first universal artistic culture, which will undoubtedly transform modern art" (VS, 638). When this happens, the West will have transformed the world's invasion of her imaginary museum into one of her "supreme conquests" (VS, 638). Malraux refers to this art struggling to be born of the resurrection of the world's past as "an unforeseeable art" (VS, 602).

But if our future remains uncertain, the closing paragraph of *Les Voix du silence* leaves us with the profound hope that the hand which will fashion it is "trembling with a secret form—one of the highest that will bear witness to the strength and honor of being a man" (VS, 640).

This hand "trembling in the twilight" (VS, 640) seems to be groping its way toward a universal art—and perhaps toward a new sacred art—and a new cycle—that will lead us farther along "our road to Paradise," let time flow to death rather than to eternity.

Note

1. According to Malraux, individualism, too, is a fundamental expression of the human soul—one common to all men.

Part V
Antimemoires

19.

The Permanence and Metamorphosis
of a Vision

The first volume of Malraux's *Antimémoires* is a simultaneous account of the genesis of the vision disclosed in the foregoing portion of this study and of the re-examination of that vision in the light of recent history and new experiences.

Although Malraux frequently dips back into a more remote past for the ideas and experiences that shaped his vision, the focus of his *Antimémoires* is on the quarter of a century that began where his last novel ended. The concentration of this analysis will be on the events which, during that twenty-five-year period, led Malraux to enter into a dialogue with some of his earlier responses to the questions defining his relationship to the world.

Antimémoires is actually a simultaneous account of two separate voyages, one beginning in 1965 and the other in 1940. The 1940 voyage, which resumes the ethical and spiritual evolution of Malraux's last fictional hero, whom we left in Chartres prison in 1940 (*supra,* p. 283), unfolds by way of memory flashbacks in the course of Malraux's 1965 journey as Minister of Culture. Corroborating the foregoing is the fact that the opening line of *Antimémoires* contains an immediate flashback from

1965 (Malraux is aboard ship "Off Crete" [1]) to 1940, which we learn was the date of Berger-Malraux's escape from prison with the chaplain of Glières. Beginning a quarter of a century apart, the two voyages gradually coincide as the volume draws to a close.

The entire first volume of *Antimémoires* is linked in some way to Malraux's last novel—both to its setting, Alsace, and to the walnut trees themselves. Part I of *Antimémoires* not only bears the same title as the novel, *Les Noyers de l'Altenburg*, but also begins with a somewhat transposed and abbreviated version of the first two panels of the novel's tryptich (*supra*, pp. 253 ff).

The reproduced section of *Les Noyers de l'Altenburg* introduces the reader of *Antimémoires* to the questions and some of the responses that composed a world view about to be reappraised in *Antimémoires*.

The central question of the novel, which was the ultimate outcome of man's perennial "struggle against the Angel" (the Angel of Death), is also that of *Antimémoires*. Malraux makes this abundantly clear in his introduction, where, in connection with the original trilogy, of which *Les Noyers de l'Altenburg* is the only extant volume, he says: "It was called *La Lutte avec l'Ange* [The Struggle with the Angel] and what else am I undertaking here" (AM, 7). The foregoing is reinforced when Malraux presents himself to his readers as a man "who is attuned to the questions that death raises about the meaning of the world" (AM, 6). In still another passage, the dominant theme of his *Antimémoires* is expressed in cyclic terms as follows: "To reflect on life—life in relation to death —is perhaps no more than to intensify one's questioning" (AM, 1).

It will be recalled that, in *Les Noyers de l'Altenburg*, both Berger-father and Berger-son had issued from "the

valley of the dead," during World War I and World
War II, respectively, with mystical intimations of man's
ultimate triumph over the Angel of Death at the end of
the human adventure. The former had seen, in the living
earth that he had espied through the line of sunflowers,
a vision of the Promised Land; the latter had viewed the
fields of the evacuated German village, into which he had
emerged after his confrontation with death in the ditch,
as an intimation of a far-off Earthly Paradise (*supra,* pp.
280–83; AM, 294–321). The image of the walnut trees
themselves had revealed the mystery of man's life in
time as one of "endless" will and metamorphosis leading,
hopefully, to the final victory. It will also be recalled that
the realization of the final victory was projected into a
far-distant future when man will have accomplished his
purpose on earth—the destruction of evil, the origin
of death.

In *Antimémoires,* which extends Malraux's history
of the human adventure from 1940 to 1965, the vision
of man's final victory is eclipsed by the reappearance of
Satan in his most hideous form, that of Torturer and
Degrador, who would destroy the very essence of man.

What is unique about *Antimémoires* is that the darkening of the vision and the emergence of a glimmer of
a new hope progress simultaneously. The reader becomes
increasingly aware of the complexity of the work's structure, which is not only cyclic but also multileveled or
stratified. While the stratified or vertical structure applies
to the realm of thought and memory into which Malraux
frequently descends when present impressions evoke past
associations, the cyclic or horizontal structure governs the
metamorphosis of his vision on the conscious level. The
book is a series of dialogues between past and present.

Like the cycle of his novels, the first book of Malraux's *Antimémoires* is, on the surface, an account of a cyclic journey from France to France. The journey begins and ends in 1965 after numerous flashbacks to earlier periods of both history and the author's own life. On the 1965 itinerary, which includes North Africa, French America, China, and India, Malraux, as Minister of Culture, is retracing not only many of his own steps but also those of his fictional hero, whose cyclic spiritual journey took him from the West to the West via the Orient.

It gradually becomes apparent that the continued interaction of East and West, with India rather than China playing the leading role this time, effects a metamorphosis of Malraux's vision of the next stage of the human adventure. If China succumbed to the temptation of the West in Malraux's early novels, we shall find the West succumbing to the ethical temptation of India in *Antimémoires*. Indeed, if there is a master-disciple relationship here, it is first between Gandhi and Nehru and then between Nehru, or perhaps India, and Malraux. But if Malraux's ethical vision undergoes a "metamorphosis" under the influence of India, his one-cycle concept of the human adventure remains intact—or "permanent" —after being set in opposition to the Eastern world of eternally recurring cosmic cycles.

Antimémoires reveals that the recent history of China and India has caused Malraux to reconsider the question of ethics in the domain of action, that is, the question of the degree to which any *end* can justify evil or unjust *means;* indeed, whether a "just end" may be achieved by any but "just means." His disillusionment with Communist ideology and methodology is voiced in connection with the resurrected China that he revisits in 1965—a China representing the betrayal of a promise: "Of the Rev-

olution, there remains nothing but museums—and operas
. . . So much death, so much hope, and so much blood,
all that I knew and dreamed about Canton ends . . .
absurdly . . . (AM, 336–37).

According to Malraux, Mao Tse-Tung wants not
peace but rather uninterrupted violent revolution, leading eventually to world revolution. In the following
passage, Malraux expresses what he believes to be Mao's
thoughts: "But there is one country dedicated to vengeance and justice, one country that will never lay down
its arms, will never lay down its spirit, before the global
confrontation" (A, 376). Malraux believes that Mao envisages a reversal of the positions of East and West in the
foreseeable future: "Three hundred years of European
energy are now on the wane; the Chinese era is dawning.
. . . Behind our entire conversation [between himself and
Mao in Peking] the hope of a twilight world stood watch"
(AM, 376).

If, in *Antimémoires*, Malraux does indeed see some
validity in the Spenglerian thesis, he does not envisage
a decline of the West but rather a metamorphosis of the
means of pursuing the Western Quest. He sees this quest,
which will hopefully culminate in the realization of the
design of history, gradually becoming that of humanity.
His hope for a universal humanism radiating from the
civilization of the West remains intact:

I'm not very convinced by theories that see in our
civilization only the end product of one culture
among others. Einstein used to say, and I believe
Oppenheimer says the same thing: there are more
researchers alive now than during the whole of
human history. Even if we are experiencing the end
of a Romano-Christian culture, or a Faustian one

[Faustian man is the Western seeker after truth: Malraux's Navigator sailing toward an unknown destination] as Spengler put it, we are also experiencing the beginning of the greatest adventure mankind has known since the birth of historical cultures (AM, 244).

Elsewhere Malraux reiterates what he had so often said in his volumes on art: "We are taking part in the most colossal resurrection the world has ever known" (AM, 235); "the first world civilization claims the world's art as its indivisible heritage" (AM, 49).

Malraux sees two forces working toward the realization of his own concept of the purpose of history: both its "immediate" purpose, the reunification of mankind, and its ultimate purpose, the destruction of evil. On the one hand he sees the "imaginary museum" of the West effecting a fusion of the world's divergent cultures into one, and on the other, the ethical lesson of India offering new hope for man's ultimate victory over Satan.

In striking contrast to the violent course currently being pursued by Mao's China, which may yet lead to the destruction of mankind, Malraux offers India's discovery of the efficacity of an alternative course: "the supreme value that India had brought to the world was non-violent action, by virtue of which the liberation of India could rank with the great revolutions of history" (AM, 137). "In a world from which the shadows of Stalin and Hitler had not yet faded, India could boast of having freed herself from England without a single English casualty" (AM, 129). In still another passage Malraux speaks of the men, especially Gandhi and Nehru, who made India's liberation possible: "Five hundred million men had lived under foreign rule; in a single generation, the moral action of a few men had liberated them . . ." (AM,

142). Speaking on the same subject during one of his dialogues with Malraux, Nehru totally repudiated the Machiavellian thesis: "It has been said that non-violent action was an illusion; here, it has been the only *real* means of political action. Even in politics, an evil action has evil consequences" (AM, 137). On the next page India's neutrality is explained on the basis of the same repudiation: "the refusal to choose between Communist and Capitalist nations, the refusal to justify the means by the end, did not spring from nineteenth-century liberalism, but from thousands of years of Hindu thought" (AM, 138). Machiavellianism is again rejected when Nehru declares that the most difficult task facing liberated India is the creation of "a just state by just means" (AM, 139).

Malraux's disillusionment with the China whose death and rebirth he had described in his novels is counterbalanced by the hope he sees in renaissant India: "After what Gandhi had called India's *dance macabre,* one of humanity's greatest adventures was under way, groping toward the establishment of a nation of four hundred million souls on the basis of faith in the ineluctable power of forgiveness" (AM, 143). This hope is reinforced, in *Antimémoires,* as the enormous hand (the glover's sign at Bône) that had announced Malraux's "return to life" after his close call with death during his flight from Sheba to France, joins, in his thoughts, the "bronze hand of Peace" over the Palace of Justice at Chandigarh (AM, 340). Together the hands communicate "life" and "peace" as the goals toward which human energies may someday be directed. The reason for projecting the achievement of the goals into the future is given in Nehru's quotation from a speech made by General Bradley in 1948: "We have unraveled the mystery of the atom and rejected the Sermon on the Mount: we know the art of killing, not the art of living . . ." (AM, 227). How soon the dream will coincide with reality depends upon how soon man-the-destroyer will make way for his positive counterpart; Nehru ventures a guess: "Once I used to think that only our sons would have a chance to be *builders* [italics mine]. Our grandsons perhaps . . ." (AM, 225). Nehru also expresses his views on how the necessary transformation of man might be effected: "in my youth I used to talk of spiritualizing politics" (AM, 227); "politics should try to fight against the destruction which science brings in its wake, and against the violence which humanity carries within itself" (AM, 227). The Indian leader was convinced that science had failed, that something more was needed to stem the tide of destruction: "humanity lacks some essential quality. What? A sort of spiritual element, which would curb the scientific power of modern man. It is now clear that science is incapable of ordering life. A life is ordered by values. Our own, but also that of nations—and perhaps that of humanity" (AM, 227). Malraux, the "tragic humanist," is not at all certain about the fate of India's contribution to the world: "The strength of non-violence lay in the fact that the enemy was a colonial empire. It remains to be seen what will happen if it encounters an Asian adversary. And the Asian adversary is waiting" (AM, 241).

Malraux's 1965 visit to India occasioned not only an exposition of the continuing interaction of East and West in the secular domain but also a setting-in-opposition of the Hindu and Christian world views. In *Antimémoires,* he places particular emphasis on the different responses of each to his central theme: the meaning of life in the face of death—"the struggle with the Angel."

It soon becomes apparent that man's response to the Angel is directly related to his concept of time. Eastern man lives in "cosmic time"; he lives in a world of eternally recurring cycles where everything, including his own being, is subject to endless death and rebirth. Western man lives in "historic time," conceived as irreversible— a time which had a beginning and will have an end, a time in which he himself lives only once.

In *Antimémoires*, the walnut trees of Altenburg symbolize the Western Christian world view, the one-cycle vision of history, while the sacred trees of India and Senegal symbolize the eternally recurring cosmic-cycle vision of the East. For Malraux, the walnut trees seem to be in harmony with the idea of the creation, to suggest an identification between the tree of nature and the tree of man, both striving toward the same goal—their "endless" will and metamorphosis directed toward the fulfillment of the Creator's design, obscure though that design may seem to man. The sacred trees, on the other hand, are symbols of eternity, of time without either a beginning or an end; they are symbols of a world in which not only the gods but also men "always were and always will be."

The image of the sacred trees inevitably evokes that of the walnut trees in Malraux's mind. In the following passage, the cyclic image around the sacred trees is contrasted with the one Malraux had so often seen around the walnut trees. While the former suggests the eternal rebirth of men in everlasting time, the latter had suggested a correspondence between the time of nature (the creation) and the time of man:

> From ocean to ocean, around sacred trees which no longer protect them from the sun, motionless men are forming rings—as around the glowing pyres of Benares—and as once, above Strasbourg, did the young shoots and the dead nuts of winter (AM, 252).

Malraux intimates that the Christian concept of one life within the one grand cycle of the human adventure enhances the importance of man's sojourn on earth, while the Indian concept of eternally recurring cycles, governing the eternal death and rebirth of the same creatures diminishes it:

> in the darkness [of India] haunted by royal and divine cosmogonies, there had *never* been a Creation. For the Fall, the Redemption and the Last Judgment that Christianity reveals, the world is a backdrop; for Brahmanism, man is an episode. Not only because of transmigration but because the fabled cycles that divide the successive returns from the shades have the gods and the elements for heroes (AM, 191).

In the Western Christian concept, man is the hero on earth, a hero with a destiny to fulfill.

The notion that the human life span seems more infinitesimal, and hence less significant, in the Indian world of cosmic cycles than in the Western world of natural cycles is communicated in another passage where Malraux contrasts the trees of Altenburg with the sacred tree of Queen Sebeth of the Casamance:

> The queen's fetish was a tree, something like the giant plane tree. An open space had been cleared around it, so that it was possible to see how it towered over the forest. . . . the rest of the clearing was covered with the silken snow of kapok which drifted down continually. In this setting of dreamlike purity, the congealed blood of sacrifices streamed from the tree.

Her tree reminded me of the walnut trees that I had not forgotten, but these were attuned to the rhythm of human life, while the sacred tree was suggestive of a geological rhythm, in which man flitted past like a butterfly (AM, 50–51).

The butterfly, suggestive of the extreme brevity of life, is one of the leitmotifs of *Antimémoires*. Of particular interest in connection with this leitmotif is Malraux's designation of "butterfly" as one of the denotations of the word *"farfelu"* of his title, *Royaume farfelu*. Charles Lucet, the French ambassador to the United States, informs us of this in his article "Malraux et ses *Antimémoires"*:

In a more or less concrete way, Malraux himself was eager to specify, so to say, the meaning of this word which recurs so often in his work and in his conversation. "I am very sensitive, he said, to the *farfelu* [bizarre, ephemeral]. You know that I reinvented this word which comes from Rabelais and which signified 'plump.' But *farfala* [2] also means butterfly." This is very enlightening–the realm of the plump butterfly. The explanation is itself bizarre [*farfelu*], and it is quite certainly what Malraux, the teaser, was seeking to prove. [3]

But Malraux's explanation is not so "bizarre" when we remember that "royaume farfelu" was the Kingdom of Death (*supra*, p. 136) and hence the realm of the ephemeral. And what creature images the ephemeral more vividly than a butterfly? Nor is the adjective "plump" (*dodu*) as mystifying as it might seem, since it suggests the shape of the earth: "royaume farfelu" is, therefore, the "plump realm of the ephemeral," or the realm in which "man flits by like a butterfly." And there can be no doubt that in *Antimémoires,* where Malraux guides his readers through the tombs of men and the tombs of the gods—museums—we are still in the Kingdom of Death, the realm where men die.

The butterfly leitmotif reappears on Malraux's stop-off at Aden where he visits the museum housing the art treasures of Sheba—treasures for which he had once risked his life: "The curator shows us some *butterflies* [italics mine]. . . . I think of the old queen of the Casamance beside her sacred tree under the silky flakes of kapok. . . . It is *midday* [italics mine]" (AM, 69). Frequently and significantly, Malraux exits from the tombs of both men and the gods either at "noon," a symbol of the ascending spirit, or in the spring of the year, symbolic of the "return to life." These exits introduce the theme of the resurrection, the hope of man's eventual triumph over the Angel of Death. Significant, too, is the fact that portions of the "return to life" scenes from both *Le Temps du mépris* and *Les Noyers de l'Altenburg (supra,* pp. 220–27, 280–83) are reproduced in *Antimémoires* along with the real-life experiences that inspired them.

While Malraux apparently interprets these experiences, which played a great role in his life (AM, 98), as reflections of what "may" come to pass at the end of time, he seems to reject the Hindu belief in eternal death and rebirth in unending time. He does so on the grounds that eternal recurrence would deny the idea of progress in human history, for "the imprisoned *maya* would go on forever bringing back the same men, the same dreams and the same gods in eternal cycles" (AM, 220).

A restatement of this refutation of the Indian world

view appears at the end of the *Antimémoires* sequel to the "return to life" experience of Berger-Malraux in *Les Noyers de l'Altenburg*. The reiterated refutation is all the more forceful because it follows the memorialist's comparison of the irreligious West with the religious East. On the one hand, Malraux expresses his disenchantment with the growing atheism of the West, especially that of his tank companions for whom neither life nor death seemed to have any meaning, and who had returned from "the valley of the dead" with no revelation of any kind: "How many Pradé's [one of the tank companions) I had known, secluded in their caverns of nothingness! Atheists about everything, even perhaps about themselves" (AM, 221). On the other hand, Malraux communicates his awareness that Indian religions render death even more meaningful than life; he makes particular mention of the Hindu god Shiva, whose dance of eternal death and rebirth projects into the next life the hope of communication with the Essence not attained in the present one. And then Malraux says: "But no god danced in the hearts of my tank companions" (AM, 220). The immediate prelude to the refutation of the Indian world view contains an enumeration of Malraux's own "return to life" experiences; the focus is on the glover's sign—the enormous hand at Bône—that had announced Malraux's "rediscovery of life" after his perilous return flight from Sheba. Earlier in the volume, Malraux had informed us that this experience became Kassner's in *Le Temps du mépris* —Kassner, who had wondered whether he might return "on such an evening after he had really been killed" (*supra*, p. 226; AM, 65). When it comes, Malraux's answer to the question of "rebirth in time" or "transmigration" is categorical: "the imperceptible coolness of the tropical dawn was mingling on my face with the eternal Hindu resurrection in which life and death were united [Malraux now remembers what Nehru had said to him]: 'Everything you spoke about was to do with man. . . .' " Then Malraux concludes: "But for Man, death has no dawn" (AM, 248).

If Malraux repudiates the Hindu belief in "eternal life in this world," both his anguish and his hope with regard to the Christian belief in "eternal life in *another* world" seem to have been deepened by the experiences recorded in *Antimémoires.*

The Christian theme of salvation begins and ends the author's 1965 voyage. The theme is introduced on the opening pages, where Malraux, still aboard ship, recalls his conversation with the chaplain of Glières on the occasion of their escape from prison in 1940. Believing that all children are saved, the chaplain said to Malraux: "And then, the fundamental fact is that there's no such thing as a grown-up person" (AM, 1). The theme reappears when Malraux's disillusionment with the atheistic tank companions with whom he had "returned to life" in 1940 brings to mind the Spanish Republican monk of *L'Espoir*—the monk who had given his own version of the Second Coming of Christ to the group of peasants gathered around him: "And when they'd all done enough killing—and when the last file of the poor had set off on their month. . . . a star that no one had ever seen rose above them . . ." (AM, 221).

We encounter the theme of salvation again in Malraux's account of his imprisonment in 1944. He was then Colonel Berger of the Alsace-Lorraine division of the Resistance and had been captured by the German Das Reich division. Almost certain that he would be condemned to death by the Gestapo, Malraux asked for a Bible. After reading the Gospel of St. John to no avail,

Malraux the agnostic poignantly declared: "I felt strongly
that all faith dissolves life in the eternal, and I was cut
off from the eternal" (AM, 155). He seemed to be reaching out for a faith that eluded him:

> Alone in the face of death I encountered that age-old
> Compassion that had enveloped so many despairs as
> the Last Judgment would roll back so many sepul-
> chres: "Lord, help us in the hour of our death. . . ."
> But faith means belief; I had great respect for the
> Christian message which had pervaded the earth in
> which I would doubtless soon be lying, but I did not
> believe in it (AM, 155–56).

In the shadow of death, Malraux referred to his life
as "a human destiny coming to an end in front of a
dozen rifles, among so many other destinies as ephemeral
as the earth" (AM, 155). The word "ephemeral" indicates
that Malraux still believes that time will end, that the
one, grand cycle of the human adventure will be completed. Thinking of Nehru at one point, he wondered:
"Why should his agnosticism cut him off from Shankara,
since mine did not cut me off from St. Augustine" (AM,
239)? With St. Augustine, Malraux also believes that the
mystery of the human adventure—and of human suffering—is impenetrable: "In what oriental text had I read:
'The meaning of the world is as inaccessible to man as
the behavior of the chariots of kings is to the scorpions
they crush'" (AM, 156)?

As he is about to return to Europe, Malraux again
recalls the chaplain of Glières who, with "his arms
raised toward the stars of Dieulefit," had said: "'There
are no grown-ups . . .'" (AM, 380). This cyclic theme
and figure of salvation which reappears as Malraux is

about to return to the West not only unifies his journey
but also adumbrates the predominance of the theme in
the concluding section of *Antimémoires,* which is set in
Paris.

On Malraux's first stop-off at Anchorage on his
homeward flight to France via the Pole, the theme of
salvation is embodied in a scene reminiscent of the
Church of Beaulieu in *Les Noyers de l'Altenburg* (*supra,*
p. 275): the Tourist Information Bureau "had set up a
crèche, taken it down and left the statues [St. Joseph and
the Virgin] behind in the lonely square at the foot of the
magic animals. There was one solitary car on the avenue.
It was December 26" (AM, 381).

In the air again, Malraux views the scene from the
plane:

> But in this polar night, over the last primordial
> waters similar to those of India, on which an *infant
> god* [italics mine] . . . lies cradled, the dialogue which
> seems to me the most agonizing of all is one I know
> only through having heard it. It is not directly linked
> with my life—although. . . . If it comes back to me
> now as the secret arbiter of so much remembrance in
> this long night, it is surely because the dialogue be-
> tween the human animal and torture is more pro-
> found than that of man and death (AM, 381).

The Christian themes of suffering, salvation, and the
resurrection are inextricably interwoven in the entire last
section of *Antimémoires,* where Malraux draws an analogy
between the Calvary of Christ—it is Christmas week of
1965 in Paris—and that of man. The spotlight is on the
martyrdom of Jean Moulin, who was tortured to death

by the Germans during the Resistance, and on the victims of the Nazi extermination camps.

The Paris that Malraux finds upon his return from the East is preparing for the ceremony which is to end with the deposition of the remains of Jean Moulin in the Pantheon. Malraux himself is scheduled to deliver the funeral oration on the following day. "The ashes are brought in a child's coffin" (AM, 382), Malraux observes. The size of the coffin is significant because all children, according to the chaplain of Glières, are saved, and because Christ, whose birthday is being celebrated concomitantly with the burial ceremonies, was the "infant god" who had come to save the world.

The analogy between Christ and man in the domain of suffering is explicitly expressed in the part of Malraux's oration dealing with Jean Moulin's martyrdom: "His mission is over, his *calvary* [italics mine] begins. Jeered at, savagely beaten, his head covered with blood, his organs shattered, he reaches the limits of human suffering without even betraying a single secret, he who knew them all" (AM, 383).

When the obsequies are over, Malraux recalls that during them

> the shadow that looms over the shadow of death passed slowly over the Pantheon—eternal Evil, which all religions have confronted in their turn, and which this child's coffin confronted . . . with its invisible guard of ghosts . . . with these survivors [of the Resistance] . . . who would perhaps never see each other again (AM, 387).

As the survivors of the Resistance leave the scene in *Antimémoires,* those of Dachau, Ravensbrück, and Auschwitz appear to give their accounts, as Malraux had earlier recorded them, of the horrors they suffered. The date of the deportees' accounts reinforces the predominance, in this section, of the three related Christian themes: suffering, salvation, and the resurrection: "Christmas Day, 1944. In the men's hospital, there is a sermon by a Resistance priest. Dysentery, typhus, tuberculosis, sores, limbs broken while working or beneath the blows of the kapos. . . . Skeletons with shriveled skin showing through striped rags. An almost silent hell" (AM, 394). This hell, says Malraux, was unlike anything yet contrived by man: "torture had existed for centuries . . ." (AM, 398). What had not yet existed was this organized degradation based on the thesis that if you "treat men like dirt . . . they really become dirt" (AM, 400). "Hell is not horror, it is being degraded to the point of death . . . Satan is the Degrador" (AM, 398).

The aim of the Degrador was to destroy in man that which made him man: "It was aimed at making you lose your soul, in the sense in which one talks about 'losing one's reason' " (AM, 405). But the Degrador did not succeed. Most of the internees resorted to sabotage: they accepted the torments to which they were subjected as they would have accepted a cancer—they did not participate in them; they retained their ability to return contempt for contempt. Malraux says that "conversions were rare, but almost all the atheist prisoners took part in the semisecret religious ceremonies, for as soon as the priest spoke of the Passion, he was speaking to them about themselves" (AM, 398).

We find a strange, or at least unexpected, metamorphosis in Malraux's attitude toward his main theme, "the meaning of life in the face of death," in his reactions to the survivors' accounts of their "rediscoveries of life" upon their liberation from the camps. It is at this point in *Antimémoires* that the dialogue between past and present moves the central theme into a new perspective. For the heroes of Malraux's early novels, death had accentuated the absurdity of life; in *Antimémoires*, the situation is reversed: life itself appears absurd to those who return from the hell of the camps—from the domain of death. There is a compelling contrast between the sacred will to live that prevailed in the domain of the Degrador and the absurd banality of everyday life which acts as a "tomb" for the memories of the survivors.

It is a deportee from Ravensbrück—a woman named Brigitte—who gives the most detailed account of her "rediscovery of life" experience in *Antimémoires*. In addition to Malraux, her listeners include Edmond Michelet, a Spanish Republican, and the priest who had read from the Gospel at Dachau. What Brigitte found upon her return was a paradoxical situation: indifference to the point of cruelty on the one hand, and, on the other, the simple comforts of family life—a family which, like her bed, was warm but strange. People, including her parents, appeared childlike to her.

At several points in her story, Brigitte mentions the difficulty she experienced in abandoning the intense feelings that had kept the prisoners alive: "In the camp we lived in a state of indignation. A steady, constant indignation. . . . And we found ourselves back here with our indignation undirected" (AM, 408).

When we came back from the moon . . . there was no longer any camp—long live sheets and Eau de Cologne! But the self-defense that had been protecting us had become purposeless. We came back expecting to find a world dominated by it. We had climbed the

Stations of the Cross, we had been crucified, and it all ended in Mary Magdalene's bed (AM, 409–10).

Upon hearing this last statement, the priest of Dachau smiled as if to say: "my poor little girl" (AM, 410).

Those who had returned from hell, one and all, were soon absorbed in the petty quarrels and simple, banal pleasures of everyday life which gradually buried their memories. Brigitte says it was the only way to survive among the living: "What did living involve? Being blind. So we all became blind again. Sooner or later" (AM, 410).

Her disillusionment parallels that of Malraux in his *Antimémoires* sequel to the intimation of the Earthly Paradise in *Les Noyers de l'Altenburg*: "It certainly *wasn't* [italics mine] the Resurrection," says Brigitte. "There was no longer a hell, and there was no longer anything to counteract hell. . . . It was like Dante's return among the indifferent" (AM, 410).

The word "wasn't," italicized in this last quotation, does not imply a denial of the resurrection but rather a distinction between what happens in the course of men's lives after sojourns in hell or realms of death, and the idea that they have of the resurrection prophesied in the New Testament.

The questioning of the Christian theme reaches a depth of intensity on the last pages of *Antimémoires* where we find Malraux the agnostic attempting to reverse Dostoëvsky's "Niet." The resurrection had been Dostoëvsky's "invincible hope" (AM, 388). Malraux speaks of the enlarged photograph of Lazarus that he had seen on the wall of the Russian writer's home in Moscow: "that Lazarus whose mantle Dostoëvsky had long ago assumed, not in order to console the murderers and the prostitutes but to shake the pillars which uphold the riddle of the world . . . the supreme riddle: 'What am I doing on this earth where sorrow reigns' " (AM, 389)? On the same page Malraux mentions the Bible that the guardian of the house had shown him—the Bible that Dostoëvsky had had in prison: "It was covered with annotations: the word *Niet* again and again" (AM, 389). Malraux elaborates:

> To foretell the future, the Russians used to open the Bible when they woke up: the first paragraph on the left-hand page foretold what was to happen. And so, always in the same handwriting, opposite some such passage as "Mary Magdalene saw that the stone had been taken away from the sepulcher," after weeks or days the prisoner had sadly written: "No" (AM, 389).

Malraux quotes from Dostoëvsky's *The Brothers Kara-mazov* to explain the "Niet": " 'If the divine will implies the torture of an innocent child by a brute, I am handing back my ticket' " (AM, 388). Then, as if to reassure both us and Dostoëvsky, Malraux, in an apostrophe to his departed "master," says:

> It is not your anguish, prophet, which fills this shabby room, even if it is the anguish of our time: all life becomes mystery when it is questioned by pain. It is the voice of Lazarus, against whom neither mystery nor death prevails, the indomitable reply of Antigone or of Joan of Arc before the tribunals of the earth: "I was not born to partake of hatred, but to partake of love"; it is the eternity of which the psalmist sang, and which Shakespeare rediscovers two

thousand years later beneath the enchanted stars of Venice . . ." (AM, 390).

The shadow of Satan which, in *Antimémoires,* had eclipsed the mystical revelation of man's return to the Earthly Paradise in *Les Noyers de l'Altenburg* is dispelled by this reaffirmation of Malraux's hope in the resurrection. The restoration of his hope is accompanied by a vision of the next stage on the way to its realization. *Antimémoires* ends with Malraux's return to Lascaux, one of the scenes of the dawn of the human adventure. The scene subtly communicates the hope that nonviolence, conservation, and construction will, in the not-too-distant future, supersede violence and destruction in human affairs. When questioned by Malraux, the guide at Lascaux identified himself as one of the boys who had found the prehistoric paintings in the cave in 1940. One of his two pals had died in the Resistance, and the other had become a *master-builder.* The "corrugated iron huts" next to the entrance of the cave were for "conscientious objectors. The conservation work had been entrusted to them" (AM, 412). The two dates associated with the cave—that of its discovery in 1940 and that of Malraux's visit in 1965—are those of the two voyages recounted in *Antimémoires.*

And when all had had their surfeit of killing . . . a star that they had never seen rose above them (E, 245; AM, 221).

Conclusion

The ubiquity of the cycle idea in all of Malraux's works, and in instances too numerous to mention in this study, leaves no doubt that the cycle is Malraux's "signature" as an artist.

The author of *Antimémoires* explicitly avows his interest in the idea on the occasion of his first stop-off at the Cairo museum. A little blue figurine attracts his fancy and he explains the reason: "(It bears the date 1965, Twelfth Empire. Time's symmetry has often haunted me. What were the events of the year 1965 B.C.?)" (AM, 40). Particularly significant is the fact that the same cycle of time—1965 B.C. to A.D. 1965—comes to mind on the next to the last page after the remains of the Resistance hero have been deposited in the Pantheon: "Those who have come to salute the ashes of Jean Moulin in memory of their own dead pass slowly against the sky of death—as in the cities of Egypt and Mesopotamia in the year 1965 before Christ. There is no coming back from hell any more than there is from death" (AM, 411). I found this last sentence disconcerting: therefore I wrote Malraux about it; it refers to what happens in the course of the human adventure rather than at the end of time. The word "death," however, does not appear in Malraux's reply. In translation, the letter, which came to me through Marcel Brandin of the Ministry of Cultural Affairs, reads: "on returning from hell (extermination camps) one *loses* the memory of what it was, and no experience of hell can be integrated with life" (January 17, 1969). The reply, which places the emphasis on memory, links the sentence, including the word "death," to Malraux's opening epigraph, which subtly rejects the idea of transmigration:

The elephant is the wisest of all animals, the only one who remembers his former lives; thus he remains motionless for long periods of time, meditating thereon (Buddhist text).

In *Antimémoires,* Malraux also mentions his fascination for the symmetry of place, especially Alsace (AM, 18–19), which played a very important role in his life.

The cycle idea is not absent from Malraux's work as Minister of Cultural Affairs either: one of his major projects is "to set up 90 houses of culture in the next 10 years." [4]

The succeeding volumes of *Antimémoires* will no doubt further enrich a literary creation which represents a unique contribution to our age—a contribution which has expanded our horizons while deepening our anguish and our hope.

Notes

1. André Malraux, *Anti-memoirs,* trans. Terence Kilmartin (New York: Holt, Rinehart, and Winston, 1968), p. 1. Henceforth cited as AM.
2. *The French Review,* XLII, No. 1 (October, 1968), 6.
3. This is the Italian word for "butterfly"; the correct spelling is *farfalla.*
4. *Newark Evening News,* December 9, 1966.

A Selected Bibliography

A. Books by André Malraux

Lunes en papier. Paris: Simon, 1921. (Consulted in Skira edition of 1945.)

La Tentation de l'Occident. Paris: Grasset, 1926. (Consulted in Skira edition of 1945.)

Les Conquérants. Paris: Grasset, 1928. (Consulted in Skira edition of 1945.)

Royaume farfelu. Paris: Gallimard, 1928. (Consulted in Skira edition of 1945.)

La Voie royale. Paris: Grasset, 1930. (Consulted in Skira edition of 1945.)

La Condition humaine. Paris: Gallimard, 1933.

Le Temps du mépris. Paris: Gallimard, 1935.

L'Espoir. Paris: Gallimard, 1937.

La Lutte avec l'ange: Les Noyers de l'Altenburg. Lausanne-Yverdon: Editions du haut pays, 1943. (Consulted in Skira edition of 1945.)

Ouevres complètes. Genève: Skira, 1945.

Esquisse d'une psychologie du cinéma. Paris: Gallimard, 1946.

Le Musée imaginaire (La Psychologie de l'art, Vol. I). Genève: Skira, 1947.

La Création artistique (La Psychologie de l'art, Vol. II). Genève: Skira, 1949.

Les Conquérants. "Version définitive," with Postface. Paris: Grasset, 1949.

The Case for De Gaulle, with James Burnham. A "dia-
logue." New York: Random House, 1949.
La Monnaie de l'absolu (La Psychologie de l'art, Vol. III).
Genève: Skira, 1950.
Saturne. Paris: Gallimard, 1950.
Les Voix du silence. Paris: Gallimard, 1951.
Le Musée imaginaire de la sculpture mondiale, Vol. I.
Paris: Gallimard, 1952.
*Le Musée imaginaire de la sculpture mondiale: Des bas-
reliefs aux grottes sacrées.* Paris: Gallimard, 1954.
*Le Musée imaginaire de la sculpture mondiale: Le Monde
chrétien.* Paris: Gallimard, 1954.
La Métamorphose des dieux. Paris: Gallimard, 1957.
Antimémoires. Paris: Gallimard, 1967.
Anti-memoirs. trans. Terence Kilmartin. New York: Holt,
Rinehart and Winston, 1968.

B. *Articles, Prefaces, and Reviews by André Malraux*

"Des Origines de la poésie cubiste," *La Connaissance,* I,
No. 1 (January, 1920), 38–43.
Review of *Trois livres de Tailhade,* by Tailhade, *La Con-
naissance,* I, No. 2 (February, 1920), 196–97.
"La Genèse des chants de Maldoror," *Action,* No. 3 (April,
1920), 33–35.
"Mobilités," *Action,* No. 4 (July, 1920), 13–14.
"Prologue," *Action,* No. 5 (October, 1920), 18–20.
"Journal d'un pompier du jeu du massacre," *Action,* No.
8 (August, 1921) 16–18.
"Aspects d'André Gide," *Action,* 3ᵉ année [not numbered]
(March–April, 1922), pp. 17–21.
Review of *L'Abbaye de Typhaines,* by Le Comte de
Gobineau, *Nouvelle Review Française,* July, 1922, pp.
97–98.

Review of *Art Poétique,* by Max Jacob, *Nouvelle Revue Française,* August, 1922, pp. 227–28.

Preface to *Mademoiselle Monk,* by Charles Maurras. Paris: Stock, 1923.

Review of *Malice,* by Pierre Mac Orlan, *Nouvelle Revue Française,* May, 1923, pp. 836–37.

"Lettres d'un Chinois," *Nouvelle Revue Française,* April, 1926, pp. 409–20.

Review of *Défense de l'Occident,* by Henri Massis, *Nouvelle Revue Française,* June, 1927, pp. 813–18.

Review of *Buddha Vivant,* by Paul Morand, *Nouvelle Revue Française,* August, 1927, pp. 253–55.

Review of *Histoire comique de Francion,* by Charles Sorel, *Nouvelle Revue Française,* No. 29 (November, 1927), pp. 686–88.

"D'une jeunesse européenne," *Ecrits* (Les Cahiers Verts, No. 70). Paris: Grasset, 1927, pp. 129–53.

Review of *Où le coeur se partage,* by Marcel Arland, *Nouvelle Revue Française,* No. 173 (February 1, 1928), pp. 250–52.

Review of *L'Imposture,* by Georges Bernanos, *Nouvelle Revue Française,* No. 174 (March, 1928), pp. 406–408.

"Contes, historiettes et fabliaux," review of *Dialogue d'un prêtre moribund,* by Le Marquis de Sade, *Nouvelle Revue Française,* 15ᵉ année, No. 177 (June 1, 1928), pp. 853–55.

Review of *L'Enfant et l'écuyère,* by Franz Hellens, *Nouvelle Revue Française,* No. 31 (August 1, 1928), pp. 291–92.

Review of *Battling le ténébreux,* by Alexandre Vialatte, *Nouvelle Revue Française,* No. 31 (December 1, 1928), pp. 869–70.

Review of *Journal de voyage d'un philosophe,* by Hermann Keyserling, *Nouvelle Revue Française,* No. 32 (June 1, 1929), pp. 884–86.

Review of *Pont-Egaré,* by Pierre Véry, *Nouvelle Revue Française,* No. 33 (December, 1929), pp. 838–39.

"Exposition Gothico-Bouddhique—Exposition Gréco-Bouddhique," *Nouvelle Revue Française,* February, 1931, pp. 298–300.

"Réponse à Trotsky" (trans. Beth Archer), *Nouvelle Revue Française,* No. 211 (April 1, 1931).

"Jeune Chine," *Nouvelle Revue Française,* No. 38 (January, 1932), pp. 5–26.

"Expositions d'oeuvres de Semirani (Galérie de la NRF)," *Nouvelle Revue Française,* No. 38 (April, 1932), pp. 771–73.

Review of *Documents Secrets,* by Franz Hellens, *Nouvelle Revue Française,* No. 38 (May 1932), pp. 915–16.

Review of *En marge d'Hymenée,* by Louis Guillout, *Europe,* June 15, 1932, pp. 304–307.

Preface to *L'Amant de Lady Chatterly,* by D. H. Lawrence. Paris: Gallimard, 1932.

"Exposition Fautrier," *Nouvelle Revue Française,* No. 40 (February 1, 1933), pp. 345–46.

Preface to *Sanctuaire,* by William Faulkner. Paris: Gallimard, 1933.

Review of *Les Traqués,* by M. Mateev, *Nouvelle Revue Française,* 22e année, No. 249 (June 1, 1934), pp. 1014–16.

"L'Art est une conquête," *Commune,* Nos. 13–14 (September–October, 1934), pp. 68–71.

"L'Attitude de l'artiste," *Commune,* No. 15 (November, 1934), pp. 166–75.

Review of *Journal d'un homme de quarante ans,* by Jean Guéhenno, *Nouvelle Revue Française,* No. 44 (January, 1935), pp. 148–51.

Reviews of *Sans Reprendre Haleine,* by Ilya Ehrenburg, *Nouvelle Revue Française,* November, 1935, pp. 770–72.

Review of *Les Nouvelles Nourritures,* by André Gide, *Nouvelle Revue Française,* December, 1935, pp. 935–37.

"Réponse aux 64," *Commune,* No. 27 (December, 1935), pp. 410–16.

Preface to *Indochine S.O.S.,* by Andrée Viollis. Paris: Gallimard, 1935.

"Sur l'héritage culturel," *Commune,* September, 1936, pp. 1–9.

"N'était-ce donc que cela," *Saisons: Almanach des lettres et des arts,* No. 3 (Winter, 1946 and 1947), pp. 9–24.

"Man and Artistic Culture," *Reflections on Our Age: Lectures Delivered at the Opening Session of Unesco at the Sorbonne University,* Paris (trans. Stuart Gilbert). New York: Columbia University Press, 1949, pp. 84–99.

Preface to *Les Liaisons dangereuses,* by Choderlos de Laclos. Paris: Gallimard, 1952.

"Three Speeches" (trans. Kenneth Douglas), *Yale French Review,* No. 18 (Winter, 1957), pp. 27–38.

"Il segreto dei grandi veneziani," *La Civiltà veneziana nell'età barocca.* Florence: Sansoni, 1958.

"When the French Lived in Darkness," *The New York Times Magazine,* January 17, 1965, pp. 12–13, 82–84.

"André Malraux répond à dix questions," *Arts,* September 29–October 5, 1965, pp. 5–7.

C. Books on André Malraux

Blend, Charles D. *André Malraux: Tragic Humanist.* Columbus: Ohio State University Press, 1963.

Blumenthal, Gerda. *André Malraux: The Conquest of Dread.* Baltimore: Johns Hopkins University Press, 1960.

Boisdeffre, Pierre de. *André Malraux* (Classiques du XXe siècle, Vol. I). Paris: Editions Universitaires, 1952.

Delhomme, Jeanne. *Temps et destin.* Paris: Gallimard, 1955.

Fitch, Brian T. *Les Deux univers romanesques d'André*

Malraux (Archives des Lettres Modernes, 52). Paris: Minard, 1964.

Frohock, Wilbur Merrill. *André Malraux and the Tragic Imagination*. Stanford, Calif.: Stanford University Press, 1952.

Gannon, Edward, S.J. *The Honor of Being a Man: The World of André Malraux*. Chicago: Loyola University Press, 1957.

Halda, Bernard. *Berenson et André Malraux*. Paris: Minard, 1964.

Hartman, Geoffrey H. *André Malraux*. London: Bowes & Bowes, 1960.

Hoffman, Joseph. *L'Humanisme de Malraux*. Paris: Klincksieck, 1963.

Langlois, W. G. *André Malraux: The Indo-China Adventure*. New York: Praeger, 1966.

Lapicque, Charles. *A Propos des "Voix du Silence."* Paris: Centre de Documentation Universitaire (Collège Philosophique).

Lewis, R. W. B., (ed.). *Malraux: A Collection of Critical Essays*. Englewood Cliffs: Prentice-Hall, 1964.

Mauriac, Claude. *Malraux ou le mal du héros*. Paris: Grasset, 1946.

Picon. Gaëtan. *André Malraux*. Paris: Gallimard, 1945.
———. *Malraux par lui-même*. Paris: Edition du Seuil, 1953.

Righter, William. *The Rhetorical Hero: An Essay on the Aesthetics of André Malraux*. New York: Chilmark Press, 1964.

Savane, Marcel. *André Malraux*. Paris: Richard-Masse, 1946.

Vandegans, André. *La Jeunesse littéraire d'André Malraux. Essai sur l'inspiration farfelue*. Paris: J.J. Pauvert, 1964.

Wilkinson, David. *Malraux: An Essay in Political Criticism*. Cambridge: Harvard University Press, 1967.

D. Books on André Malraux and Other Authors

Benson, Frederick R. *Writers in Arms: The Literary Impact of The Spanish Civil War.* New York: New York University Press, 1967.

Bespaloff, Rachel. "Notes sur André Malraux," in *Cheminements et carrefours.* Paris: Vrin, 1938.

Blanchot, Maurice. "Notes sur Malraux," in *La Part du feu.* Paris: Gallimard, 1949.

Brée, Germaine, and Margaret Guiton. *The French Novel from Gide to Camus.* New York: Harcourt, Brace & World, 1962.

Brombert, Victor. "Malraux: Passion and Intellect," in *The Intellectual Hero: Studies in the French Novel.* Philadelphia, Pa.: J. B. Lippincott, 1961.

Frank, Joseph. "Malraux's Image of Man," in *The Widening Gyre.* New Brunswick, N.J.: Rutgers University Press, 1963.

Garaudy, Roger. *Literature of the Graveyard: Jean-Paul Sartre, François Mauriac, André Malraux, Arthur Koestler.* New York: International Publishers, 1948.

Goldberger, A. *Visions of a New Hero; The Heroic Life According to André Malraux and Earlier Advocates of Human Grandeur.* Paris: Minard, 1965.

Goldmann, Lucien. *Pour une sociologie du roman.* Paris: Gallimard, 1964.

Howe, Irving. "Malraux, Silone, Koestler: The Twentieth Century," in *Politics and the Novel.* New York: Meridian Books, A Horizon Press Book, 1957.

Knight, Everett W. *Literature Considered as Philosophy: The French Example.* New York: Collier Books, 1962.

Simon, Pierre-Henri. "André Malraux ou le défi de la mort," in *L'Homme en procès.* Neuchatel (Switz.): Editions de la Baconnière, 1950.

Stéphane, Roger. *Portrait de l'aventurier: T. E. Lawrence, Malraux, Von Salomon,* précédé d'une étude de Jean-Paul Sartre. Paris: Sagittaire, 1950.

E. Articles on André Malraux

Albérès, R. M. "André Malraux and the 'Abridged Abyss'" (trans. Kevin Neilson), *Yale French Studies,* No. 18 (Winter, 1957), pp. 45–54.

Ball, Bertrand Logan, Jr. "Nature, Symbol of Death in *La Voie royale,*" *French Review,* XXXV, No. 4 (February, 1962), 390–95.

Barrett, Wm. "Of Man's Greatness," *Twilight of the Absolute,* by André Malraux, *Saturday Review,* May 5, 1951, p. 37.

————. "3,000 Years of Triumph; with biographical sketch by B. Kalb," *Saturday Review,* November 21, 1953, pp. 17–19.

Baumgartner, Paul. "Solitude and Involvement: Two Aspects of Tragedy in Malraux's Novels," *French Review,* XXXVIII, No. 6 (May, 1965), 766–76.

"Black Sun," *Time,* August 19, 1957, p. 65.

Blanchot, Maurice. "Time, Art, and the Museum," from "Le Musée, l'Art, et le Temps" (trans. Beth Archer), *Critique,* Vols. VI and VIII, Nos. 43 and 44 (December, 1950, and January, 1951). (Consulted in R. W. B. Lewis, ed. Englewood Cliffs: Prentice Hall, 1946.)

Blend, Charles D. "Early Expressions of Malraux's Art Theory," *Romanic Review,* LIII, No. 3 (October, 1962), 199–213.

Brée, Germaine. "Glimpses of an Inhuman Future," *Saturday Review,* No. 44 (December 9, 1961), p. 19.

Cabane, Pierre. "Encore un beau discours," *Arts,* October 20–26, 1965, p. 18.

Chevalier, Haakon M. "André Malraux; The Return of the Hero," *Kenyon Review,* II (Winter, 1940), 35–46.

Chiaromonte, Nicola. "Malraux and the Demons of Action," Part I, *Partisan Review,* July, 1948, pp. 776–89; Part II, *Partisan Review,* August, 1948, pp. 912–23.

Cordle, Thomas. "The Royal Way," *Yale French Studies,* No. 18 (Winter, 1957), pp. 20–26.

D'Aubarède, Gabriel. "Rencontre avec Malraux," *Les Nouvelles Littéraires,* No. 1283 (April 3, 1952), pp. 1, 4.

Drieu la Rochelle. "Malraux, L'homme nouveau," *Nouvelle Revue Française,* No. 35 (December, 1930), pp. 879–85.

Dupée, F. W. "André Malraux," *Partisan Review,* IV, No. 4 (March, 1938), 24–35.

Flanner, J. "Profiles," *New Yorker,* No. 30 (November 6, 1954), pp. 45–81.

———. "Profiles," *New Yorker,* No. 30 (November 13, 1954), pp. 46–100.

Genet. "Letter from Paris," *New Yorker,* No. 35 (April 18, 1959), pp. 154–156.

———. "Letter from Paris," *New Yorker,* No. 33 (January 18, 1958), pp. 80–83.

Herz, Micheline. "Woman's Fate," *Yale French Studies,* No. 18 (Winter, 1957), pp. 7–19.

Hoog, Armand. "Malraux, Möllberg, and Frobenius," *Yale French Studies,* No. 18 (1957), pp. 87–96.

"Hopeful Twilight," *Time,* No. 57 (March 19, 1951), p. 65.

Kaufman, W. "Malraux's Paris Revolution," *Saturday Review,* No. 42 (December 5, 1959), p. 58.

"Keep Smiling; unveiling of Da Vinci's Mona Lisa in Washington," *Time,* January 18, 1963, pp. 16–17.

Langlois, Walter. "The Debut of André Malraux, Editor Kra, 1920–22)," *PMLA,* LXXX, No. 1 March, 1965), 111–22.

Leefmans, B. M. P. "Malraux and Tragedy: The Structure of 'La Condition humaine,'" *Romanic Review,* XLIV, No. 3 (October, 1953), 208–14.

Lucet, Charles. "Malraux et ses *Antimémoires,*" *French Review,* XLII, No. 1 (October, 1968), pp. 1–15.

Magny, Claude-Edmonde. "Malraux le fascinateur," *Esprit,* No. 149 (October 1948), pp. 513–34.

"Man's Quest," *Time,* No. 66 (July 18, 1955), pp. 24–26.

Mauriac, C. "Malraux: Again From Letters to Action," *The New York Times Magazine,* July 6, 1958, pp. 9–17.

Monnerot, Jules. "Sur André Malraux," *Confluences,* No. 2 (April, 1946), pp. 216–25.

Picon, Gaëtan. "Man's Hope" (trans. Rima Drell Reck), *Yale French Studies,* No 18 (Winter, 1957), pp. 3–6.

Reck, Rima Drell. "Malraux's Transitional Novel: *Les Noyers de L'Altenburg,*" *French Review,* XXXIV, No. 6 (May, 1961), 537–44.

"Rise of Mass Culture," *Time,* No. 79 (May 25, 1962), pp. 56–60.

Rodriguez Pintos, Carlos. "Saludo a André Malraux," *Revista Nacional* (Montevideo), IV, No. 202 (October–December, 1959), pp. 512–13.

Roedig, Charles F. "Malraux on the Novel (1930–1945)," *Yale French Studies,* No. 18 (Winter, 1957), pp. 39–44.

Roudiez, Leon S. "Schème et vocabulaire chez Malraux," *French Review,* XLI, No. 3 (December, 1967), 304–18.

Sonnenfeld, Albert. "Malraux and the Tyranny of Time: the Circle and the Gesture," *Romanic Review,* LIV, No. 3 (October, 1963), 198–212.

Sperber, Manes. "Dialogue Between Past and Present," *The New York Times Book Review,* October 20, 1968, pp. 1, 40–44.

"Telling Voice," *Time,* No. 62 (November 23, 1953), p. 86.

Trotsky, Leon. "La Révolution Etranglée," *Nouvelle Revue Française,* No. 211 (April, 1931), pp. 501–507.

"Vision of Victory," *Time,* No. 72 (July 7, 1958), p. 20.

Wilson, Edmund. "André Malraux," *New Republic,* August 9, 1933. (Consulted in R. W. B. Lewis, ed., *Malraux: A Collection of Critical Essays.* Englewood Cliffs: Prentice Hall, 1946.)

F. Background Materials

Albérès, R. M. *La Révolte des écrivains d'aujourd'hui.* Paris: Correa, 1949.

Arland, Marcel. "Sur un nouveau mal du siècle," *Nouvelle Revue Française,* February, 1924, pp. 149–55.

Cairns, Grace E. *Philosophies of History: Meeting of East and West in Cycle-pattern Theories of History.* New York: Philosophical Library, 1962.

Chassang, A., and Ch. Senninger. *Les Textes littéraires généraux.* Paris: Librairie Hachette, 1958.

Cirlot, J. E. *A Dictionary of Symbols* (trans. Jack Sage). New York: Philosophical Library, 1962.

Malraux, Clara. *Portrait de Griselidis.* Paris: Editions Colbert, 1945.

——. *Le Bruit de nos pas* (Apprendre à vivre, Vol. I). Paris: Grasset, 1963.

Mumford, Lewis. *The Conduct of Life.* New York: Harcourt, Brace & World, 1951.

Nietzsche, F. *The Works of Friedrich Nietzsche: Thus Spoke Zarathustra.* New York: Tudor, 1931.

Raymond, Marcel. *De Baudelaire au surréalisme.* Paris: Jose Corti, 1952.

Rougemont, Denis de. *L'Aventure occidentale de l'homme.* Paris: A. Michel, 1957.

St. Augustine. *The City of God* (trans. Marcus Dods, D.D.). New York: Modern Library, 1950.

Index

333